◇ 21 世纪经济学类管理学类专业主干课程系列教材

国际贸易单证实务

（修订本）

白 云　张 苗　冯晓宁　王莉娟　编著

清华大学出版社
北京交通大学出版社
·北京·

内 容 简 介

全书共 10 章，内容主要包含国际贸易单证的基本要求，交易磋商和合同的签订，信用证开立与审核，进出口货物托运、报检、报关、投保，汇票，结汇单据制作，以及外汇核销和退税。

本书集专业知识和实践应用于一体，通过学习，可以延伸读者的国际贸易实务知识，帮助读者将有关理论及实践操作技巧运用到国际贸易单证工作实践中，避免可能出现的错误和贸易环节上的问题。本书可供各本专科院校作为教材使用或从事相关专业的在职人员作为参考书使用，也可作为进出口贸易模拟操作的实训教程。

本书封面贴有清华大学出版社防伪标签，无标签者不得销售。
版权所有，侵权必究。侵权举报电话：010-62782989　13501256678　13801310933

图书在版编目（CIP）数据

国际贸易单证实务/白云等编著．—北京：清华大学出版社；北京交通大学出版社，2009.12（2020.7重印）
（21 世纪经济学类管理学类专业主干课程系列教材）
ISBN 978-7-81123-982-9

Ⅰ.①国…　Ⅱ.①白…　Ⅲ.①国际贸易—票据—高等学校—教材　Ⅳ.①F740.44

中国版本图书馆 CIP 数据核字（2009）第 220142 号

责任编辑：赵彩云　　特邀编辑：吕宏
出版发行：清 华 大 学 出 版 社　　邮编：100084　　电话：010-62776969
　　　　　北京交通大学出版社　　邮编：100044　　电话：010-51686414
印　刷　者：北京鑫海金澳胶印有限公司
经　　　销：全国新华书店
开　　　本：185×260　　印张：15.25　　字数：362 千字
版　　　次：2010 年 1 月第 1 版　　2020 年 7 月第 1 次修订　　2020 年 7 月第 5 次印刷
书　　　号：ISBN 978-7-81123-982-9/F·573
定　　　价：42.00 元

本书如有质量问题，请向北京交通大学出版社质监组反映。对您的意见和批评，我们表示欢迎和感谢。
投诉电话：010-51686043，51686008；传真：010-62225406；E-mail：press@bjtu.edu.cn。

前　言

国际货物买卖合同的磋商、签订和履行都离不开大量贸易单证的签发、制作、组合和流转,单证是国际贸易交易的核心。因此,了解国际贸易单证的基本知识,熟悉国际贸易单证工作的操作与管理,掌握国际贸易单证的审核和制作技能,这些对外贸从业人员尤为重要。基于此,我们组织编写了《国际贸易单证实务》一书。全书共10章,内容主要包含国际贸易单证的基本要求,交易磋商和合同的签订,信用证开立与审核,进出口货物托运、报检、报关、投保,汇票,结汇单据制作,以及外汇核销和退税。其主要特点如下。

1．结构新颖、内容全面、重点突出。本书在国际贸易单证各个业务重点和难点上均设置操作示例和技能实训,边讲边做,通过单证"实例"、点评、常见信用证单据条款示例及释疑等具体形式来帮助学生加深理解和掌握。

2．紧贴现实,"教、学、做"合一。本书以一个虚拟的大学毕业生从事的第一笔出口交易为背景,从进出口贸易磋商、签订合同、申请开立信用证、审证、改证、租船订舱、报关、报检、制作单据等方面入手,系统地阐述了各项主要单证的种类、作用、格式、内容和缮制方法,为学生提供了一个在仿真模拟实践中全面了解国际贸易单证的业务流程和操作技能的有效途径。

3．应用性和操作性强。本书直接针对国际商务单证员资格证考试而设,教学内容随考证要求及时跟进更新,书中配备了大量的模拟练习题,为学生顺利通过考证提供了有效的教学保障。

4．取材新颖。收录单据均源于外贸部门、银行、海关、保险公司、运输公司、国家相关部门和国际相关组织的最新规定;所有相关国际惯例、法律、规章制度均为最新版本。

本书由白云、张苗、冯晓宁、王莉娟编写,具体分工如下:白云编写了第3章、第8章、第9章;张苗编写了第2章、第6章、第10章;冯晓宁编写了第4章、第7章;王莉娟编写了第1章、第5章。

本教程在编写过程中,借鉴和吸收了国内专家、学者的大量研究成果,在此一并致谢。因编者水平所限,书中疏漏、不足之处在所避免,敬请读者批评指正。

编　者
2020年7月

目 录

第 1 章　国际贸易单证概述

1.1　国际贸易单证的概念　/2
1.2　单证缮制的基本要求　/2

第 2 章　国际贸易基本程序与单据流程

2.1　业务关系的建立及合同的商订　/8
2.2　报价及还价核算　/24
2.3　合同的履行　/30
2.4　业务善后　/35

第 3 章　信用证

3.1　信用证概述　/42
3.2　催证　/46
3.3　申请开立信用证　/48
3.4　信用证的审核　/57
3.5　信用证的修改　/74

第 4 章　进出口货物运输

4.1　进出口货物托运工作概述　/84
4.2　海洋运输托运流程及托运单缮制　/85
4.3　航空运输托运流程及托运单缮制　/98

第 5 章　货物出入境检验检疫

5.1　进出口货物报检程序　/116
5.2　进出口货物报检单据　/121
5.3　商品检验证书　/122

第 6 章　货物进出境报关

6.1　货物进出境报关程序　/136
6.2　进出口货物报关单　/138

I

第7章 进出口货物运输保险

7.1 进出口货物运输保险概述 /152
7.2 投保单 /156
7.3 保险单 /161

第8章 原产地证书

8.1 原产地证书 /172
8.2 一般原产地证书 /175
8.3 普惠制原产地证书 /177

第9章 主要结汇单据

9.1 结汇单据概述 /186
9.2 汇票 /187
9.3 商业发票 /193
9.4 包装单据 /200
9.5 海运提单 /205
9.6 装运通知 /216
9.7 受益人证明 /220
9.8 其他单据 /223

第10章 出口收汇核销及出口退税

10.1 出口收汇核销 /228
10.2 出口退税 /234

参考文献 /238

第1章

【本章导读】
国际贸易单证的概念
单证缮制的基本要求

【学习目标和要点】
通过本章学习,学生应了解单证制作的基本要求。

国际贸易是跨国界、跨市场的国际商品流动。要顺利完成一笔国际贸易业务,除了买卖双方外,还必须由进出口两国的海关、商检机构、银行、保险公司、航运或航空公司等十几家乃至几十家国家机关、企业单位一起参与方能实现。因此,国际贸易单证是国际贸易活动中的一个重要组成部分。

国际贸易单证概述

1.1 国际贸易单证的概念

国际贸易单证是指国际间的经济贸易中所应用的各类单据和证书(包括信用证和国际结算中的其他单据和证书)。国际贸易单证在国际经济贸易中处于十分重要的地位。国际间的货物买卖,通常要经过成交、备货、出运和收汇4个阶段。当双方当事人达成交易、履行合同时,无论是进出口企业内部各部门——进出口业务部、财务部、单证部、储运部等之间的衔接,还是进出口企业与外部各有关方面——运输公司、保险公司、商检机构、海关、贸易主管部门等之间的联系;无论是货物的托运、交付,还是货款的结算和支付,都是通过单证的制作和流转来进行的。单证贯穿于整个交易的全过程。

1.2 单证缮制的基本要求

国际贸易单证是维系参与贸易各方权利和义务的重要凭证。单证工作质量的好坏,关系到国际贸易能否顺利进行,关系到能否安全、迅速地收汇或收货,体现了一个进出口企业的业务素质和管理水平。所以,单证的制作,不仅要符合国际贸易的有关法律、惯例和规则,并与之相适应,还要符合国际商业习惯和实际需要。

国际贸易单证的缮制应做到正确、完整、及时、简明、整洁。

1.2.1 正确

在缮制单证的基本要求中,正确是前提。它包含两个方面的内容:一是要与国际贸易合同或信用证相符,二是要符合国际贸易法规或惯例的规定。

在信用证结汇方式下,正确性要求做到"三相符",即单证相符、单单相符、单货相符。单证的正确性要求精确到不能有一字之讹。例如,某公司出口毛浴巾一批,信用证中规定商品的规格为"13×30",实际出运的是与规定的规格相符的货物,但工作人员在制单时,误将30打成39,出口商和出口地银行事先没有发现,单证寄到国外,因国外市场行情不好,客户抓住该公司发票上的一字之错,拒付货款。几经磋商调解不成,最后只好把货物运回,造成货价和来回运费损失。因此,单证上任何细小的错漏都会造成重大的经济损失,不可掉以轻心。即使在跟单托收业务中,虽然单据的正确性不像信用证业务要求的那样严格,但如果单据不符合买卖合同的有关规定,也可能被进口商找到借口,迟付或拒付货款。

单据还必须与有关国际法令或惯例的规定相符。目前,各国银行开证时,绝大多数都在信用证中明确注明:该信用证系根据《跟单信用证统一惯例》(2007年修订本)即国际商会第600号出版物的规定执行(THIS LETTER OF CREDIT IS SUBJECT TO UNIFORM CUSTOMS AND PRACTICE 2007 REVISION, ICC PUBLICATION NO.600)。该惯例自1933年第一次正式发布至今,已进行了7次修订。最近一次是2006年修订的国际商会第600号出版物(以下简称《UCP600》),于2007年7月1日起施行。银行在审单时,凡信用证中有上述规定者,除信用证另有特殊规定外,都以

《UCP600》作为审单的依据。因此,在缮制单据时,应注意不要与《UCP600》的规定抵触,否则就会被银行认定出单不符而退还或拒付。

此外,还要注意了解进口国的国家法律规定以及与国际惯例不同的习惯做法、对单据的特殊要求等,注意随时了解各国在做法上的变动,尽量做到出单内容与其规定一致,以避免进口国当局的拒绝接受。

1.2.2 完整

单证的完整性一是指出口人向银行或进口商提交出口单证时,必须是全套的、齐全的;二是指除上述单据种类齐全外,单据本身内容必须完备齐全;三是指出口人所提供的各种单据的份数要齐全。

(1) 在信用证支付方式下,进口商需要哪些单证,通常都在信用证上明确规定。因此,出口商只有按信用证规定备齐所需单据,银行才能履行议付、付款或承兑的责任。目前国际贸易中信用证所要求的单据种类较多,一般除商业发票、装箱单、提单、保险单等主要单据外,还有其他证明文件,如检验证书、重量单、产地证,船龄证明书、航程证明书、邮政收据等。这些单据都需要花费时间和一定手续进行事先联系、申请才能取得,在单证制作和审核过程中,必须严密注意各环节的衔接以及单据申领的时间,注意催办,防止误期或遗漏,保证在信用证有效期内提交全套的、完整的单据。

(2) 每一种单据本身都有固定的格式、项目、文字、签章要求等,如果格式使用不当,项目漏填,文字不通或签章不全,都不能构成有效文件,因而也不能被银行接受。例如,背书是使单据的转移得以实现的手段,如果应该背书的单据漏掉背书,就会影响单据作为流通手段的作用。又如,普惠制原产地证书格式A"原产地标准"一栏,虽仅需填一个字母或加上税则号或进口成分,但如果漏填或填的不正确,便会使证明书成为一张废纸,失去其应有的作用。

(3) 要严格按照信用证的要求提交单据的份数。这项工作往往要求在审证时落实,提前了解相关部门出单份数是否能够满足要求。例如,买方开来信用证要求出具一套提单正本三份,副本三份。但买方所指定的船务公司所签发的提单文本只有两份正本为一套,而卖方事先没想到会要三份,造成交单时的被动。而当信用证规定提交全套正本时(full sets of),份数则可以灵活。根据以前国际商会第400号出版物的规定以及船运业上的习惯做法,应提供两份以上海运提单正本时称为全套正本,银行才予以受理。《UCP600》第17条"正本单据与副本"指出:信用证规定的每一种单据须至少提交一份正本;如果信用证使用"in duplicate"、"in two fold"或"in two copies"等用于要求多份单据,则提交至少一份正本,其余使用副本即可满足要求,除非单据本身另有说明。

1.2.3 及时

单证的及时性一是指出单及时;二是指交单及时。

(1) 出口单证工作的时间性很强,每一种单据都有一个适当的出单日期,因此,外贸业务人员需要了解各种单证的出单规定,以便合理安排申领时间,在取得运输单据后尽早备齐全部单据向银行提交。按国际惯例,单据出单日期之间有一定的关系。如提单日期不得迟于装运期限；保险单据不得在装运日期后签发；在 CFR 和 FOB 等交货条件下，必须在装运后立即以要求的方式发送装运通知，以便买方及时办理保险等。

(2) 在及时出单的基础上，单据缮制完成后，要仔细审核单据，确保单证相符，尽早向银行交单，达到及时出单、尽早交单、尽早结汇的目的。因此，制单工作不允许有拖延时间的现象。特别是信用证支付方式下，一般都有在装运货物后限制多少天交单议付的规定，即信用证的交单期（presentation period）。《UCP600》就交单时间的规定在第 6 条 d 款说明：信用证必须规定一个交单的截止日。规定的承付或议付的截止日将被视为交单的截止日。另外，在第 33 条"交单时间"中规定：银行在营业时间外无接受交单的义务。同时在第 29 条"截止日或最迟交单日的顺延"中又规定：如果信用证的截止日或最迟交单日适逢接收交单的银行非营业日，则截止日或最迟交单日将顺延至其重新开业的第一个银行工作日。因此，要注意信用证规定的最后交单的截止日以及该日如果是银行非营业日则不能交单，而应在开业后的第一个营业日提交单据。

1.2.4 简明

单据制作要求简明，是指单证内容应力求简洁、明了，力戒烦琐。《UCP500》第 5 条规定：为了防止混乱和误解，银行应劝阻下列意图：在 L/C 或其任何修改书中罗列过多细节。其目的在于避免单证的复杂化，这样可以减少工作量，提高效率，有利于提高单证的质量。虽然新修订的《UCP600》删除了上面的规定，但是由于各种单据性质和作用不同，所要求的内容各有侧重，《UCP600》从第 18 条到第 28 条用了大量篇幅，对信用证项下主要单据的要求作了明确规定，重点强调单据要与信用证中的描述严格一致。因此，要根据管理规定和实际业务中对单据的制作习惯填写单据中各项内容，描述要简洁、明了。如商业发票重点说明出运货物的品名、规格、价格、数量和包装等货物的详细情况，除信用证特别规定或指明外，其他单据就货物品名而言均可以使用大类或统称。例如，轻工产品中的餐具，有不锈钢餐具、陶瓷餐具之别，又有餐刀、餐叉之分，一般商业发票上需详细列明每一种餐具的具体名称、规格、单价和数量，而提单或保险单等单据上则可以使用统称"TABLEWARES"，这样可以大大减少出口单据的差错，提高单证的质量。

1.2.5 整洁

单证是否整洁、美观，不仅反映单证的外观质量，而且也反映一个国家、一个企业的业务技术水平和熟练程度。

(1) 单证格式的设计和缮制力求标准化和规范化。目前，国际贸易电子化、"无纸贸易"和电子商务发展的要求越来越高，客观上要求各国的单据格式和填制的要求一定要统一、规范。为此，早在 1978 年联合国国际贸易简化程序委员会就出版并向世界发行、推广了《联合国贸易单证设计样式》（U.N. Layout Key for Trade Documents）。目前，我国对外贸易企业的单据格式仍存在不同程度的差异，如商业发票、装箱单、备货通知等，随着国际贸易的发展变化，国际标准化格式正在慢慢取代以往的传统格式，因此，公司只有适应这一变化的需要，逐步使用标准化格式的单据，才能与电子商务新技术的使用相配合。

（2）单据内容的排列要行列整齐，字迹清晰。这是指在具体单据的填写时，必须填写整齐，力求表面的整洁。

（3）尽量减少差错和涂改。单证即使内容上正确无误，但涂改过多，不但不雅观，而且说明制单的水平低。偶有错误，在更改时必须在改正处进行签署或加盖更正章，不能遗漏。对于单据的修改，国际上有一定的规定和习惯做法，不能随意修改。一般的单据如提单最好不要超过三处修改。而一些有特殊要求的单据不能有一字之错，或不能有一处涂改，如普惠制原产地证书表格 A（G.S.P. Form A）和汇票等。

第 2 章

【本章导读】
业务关系的建立及合同的商订
报价及还价核算
合同的履行
业务善后

【学习目标和要点】
通过本章学习，学生应了解国际商品交易中合同履行的一般程序，掌握建交函的撰写，交易磋商的形式、内容和程序，出口报价还价核算，书面合同的内容，业务善后的处理，并对建交及磋商技巧有一定的了解。

国际贸易基本程序与单据流程

2.1 业务关系的建立及合同的商订

在国际贸易中,交易磋商是进行对外经济贸易活动的一个极其重要的环节。一笔交易,无论是进口还是出口,都要经过反复磋商才能做成。然而,在正式磋商前,寻找潜在客户,选择有经营能力,资信良好的客户并与之建立业务关系是极为关键的一步。

2.1.1 寻找潜在客户

企业拓展国际贸易业务,面临的首要问题往往是寻找国外客户。国际贸易中,寻找客户关系的途径方法很多,归纳起来大体有以下类型。

1. 平面媒体

通过报纸杂志发布的供求信息、国内外商会、工商团体等出版的企业名录,以函电或发送资料(产品目录、样本册等)的方式,进行沟通联系。

2. 机构或他人介绍

通过国外的亲戚、朋友或利用银行、各国贸易促进机构(如我国贸促会)和我国驻各国(地区)使领馆、商务处及其他驻外机构的介绍、沟通、联系客户。

3. 国内外交易会和博览会

这种途径的优点是能和客户当面交流,容易迅速达成交易,缺点是花费较大。国内最著名的是广州出口商品交易会;国外的主要有美国芝加哥国际日用品博览会,亚特兰大国际体育用品博览会,加拿大多伦多国际礼品博览会,英国伯明翰国际花园产品及五金工具与休闲用品博览会,德国科隆国际休闲用品及户外家具展览会,意大利马契夫秋季国际贸易博览会,澳大利亚墨尔本国际礼品、家庭用品及纺织服装展览会。

4. 国际互联网

国际互联网具有方便、快捷、经济的特点,网络上信息丰富、时效性强,网络 B2B 市场的规模在逐年扩大,是目前各类企业开发海外客户用得最多的一种方法,是发展的趋势和必然。通过网络,企业可以找到贸易机会,设置企业网页,介绍宣传本企业经营的商品,了解目标市场需求状况、价格水平以及相关政策法规等。

1) 网上信息搜索

常用的搜索引擎有以下几个。

百度(http://www.baidu.com)

Google(http://www.google.com)

中文雅虎(http://cn.yahoo.com)

Excite(http://www.excite.com)

Lycos(http://www.lycos.com)

Infoseek(http://www.infoseek.com)

AltaVista(http://www.altavista.com)

2) 网上宣传推广

企业可以自己建立网站或利用第三方 B2B 平台建立自己的主页,外商可以通过网上搜索找到该企业。如果想获得更好的推广效果,则可通过 BAIDU、YAHOO、GOOGLE 等的搜索排名方式来推广自己的产品,增加自己的贸易机会。

3) 网上搜集客户信息

利用网络可以迅速获取客户的有关信息,并廉价地与他们取得联系。国内外这方面的平台有很多,比较著名的有以下几个。

阿里巴巴 (http://china.alibaba.com)

在线广交会 (http://www.chinamarket.com.cn/web/zh_CN/cecf)

环球资源网 (http://www.globalsources.com)

欧洲之页 (http://www.europages.com)

德国商业网 (http://www.german-business.de)

加拿大黄页 (http://www.yellowpages.ca)

美国大黄页 (http://www.superpages.com)

Tradeindia (http://www.tradeindia.com)

Tradekey (http://www.tradekey.com)——在欧美和中东的影响力很大

上述平台有官方的,也有民间的,若要享有全部增值服务,需申请注册交费成为正式会员,然后再与客户直接取得联系。企业应本着最小投资获得最大收益的原则,选取那些知名度高、注册会员多、规模大的第三方平台。

4) 国际贸易常用信息查询网站

国际贸易常用信息查询网站有以下几个。

中华人民共和国商务部 (http://www.mofcom.gov.cn)

中国国际电子商务网 (http://www.ec.com.cn)

海关税则、编码、税率查询 (http://www.china-customs.com/customs-tax)

【案例】

河北恒泰进出口贸易公司是一家主营家用棉纺织品的外贸公司,其客户遍布欧美和中东地区,年出口额达500多万美元,该公司有自己的设计部门,并能按照客户的要求进行设计生产。现公司想进一步开拓美国市场,给新来的大学生杨光分配任务,从互联网上查询有关全棉毛巾的国外购买信息,并与国外客户进行沟通、联系。

(1) 登录阿里巴巴中文网主页,单击上方"出口服务"链接(见图2-1)。

图2-1 阿里巴巴中文网主页

(2) 进入出口服务首页后，在搜索栏选择要查询的国家和地区，输入查询英文关键字"TOWEL"，单击"查询海外买家"按钮（见图 2-2）。

图 2-2　阿里巴巴出口服务首页

(3) 进入查询海外买家首页后，是查询结果列表（见图 2-3）。当然，我们也可按阿里巴巴提供的搜索条件缩小搜索范围。点击查询结果，就可以看到客户具体的需求信息（见图 2-4）。

图 2-3　查询海外买家首页

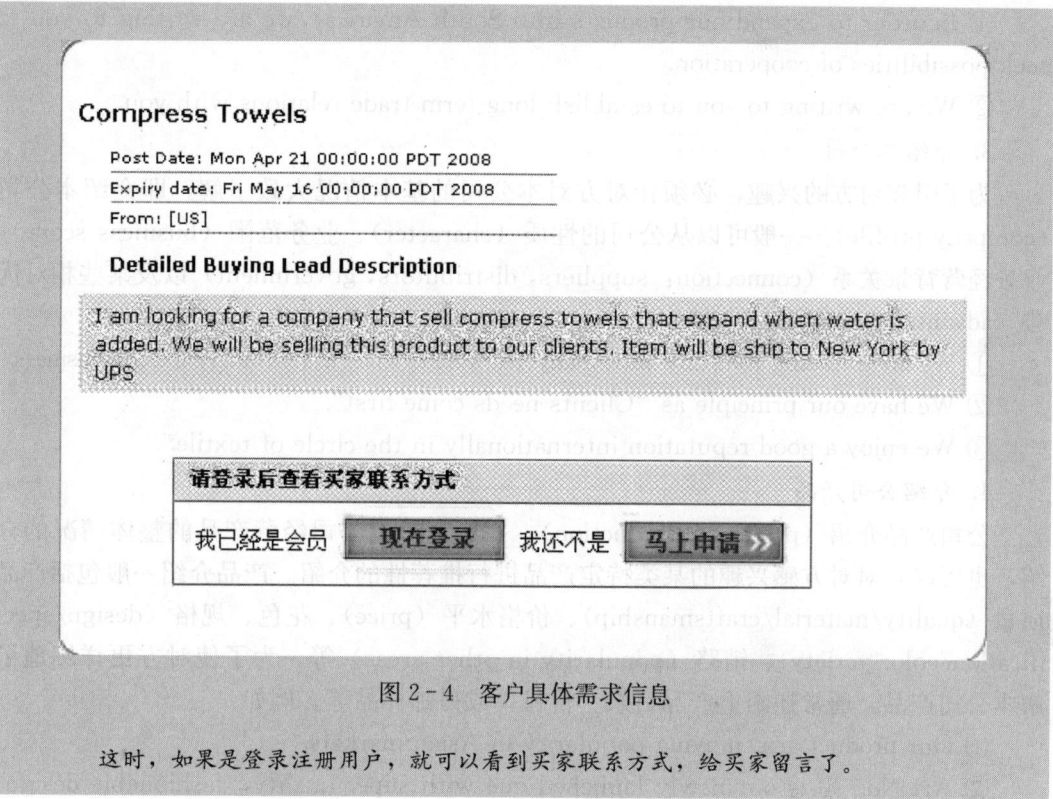

图 2-4　客户具体需求信息

这时，如果是登录注册用户，就可以看到买家联系方式，给买家留言了。

2.1.2　撰写建交函

建立业务关系通常是从进出口商的一方主动向潜在的客户发出信件、传真或 E-mail 开始，撰写建立业务联系的信函是每个外贸业务人员必须掌握的操作技能。一般来说，一份标准规范的建交函应包括以下内容。

1. 信息来源

信息来源（source of information）就是要说明你是如何取得对方资料的。由于是首次主动与对方进行交往，说明信息来源非常必要。作为进出口商，贸易信息来源的渠道很多，主要有通过驻外商务参赞（The Commercial Counselor's Office of the Embassy in foreign country）、商会、银行（bank/chamber of commerce/trade Union）、第三家公司介绍（common clients）、市场调查（market research）、互联网获悉（Internet），或在交易会（trade fair, exhibitions）上结识等。例如：

① We learned from the commercial counselor's office in your country that you are interested in Chinese handicraft.

② We have obtained your name and address from the Internet.

2. 说明致函目的

说明致函目的（purpose of writing），一般来说，建交函都是以扩大交易或地区（expanding market）、建立长期业务关系（to establish long-term relationship）为目的的。例如：

① In order to expand our products into South America, we are writing to you to seek possibilities of cooperation.

② We are writing to you to establish long-term trade relations with you.

3. 介绍本公司

为了引起对方的兴趣，必须让对方对本公司的基本情况大致了解，即介绍本公司（company profile）。一般可以从公司的性质（character）、业务范围（business scope）、业务经营背景关系（connection：suppliers，distributors，government）以及某些相对优势（advantages）。例如：

① We are a leading company with many years experience in machinery export business.

② We have our principle as "Clients needs come first".

③ We enjoy a good reputation internationally in the circle of textile.

4. 介绍公司产品

公司产品介绍（product introduction），一般是对本公司经营产品的整体情况的介绍，也可以是对对方感兴趣的某类特定产品进行推荐性的介绍。产品介绍一般包括产品质量（quality/material/craftsmanship）、价格水平（price）、花色、规格（design/specification/color variety）、销路（popularity in other areas）等。为了使对方更详细地了解本公司产品，通常还附上产品目录、价目单或另邮样品等。例如：

① Our product are enjoying popularity in Asian markets.

② Art No. 90 is our newly launched one with super quality, fashionable design, and competitive price.

③ To give you a general idea of our products, we are enclosing our catalogue for your reference.

5. 激励性结尾

激励性结尾（a pushing end），包括盼对方尽快回音、下订单或告知意见并表示敬意等语句。例如：

① We are looking forward to your specific inquires.

② Your comments on our products or any information on your market demand will be really appreciated.

③ Your early reply will be really appreciated.

【案例】

恒泰公司业务员杨光看到阿里巴巴提供的美国 PACIFIC INTERNATIONAL INC. 毛巾求购广告后，开始着手撰写建交函。下面是杨光所在公司有关情况介绍。

河北恒泰进出口贸易公司是一家国营外贸企业，主要经营各类纺织品进出口业务，产品行销东南亚、欧洲、美国市场，全棉毛巾是公司的主要出口产品之一，公司拥有经验丰富的各类型专业人员，货源及质量稳定可靠。公司在国际市场上竭诚地寻求合作机会，并愿意按照互利互惠、共同发展的原则同世界各地的客商进行业务往来。近年来，随着公司内部管理体制的改革及外贸业务的高速发展，公司已经取得了巨大的成绩。

根据上述资料拟写的建交函如下。

Dear Sir or Madam,

We learned from the Internet that you are in the market for towels, which just fall in to our business scope. We are writing to enter into business relations with you on a basis of mutual benefits and common developments.

We are a state-owned foreign trade enterprise, deals in the export of textiles. We have a home textiles department, which specialize in the export of various kinds of towels made in China of fashionable designs, comfortable feeling, and high popularity in America, Europe and Asia. We have established close business relationship with many manufacturers so that the stable supplies, the quality guarantee as well as the flexible ways of doing business can be reached.

If you need, we can send you our catalogue for towels now available for our regular export. We can also produce according to your designated styles.

It will be a great pleasure to receive your inquiries against which we will send you our best quotations.

Yours faithfully
Hebei HengTai Import & Export Corporation
Yang Guang

2.1.3 磋商签约

建立业务关系后,双方需就有关具体交易条件进行磋商。交易磋商的好坏,直接影响到合同的签订及履行,关系到买卖双方各自权利、义务和经济利益。

交易磋商的形式有口头和书面两种,书面磋商主要是通过进出口贸易英语函电,如电报、电传、传真、电子邮件等进行;磋商内容涉及买卖合同各项条款,包括品名、品质、数量、包装、价格、装运、支付、保险以及商品检验、索赔、仲裁和不可抗力等;磋商过程就是询盘、发盘、还盘、接受(其中发盘和接受是必经的两个环节),直至最终达成交易,签订合同。

1. 询盘

交易磋商往往从询盘开始,询盘(Enquiry)是指交易一方意欲购买或出售某一商品,向对方探询买卖该商品的有关交易条件的口头或书面意思表示。实际业务中,询盘常被交易一方用来试探对方对交易的诚意,询问价格以及其他交易条件,在法律上对询盘人和被询盘人都没有约束力,也并非交易磋商的必经步骤。外贸询盘函的主要内容大致包括以下几个方面。

(1) 起首:包括信息来源、自我介绍、感谢对方来函等。例如:

① We have seen your advertisement in the New Asia Journal and are particularly interested in...

② We are a leading dealer in waterproof garments in this city.

③ We are pleased to receive your fax of …

(2) 解释去函目的，提出感兴趣的商品，并索取有关资料。例如：

① We'd like to know what you can offer as well as your sales conditions.

② We take an interest in various kinds of Men's shirts.

③ Our customers have expressed interest in your raincoats and enquired about their quality.

④ It will give us much pleasure if you could send us the catalogues asked for in your letter last time.

(3) 要求报价：可笼统提出报价要求，也可根据给出的价格条件或成交数量要求报价。例如：

① Please let us know your lowest possible prices for the relevant goods.

② If your prices are favorable, I can place the order right away…

③ We shall appreciate it if you could make us the best offer for 500 tons of Walnuts on CIF New York basis.

④ We have to point out that we intend to place a large order with you if your price is competitive.

(4) 询问其他交易条件。例如：

① Could you make prompt delivery?

② Will you please tell us the earliest possible date you can make shipment?

③ Could you tell me which kind of payment terms you will accept?

2. 发盘

发盘（Offer）是交易一方（发盘人）向另一方（受盘人）提出各项交易条件并愿意按这些条件与受盘人达成交易、订立合同的口头或书面意思表示。发盘是交易磋商必经的法律步骤。发盘可以由交易一方在收到另一方询盘后发出，也可直接向对方主动提出。发盘内容必须明确无误，无含糊之词，其语气则需诚恳、委婉，并且有说服力，以赢得客户信任，最终取得订单。外贸发盘函一般由以下内容构成。

(1) 确认并感谢对方来函 (acknowledgement of inquiry)。例如：

① We are very pleased to receive your letter of 5th April answering our advertisement for…

② We've received your letter of May 9th, and as requested, we are offering you the following subject to our final confirmation.

③ Thank you for your letter of 10th March. We are gratified to receive your request for men and women's raincoat on approval.

(2) 准确阐明各项交易条件 (main trade terms)。明确答复品名、规格、价格、数量、包装、付款方式、装运、保险等条件，以供对方参考。例如：

① We are making you an offer for 500 Doz Men's Shirts at USD100 per Doz CIFC5 London for shipment in May.

② For the Fancy Brand AGT-4 Garment Sewing Machine, the best price is USD78.00 per set FOB Shanghai.

③ Our usual terms of payment are by confirmed irrevocable L/C available by draft at sight.

④ All these blankets are packed in plastic bags, 20 pieces to a carton.

（3）声明发盘的有效期或约束条件。例如：

① This offer is valid for ten days.

② For acceptance within two weeks.

③ This quotation is effective while stocks last.

④ This offer is subject to our final confirmation.

（4）鼓励对方早日订货。例如：

① As we have been receiving a rush of orders now, we would advise you to place your order as soon as possible.

② We hope you will agree that our prices are very competitive for these good quality clothes, and we look forward to receiving your initial order.

③ This favorite offer will not be repeated for some time, and we accordingly look forward to an early order from you.

3. 还盘

还盘（Counter Offer）是指受盘人在接到发盘后，不同意或不完全同意发盘人在发盘中提出的条件，为进一步磋商交易对发盘提出修改意见。还盘可以用口头或书面方式表示。从法律性质上说，还盘是一项新的发盘，原发盘一经还盘即告失效，原发盘人可不再受原发盘的约束。还盘虽然不是交易磋商必经环节，但实际业务中，很少有一方发盘即被对方无条件全部接受的情况。有时，一项交易须经过还盘、再还盘等多次反复，才能做成。

1）还盘的主要内容

（1）告知对方发盘收悉，并感谢对方发盘。例如：

① Thank you for your fax offer of March 20th for 2 000 Doz Men's Shirts.

② We are in receipt of your letter of May 9th offering us 100 tons of...

（2）说明对发盘的态度，指出变更的内容及理由（通常是抱怨价格太高）。例如：

① We regret to inform you that your price is rather on the high side though we appreciate the good quality of your products.

② We have received offers recently, most of which are below 100 US dollars.

③ Your price compares much higher than that we can get from elsewhere.

（3）提出还盘建议，给出新的交易条件，并希望对方让步。例如：

① We can't accept your offer unless the price is reduced by 5%.

② To step up trade, we counter-offer as follows: 500 tons of Walnuts at USD 900/ton CIF EMP.

③ Please extend your offer for two days further.

（4）鼓励性结尾。例如：

We wish you would seriously take this matter into consideration and let us have your favorable reply.

2) 再还盘的主要内容

(1) 对对方的还盘表示感谢，表明是否接受。例如：

① Thank for your E-mail of July 5th. We regret to say that we cannot accept your counter offer.

② Thank for your E-mail of July 5th. We think your counter offer is difficult for us to accept.

(2) 强调原发盘条件的合理性，并列举理由。如由于原料价格上涨，或工厂成本上升造成出口成本提高；强调本公司报价只含最少利润；请对方调查目前的市价等。例如：

① Our offer is reasonable and realistic. It comes in line with the prevailing market.

② Although costs have been rising since March, we have not yet raised our prices, but may have to do so when present stocks run out. We therefore advise you to place your order with us at once.

③ This offer is competitive and based on an expanding market.

④ We believe our prices are quite realistic, it is impossible that any other suppliers can quote lower than us if their products are as good as ours in quality.

⑤ Although we are desirous of meeting your requirements, we regret being unable to comply with your request for price reduction. The price we quoted is accurately calculated. We have cut our profit to the minimum.

(3) 作出让步姿态，进一步提出新的条件，并催促对方早日下订单。如由于期望与对方建立业务关系，故若对方的订单超过多少数量或多少金额，将给对方多少折扣；或提出其他条件上有所变化；或推荐一些其他替代品，以寻求新的商机。例如：

① Still, I think it unwise for either of us to insist on his own price.

② In order to assist you to compete with dealers in the market, we have decided to reduce 2% of the previous letter, if your order reaches 5 000 sets at one time.

③ I'll respond to your counter-offer by reducing our price by three dollars.

④ In view of our future business, we accept the payment half by D/P and half by L/C.

(4) 鼓励对方接受新的条件，及早订货。例如：

① My offer was based on reasonable profit, not on wild speculations, and look forward to your reply.

② Please note this is the best we can do and we hope you will accept it.

③ We sincerely hope this will be the beginning of a long and pleasant business association. We shall do our best to make it so.

4. 接受、成交签约

经过若干回合的反复磋商后，双方同意就各项交易条件达成一致，并愿意与对方达成交易、订立合同，即进入交易磋商的最后阶段——接受和成交签约（Acceptance, Conclusion of Business and Sign the Contract）阶段。

1) 接受

接受是指买方和卖方同意对方在发盘中提出的各项交易条件，并愿按这些条件与对方达成交易、订立合同的一种肯定的表示。接受是交易磋商必经环节，一方发盘经另一方接受,合同关系即告成立,此后,双方应分别履行其所承担的合同义务。如果是由我方表示接受,应慎重地对洽商的函电或谈判记录进行认真核对,经核对认为对方提出的各项交易条件确已明确、肯定、无保留条件时,再予接受;接受可以简单表示,例如:"你10日电接受",也可详细表示,即将洽商的主要交易条件再重述一下,表示接受。表示接受应在对方报价规定的有效期之内进行。

2) 会签函

在我国,出口合同一般由出口商寄送进口商会签,此时,往往随附一份短信,即会签函,其内容主要是告知对方发盘(还盘)条件可接受,销售合同已经寄出,希望对方予以签字。有时,也可附带要求买方尽快履行开证义务等。例如:

① We are glad that through our mutual effort finally we have reached the agreement.

② We believe the first transaction will turn out to be profitable to both of us.

③ We are sending you Sales Confirmation No. 990123 in duplicate. Please sign it and return one copy for our file.

④ It is understood that a letter of credit in our favor covering the above mentioned goods will be established promptly.

⑤ Please instruct your banker to issue the letter of credit as early as possible in order that we may process with the goods immediately.

3) 缮制出口合同

虽然口头表示接受在法律上是有效力的,但在出口业务中,签署一份书面合同是非常有必要的。合同是买卖双方经过反复磋商达成交易条件的书面证明,是进出口贸易中最重要的文件之一。合同需根据磋商确定的各项交易条件缮制,合同条款包括品名、品质(规格)、数量、包装、单价、装运、支付、保险、商品检验、索赔、仲裁、不可抗力等。

【相关单证】

单证 1-1 销售合同

销 售 合 同
SALES CONTRACT

卖方
SELLER:

编号 NO.:
日期 DATE:
地点 SIGNED IN:

买方
BUYER:

买卖双方同意以下条款达成交易:

This contract is made by and agreed between the BUYER and SELLER, in accordance with the terms and conditions stipulated below.

1. 商品号 Art No.	2. 品名及规格 Commodity & Specification	3. 数量 Quantity	4. 单价及价格条款 Unit Price & Trade Terms	5. 金额 Amount

允许　　溢短装，由卖方决定
With　　More or less of shipment allowed at the sellers' option

6. 总值
Total Value

7. 包装
Packing

8. 唛头
Shipping Marks

9. 装运期及运输方式
Time of Shipment & means of Transportation

10. 装运港及目的地
Port of Loading & Destination

11. 保险
Insurance

12. 付款方式
Terms of Payment

13. 备注
Remarks

The Buyer　　　　　　　　　　　　　　The Seller

【案例】

1. 询盘

河北恒泰公司业务员杨光发出建交函后，很快收到了美国 PACIFIC INTERNATIONAL INC. 的询盘。

PACIFIC INTERNATIONAL INC.
129 HAYWARD WAY STREET, MONTE, CA 91513
TEL: 1-213-2891024　　FAX: 1-213-2891025

TO: HEBEI HENGTAI IMPORT & EXPORT CORPORATION
FM: PACIFIC INTERNATIONAL INC.
DT: April 23th, 2008

Dear Mr. Yang,

Thank you for your interest in our advertisement in Alibaba. We are importers of textiles and manufactured cotton goods. We have recently conclude some satisfactory business with Chinese company and therefor write to you in the hope of establishing business relations.

From your letter, we notice that you are able to supply home textiles. We now have a good demand for 4 000 Doz 100% cotton stripe towel. We should be grateful if you would kindly send us some samples of the above mentioned goods which you can supply together with a comprehensive price list giving details of packing, specification and the time of shipment so as to enable us to go fully into the possibilities of business. We look forward to your early news and trust that through our mutual cooperation we shall be able to conclude some transactions with you in the near feature.

Yours truly
PACIFIC INTERNATIONAL INC.
Paul Smith

2. 发盘

杨光没想到新结识的美国客户这么快就有了回复,立即着手准备有关资料,确定报价,索取有关样品后,于4月25日发盘,并建议客户增加订货数量为4 500打以便凑成一整20'集装箱。

HEBEI HENGTAI IMPORT&EXPORT CORPORATION
NO. 231 HEPING ROAD, SHIJIAZHUANG, HEBEI, CHINA
TEL: 86-0311-84576936　　FAX: 86-0311-84576937

TO: PACIFIC INTERNATIONAL INC.
FM: HEBEI HENGTAI IMPORT&EXPORT CORPORATION
DT: April 25th, 2008
Dear Sirs,

We are very pleased to receive your enquiry of April 23rd and enclose our price list giving the details you ask for. Also by separate post we are sending you some samples and feel confident that when you have examined you will agree that the goods are both excellent in quality and reasonable in price.

Because of their softness and durability, our products are rapidly selling in overseas market because of their reasonable price, which will meet your demand also.

If possible, please increase the quantities to 4 500 Doz so that we can put them in a container of 20'.

We look forward very much to the pleasure of receiving an order from you.

Yours sincerely
HEBEI HENGTAI IMPORT&EXPORT CORPORATION
Yang Guang

3. 还盘

数日后,美国 PACIFIC INTERNATIONAL INC. 收到恒泰公司的样品和报价单后,给出了还盘函。

PACIFIC INTERNATIONAL INC.
129 HAYWARD WAY STREET, MONTE, CA 91513
TEL: 1-213-2891024　　FAX: 1-213-2891025

TO: HEBEI HENGTAI IMPORT&EXPORT CORPORATION
FM: PACIFIC INTERNATIONAL INC.
DT: May 9th, 2008
Dear Mr. Yang,

Thank you for your quotation and samples you kindly sent us dated April 25th, 2008.

Firstly, We think it is acceptable to increase the quantities to 4 500 Doz in a container of 20'. But after careful examining and comparison with other similar products, we found that your price is higher than the average in the market. In order to allow us a better competing position, we shall be grateful if you could reduce the price to USD 4.6 per Doz CIF Los Angeles. Moreover, we advise you to make some adjustment of your terms of payment L/C to D/P at sight and that the time of shipment should be on or before the end of August, 2008.

We hope we can enter into a lasting business relationship with you and look forward to receiving your reply.

Yours Faithfully
PACIFIC INTERNATIONAL INC.
Paul Smith

4. 再还盘

杨光认真研究了美国 PACIFIC INTERNATIONAL INC. 的降价等建议，经过与公司经理和有关加工厂协商以及市场调查后，认为由于棉花等原材料价格上涨，已没有多少降价余地，但考虑到首次合作因素，同意适当降价，对于新开发客户，我方仍坚持即期L/C的结算方式，收到信用证后2个月内发货。

HEBEI HENGTAI IMPORT&EXPORT CORPORATION
NO. 231 HEPING ROAD, SHIJIAZHUANG, HEBEI, CHINA
TEL: 86-0311-84576936   FAX: 86-0311-84576937

TO: PACIFIC INTERNATIONAL INC.
FM: HEBEI HENGTAI IMPORT&EXPORT CORPORATION
DT: May 12th, 2008
Dear Mr. Smith,
We have received your letter of May 9th, 2008.

We would like to inform you that your price are not appropriate to us, and we always sell these items at the prices we quoted in your country. As you know, wages and materials have risen considerably these days. We are compelled to adjust our prices to cover the increasing cost. USD 5.0 per Doz is our lowest level, which leaves us with only the smallest profit. But considerable the first order between us, we are willing to bring down our price to USD 4.9 per Doz.

Although we have confidence in your integrity, our usual terms of payment by sight L/C remain unchanged in all cases with new clients. So for the time being, we regret our inability to accept your D/P terms. Maybe after several smooth and satisfactory transactions, we can consider other flexible ways.

The time of shipment should be effected within 2 months from receipt of the relevant L/C.

For your information, the demand for our products has been extremely great recently. This offer is valid for 5 days and we looking forward to receiving your order at the earliest date.
Yours sincerely
HEBEI HENGTAI IMPORT&EXPORT CORPORATION
Yang Guang

5. 接受、成交签约

美国 PACIFIC INTERNATIONAL INC. 收到杨光的回函后，于5月16日表示接受，17日，杨光回函确认，并要求对方尽快开立信用证。

HEBEI HENGTAI IMPORT&EXPORT CORPORATION
NO. 231 HEPING ROAD, SHIJIAZHUANG, HEBEI, CHINA
TEL: 86-0311-84576936   FAX: 86-0311-84576937

TO: PACIFIC INTERNATIONAL INC.
FM: HEBEI HENGTAI IMPORT&EXPORT CORPORATION
DT: May 17th, 2008

Dear Mr. Smith,

Thank you for your kind of acceptance dated May 16th, 2008.

Enclosed are two copies of your Sales Confirmation No. 02AG18185. Please sign and return one copy for our file.

It is understood that the relevant L/C in our favor should be issued not later than 60 days before the stipulated time of shipment. We suppose the conclusion of this transaction will lead to more business in future.

We appreciate your cooperation and look forward to receiving your further orders.

Yours sincerely
HEBEI HENGTAI IMPORT&EXPORT CORPORATION
Yang Guang
Enclosures:

销 售 合 同
SALES CONTRACT

合同号码：
Contract No.: 02AG18185
日期：
Date: JUN. 20, 2008

卖方：   电话：
The Sellers: HEBEI HENGTAI IMPORT&EXPORT CORPORATION   TEL: 86-0311-84576936
地址：   传真：
Address: NO. 231 HEPING ROAD, SHIJIAZHUANG, HEBEI, CHINA   FAX: 86-0311-84576937

买方：   电话：
The Buyers: PACIFIC INTERNATIONAL INC.   TEL: 1-213-2891024
地址：   传真：
Address: 129 HAYWARD WAY STREET, MONTE, CA 91513   FAX: 1-213-2891025

兹经买卖双方同意，由买方购进，卖方出售下列货物，并按下列条款签订本合同：
This Contract is made by and between the Buyers and the Sellers; whereby the Buyers agree to buy and the Sellers agree to sell the undermentioned goods on the terms and conditions stated below:

(1) 货物名称、规格 Name of Commodity, Specifications	(2) 数量 Quantity	(3) 单价 Unit Price	(4) 总值 Amount
100% COTTON STRIPE TOWEL ART NO. ABC69 SIZE: 30″×60″	4 500 DOZS	CIF LOS ANGELES USD 4.90/DOZ	USD22 050.00
5% more or less both in amount and quantity allowed		Total Amount	USD22 050.00

合同总额 Total Contract Value:
SAY U.S. DOLLARS TWENTY TWO THOUSAND AND FIFTY ONLY

(5) 包装:
Packing Terms: To be packed in bale. One dozen to a polybag, 20 dozens in a bale

(6) 装运口岸:
Port of Loading: CHINESE PORT

(7) 目的口岸:
Port of Destination: LOS ANGELES PORT, USA

(8) 唛头:
Shipping Marks: PACIFIC
　　　　　　　　18185
　　　　　　　　LOS ANGELES
　　　　　　　　1-225

(9) 装运期限:
Time of Shipment: Not later than AUG. 31, 2008, allowing transshipment and partial shipment

(10) 付款条件:
Terms of Payment: The Buyer shall open through a bank acceptable to the seller an irrevocable Letter of Credit at sight to reach the seller 20 days before the month of shipment valid for negotiation in China until the 15th day after the date of shipment.

(11) 保险:
Insurance: The Seller shall cover insurance against All Risks and War Risk for 110% of invoice value as per Ocean Marine Cargo Clause of the People's Insurance Company of China dated 1/1/1981.

(12) 单据:
Documents:
议付时卖方应提交如下单据:
The Seller shall present the following documents to the bank for negotiation:

① Manually signed commercial invoice in triplicate certifying the origin of goods and contents to be true and correct.

② Full set of clean on board ocean bills of lading made out to order and blank endorsed and marked "Freight Prepaid" and notify applicant showing contract No. and this credit No..

③ Packing list in triplicate indicating quantity/gross and net weight of each package and packing conditions as called for by the L/C.

④ Manually signed certificate of China origin in triplicate issued by authority institution.

(13) 装运通知:
Advice of Shipment: The Sellers shall upon competition of loading, advise immediately the Buyers by cable of the contract number, name of commodity, number of packages, gross and net weights,

invoice value, name of vessel and loading date.

(14) 品质/数量异议：如买方提出索赔，凡属品质异议须于货到目的口岸之日起 30 天内提出，凡属数量异议须于货到目的口岸之日起 15 天内提出，对所装货物所提任何异议于保险公司、轮船公司、其他有关运输机构或邮递机构所负责者，卖方不负任何责任。

Quality/Quantity Discrepancy: In case of quality discrepancy, claim should be filed by the Buyer within 30 days after the arrival of the goods at port of destination, while for quantity discrepancy, claim should be filed by the Buyer within 15 days after the arrival of the goods at port of destination. It is understood that the Seller shall not be liable for any discrepancy of the goods shipped due to causes for which the Insurance Company, Shipping Company, other Transportation Organization /or Post Office are liable.

(15) 不可抗力：由于人力不可抗拒事故，使卖方不能在合同规定期限内交货或者不能交货，卖方不负责任。但卖方必须立即通知买方，并以挂号函向买方提出有关政府机关或者商会所出具的证明，以证明事故的存在。由于人力不可抗拒事故致使交货期限延期一个月以上时，买方有权撤销合同。卖方不能取得出口许可证不得作为不可抗力。

Force Majeure: In case of Force Majeure the Sellers shall not held responsible for delay in delivery or non-delivery of the goods but shall notify immediately the Buyers and deliver to the Buyers by registered mail a certificate issued by government authorities or Chamber of Commerce as evidence thereof. If the shipment is delayed over one month as the consequence of the said Force Majeure, the Buyers shall have the right to cancel this Contract. Sellers' inability in obtaining export licence shall not be considered as Force Majeure.

(16) 延期交货及罚款：除本合同第（15）条人力不可抗拒原因外，如卖方不能如期交货，买方有权撤销该部分的合同，或经买方同意在卖方缴纳罚款的条件下延期交货。买方可同意给予卖方 15 天优惠期，罚款率为每 10 天按货款总额的 1%，不足 10 天者按 10 天计算。罚款自第 16 天起计算。最多不超过延期货款总额的 5%。

Delayed Delivery and Penalty: Should the Sellers fail to effect delivery on time as stipulated in this Contract owing to causes other than Force Majeure as provided for in Clause (15) of this Contract, the Buyers shall have the right to cancel the relative quantity of the contract, or alternatively, the Sellers may, with the Buyers' consent, postpone delivery on payment of penalty to the Buyers. The Buyers may agree to grant the Sellers a grace period of 15 days. Penalty shall be charged at the rate of 1% of the total value for every 10 days, odd days less than 10 days should be counted 10 days. The total penalty shall be calculated from the 16th day and shall not exceed 5% of the total value of the goods involved.

(17) 仲裁：一切因执行本合同或与本合同有关的争执，应由双方通过友好方式协商解决。如经协商不能得到解决时，应提交北京中国国际贸易促进委员会对外经济贸易仲裁委员会。按照中国国际贸易促进委员会对外经济贸易仲裁委员会仲裁程序暂行规定进行仲裁。仲裁委员会的裁决为终局裁决，对双方均有约束力。仲裁费用除非仲裁委员会另有决定外，由败诉一方负担。

Arbitration: All disputes in connection with this Contract or the execution thereof shall be friendly negotiation. If no settlement can be reached, the case in dispute shall then be submitted for arbitration to the Foreign Economic and Trade Arbitration Commission of the China Council for the Promotion of International Trade in accordance with the Provisional Rules of Procedure of the Foreign Economic and Trade Arbitration Commission of the China Council for the Promotion of International Trade. The Award made by the Commission shall be accepted as final and binding upon both parties. The fees for arbitration shall be borne by the losing party unless otherwise awarded by the Commission.

买方	卖方
The Buyers	The Sellers

【技能实训】

1. 请根据以下资料撰写发盘、还盘函电

河北东方轻工业品进出口公司（石家庄和平西路198号，邮政编码050000）在接到美国太平洋国际贸易有限公司（PACIFIC INTERNATIONAL INC.，129 HAYWARD WAY STREET, MONTE, CA 91513）2008年1月初的询盘后，1月15日做出发盘：

货号TS01瓷器的CIF洛杉矶价为20.50美元；

货号TS02瓷器的CIF洛杉矶价为29.99美元；

付款方式：不可撤销、保兑、可转让即期信用证支付；

装运期：收到相关信用证后45天装运；

报盘有效期10天。

应美国公司要求，随附销售说明书、插图目录。

5天后，美国公司发来电子邮件，表明中方价格偏高，还价为货号TS01瓷器的CIF洛杉矶价为19.35美元，货号TS02瓷器的CIF洛杉矶价为25.50美元，并要求以付款交单的方式付款。

1月25日，中方拒绝美方的还价，强调中国瓷器质量上乘，在世界市场上享有盛誉。但为开发市场，同意给予特别报价：货号TS01瓷器的CIF洛杉矶价为20.00美元，货号TS02瓷器的CIF洛杉矶价为28.50美元，但坚持以信用证付款。

请根据上述信息撰写发盘函、还盘函、反还盘函。

2. 根据以下资料填写合同

河北粮油进出口公司经过多次交易磋商，2008年1月12日，与加拿大NIVADA TRADING CO., LTD.（Address：#389 JALAN STREET, TORONTO, CANADA；Tel No.：01-7787910；Fax No.：01-7789910）签约，合同编号为SC20080112。合同标的：36 000公吨中国花生，允许数量、金额溢短装10%，规格为长粒大米，碎粒（BROKEN GRAINS）不超过35%，水分（MOISURE）不超过15%，含油量（OIL CONTENT）不低于45%。双方商定的交易条件如下：

Unit Price：FOB天津，以毛作净（GROSS FOR NET）每吨300美元。

Shipment：2008年3月、4月、5月分三批等量交货，自中国天津经中国香港运至加拿大多伦多。

Payment：按发票总额以保兑的不可撤销的信用证支付，凭即期汇票付款，在中国议付有效期为装运期后第15天，信用证不迟于2008年2月15日开抵卖方。

Packing：单层新麻袋（GUNNY）包装，每袋约50千克。

Shipping Marks：由卖方决定。

Insurance：由买方安排投保。

根据以上内容，为河北粮油进出口公司填制出口销售合同。

2.2 报价及还价核算

交易磋商环节，价格往往是核心，价格的高低，直接关系到交易磋商的成败和买卖双方的利益，因此，准确合理地核算出口价格是外贸业务人员必须掌握的一项基本技能。

2.2.1 出口报价

《联合国国际销售合同公约》规定，一项有效的发盘至少要包括品名、价格和数量3项基本条件。在发盘中，一个完整的出口报价由4部分表示，缺一不可，即计量单位、单位价格金额、计价货币和贸易术语。例如：

$$\underset{①}{\text{大米}} \quad \underset{②}{\underline{\text{每公吨}}} \quad \underset{③}{\underline{350}} \quad \underset{④}{\underline{\text{美元}}} \quad \underset{}{\underline{\text{CIF 香港}}}$$

核算商品报价应首先明确报出的价格是由哪些部分组成的，然后了解各组成部分的计算方法，最后才能得出合理准确的报价。出口价格的构成包括三大要素：商品成本、费用和预期利润。

1. 成本

成本（cost）是出口商品价格的核心，包括生产成本、加工成本和采购成本。生产成本也称产品的出厂价格，是指制造企业生产某一产品所需的成本；加工成本是指加工企业对原辅材料进行加工所需的成本；采购成本是指贸易商向制造商、加工商采购出口商品所需的成本。

进出口公司采购国内出口商品的成本一般表现为含税价格，即包含增值税在内，生产厂家向出口公司提供增值税发票（见图 2-5），产品出口后，国家再按退税税率向出口公司退税。因此，在对外报价核算出口商品实际成本时，应考虑退税因素，扣除出口退税额。

上海增值税专用发票

3100961141　　　　发　票　联　　　　　　No.

开票日期：　年　月　日

购货单位	名称		税务登记号	
	地址、电话		开户银行及账号	

货物或应税劳务名称	规格型号	计量单位	数量	单价	金额 万千百十元角分	税率/%	税额 万千百十元角分
合　计							

价税合计	拾　万　仟　佰　拾　元　角　分　RMB————
备　注	

销货单位	名称		税务登记号	
	地址、电话		开户银行及账号	

销货单位（章）：　　收款人：_____　　复核：_____　　开票人：_____

图 2-5　增值税发票

成本计算公式为

采购成本＝含税成本(发票金额)＝不含税成本＋增值税额＝不含税成本×(1＋增值税税率)

增值税额＝不含税成本×增值税税率(取 17％)

$$\text{不含税成本} = \frac{\text{含税成本}}{1 + \text{增值税税率}}$$

$$出口退税收入=不含税成本\times 退税税率=\frac{含税成本}{1+增值税税率}\times 退税税率$$

$$出口商品实际成本=含税成本-出口退税收入=含税成本-\frac{含税成本\times 退税税率}{1+增值税税率}$$

$$=\frac{含税成本\times (1+增值税税率-退税税率)}{1+增值税税率}$$

例 2-1 某产品购货成本是 90 元人民币（含 17% 增值税），若该产品出口有 10% 的退税，则该产品每单位的实际成本为多少？

解 该产品每单位的实际成本 $=\dfrac{含税成本\times (1+增值税率-出口退税税率)}{1+增值税税率}$

$=\dfrac{90\times (1+17\%-10\%)}{1+17\%}=82.31$ 元人民币/单位

2. 费用

出口业务中发生的费用（expenses）比一般国内贸易要复杂得多，主要有国内费用和国外费用两部分。国内费用是指卖方将货物装上出口运输工具前所发生的一切费用，包括包装费、仓储费、国内运输费、认证费（许可证、产地证）、港区港杂费、商检报关费、捐税、垫款利息、银行费用、业务费用和其他费用等；国外费用是指装运港至目的港的运输费用、保险费用和客户佣金。

需要注意的是，如果是 FOB 价格，只需核算国内费用和客户佣金即可；如果是 CFR 价格，还需核算国外运费和佣金；如果是 CIF 价格，则需要核算国外运费、保险费和佣金。

1) 出口运费的计算

我国出口货物大部分都采用海洋运输，海洋运费的计算比较复杂，计费方式主要有以下两种。

(1) 件杂货物（散货）运费。即按货物的运费吨（F）（体积吨（M）、重量吨（W））核算基本运费，再加一定的附加费。计算公式为

班轮运费 = 基本运费 + 附加运费 = 基本运费 × 运费吨 × (1 + 各种附加费率之和)

计算步骤如下：

① 根据货物名称，在运价表的货物分级表查到货物的等级（CLASS）和运费计算标准（BASIS）；

② 根据货物的装运港、目的港，找到相应的航线，按货物的等级查到基本运价；

③ 查出该航线和港口所要收取的附加费项目和数额（或百分比）及货币种类；

④ 根据基本运价和附加费算出实际运价（单位运价）；

⑤ 根据货物的托运数量算出应付运费总额。

(2) 集装箱运费。集装箱货物可分为拼箱货物（LCL）和整箱货物（FCL），若为拼箱货物，应先算出所装箱的确切数量，再按上述件杂货的计算方法查表计算运费；若为整箱货物，直接按包厢费率（Box Rate）计算即可。计算公式为

集装箱运费 = 包箱费率 × 集装箱数量

$$集装箱数量=\frac{货物的总重量(或体积)}{集装箱有效载货重量(容积)}$$

上式所得结果应取整数,且选数值较高者。

$$每箱所装货物数量=\frac{集装箱有效载货重量(容积)}{单件运输包装货物的重量(或体积)}$$

目前,国际上两种最为通用的集装箱规格及有效容积和载货重量如下。

① 20 英尺集装箱规格为 8'×8'×20'(238 厘米×234 厘米×590 厘米),有效容积为 25 立方米,载货重量 17 500 千克。

② 40 英尺集装箱规格为 8'×8'×40'(238 厘米×230 厘米×1 205 厘米),有效容积为 55 立方米,载货重量为 24 500 千克。

例 2-2 纸箱包装货物,尺码为 50 厘米×50 厘米×30 厘米(0.075 立方米),毛重每箱 60 千克,则 20' 集装箱能装的最大数量为多少?

解 按体积计算:$\frac{25 \text{ 立方米}}{0.075 \text{ 立方米/箱}}=333.333$ 箱,取整后能装 333 箱;

按重量计算:$\frac{17\,500 \text{ 千克}}{60 \text{ 千克/箱}}=291.666$ 箱,取整后能装 291 箱。

因此,该货物实际装箱数量为 291 箱。

2) 出口保险费、佣金的计算

(1) 保险费。如采用 CIF 或 CIP 术语,在报价中应计算保险费。计算公式为

投保金额=CIF(或 CIP)×(1+投保加成),投保加成一般取 10%。

保险费=投保金额×保险费率=CIF(或 CIP)×(1+投保加成)×保险费率

$$CIF(或 CIP)=\frac{CFR(或 CPT)}{1-(1+投保加成)\times 保险费率}$$

(2) 佣金。计算公式为

佣金=含佣价(成交金额)×佣金率

净价=含佣价-佣金

净价=含佣价×(1-佣金率)

3. 预期利润

预期利润(expected profit)的大小由出口企业自行决定。利润既可以用定额表示,也可以用利润率表示。用利润率计算的基数,可以是成本,也可以是出口销售价格。公式为

利润=成本(销售价格)×利润率

例 2-3 出口某商品,生产成本为每单位 200 元,出口的国内费用为 10 元,如果公司的利润率为 10%,公司对外报 FOB 价,要求分别按照生产成本、出口成本和 FOB 出口价格为基数计算利润额。

解 按生产成本为基数计算的利润额为 200×10%=20(元);

按出口成本为基数计算的利润额为(200+10)×10%=21(元);

按 FOB 出口价格为基数计算的利润额为 $\frac{(200+10)\times 10\%}{1-10\%}=23.33$(元)。

2.2.2 出口报价核算

出口报价可以分别采用 FOB、CFR 和 CIF 术语,采用不同的术语,报价核算方法

也不尽相同，但无论采用何种术语报价，均由成本、费用和利润三大要素构成，只要将这三大部分分别计算出来，最后加以汇总，出口报价核算就不再困难，现分别予以说明。

1. FOB 报价核算

FOB 术语由进口商承担国外运保费，因此在报价中无须考虑国外运保费，只需计算成本、国内费用、佣金和利润。计算公式为

$$FOB = \frac{商品含税进价 + 国内费用 - 退税}{汇率} + 利润 + 佣金$$

$$FOB = \frac{\frac{商品进价 + 国内费用 - 退税}{汇率}}{1 - 利润率 - 佣金率}$$

2. CFR 报价核算

CFR 术语由出口商承担国外运费，但不需承担保险费，因此在报价中，除计算成本、各项国内费用、佣金和利润外，还应考虑国外运费。计算公式为

$$CFR = \frac{商品含税进价 + 国内费用 - 退税}{汇率} + 利润 + 佣金 + 国外运费$$

$$CFR = \frac{\frac{商品进价 + 国内费用 - 退税}{汇率}}{1 - 利润率 - 佣金率} + 国外运费$$

3. CIF 报价核算

CIF 术语由出口商承担所有国内外费用，因此，在报价中，应将成本、国内外各项费用、佣金和利润一并考虑计入，投保加成一般取 10%。计算公式为

由

$$CIF = \frac{商品含税进价 + 国内费用 - 退税}{汇率} + 利润 + 佣金 + 国外运费 + 保险费$$

有

$$CIF \times (1 - 佣金率 - 利润率) - CIF \times (1 + 投保加成) \times 保险费率 = \frac{商品进价 + 国内费用 - 退税}{汇率} + 国外运费$$

则

$$CIF = \frac{\frac{商品进价 + 国内费用 - 退税}{汇率}}{1 - 利润率 - 佣金率 - (1 + 投保加成) \times 保险费率} + 国外运费$$

例 2-4 根据下列信息，进行出口报价核算。

某公司接到日本客户询价购买"健康"牌运动鞋，装一20'货柜，CIFC3 东京。

商品货名："健康"牌运动鞋；

型号、规格：S-M-L-XL；

包装：16 双/箱；

净重：20 千克/箱；毛重：25 千克/箱；尺码：(90×50×30) 立方厘米/箱；

出口运费：880 美元/20'集装箱；

保险费率：0.50%；

国内购货价:120元/双(含17%增值税);

国内费用:办公费500元人民币;开证通知费200元人民币;贷款年利率6%(期限2个月);议付费率1‰(按成交金额计);商检费、拖车费、报关费和码头费合计2 500元人民币;佣金率3%;

出口退税率:10%;

预期利润率:10%;

汇率:1美元=7元人民币。

报价核算如下。

(1) 实际成本

$$实际成本 = 含税进价 - \frac{含税成本 \times 出口退税率}{1+17\%} = 120 - \frac{120 \times 10\%}{1.17} = 110(元)$$

(2) 国内费用

① 20′集装箱出口数量:

$$按毛重计 = \frac{17\ 500\ 千克}{25\ 千克/箱} = 700(箱)$$

$$按尺码计 = \frac{25\ 立方米}{(0.9 \times 0.5 \times 0.3)立方米/箱} = 185(箱)$$

取185箱,共计装运185×16=2 960(双)

② 国内费用(未包括议付费)

$$国内费用 = \frac{500+200+2\ 500}{2\ 960} + \frac{120 \times 6\%}{6}$$

$$= 1.08 + 1.2 = 2.28(元/双)$$

(3) 出口运费

$$出口运费 = \frac{880}{2\ 960} = 0.30(美元/双)$$

根据以上计算,得出CIFC3报价为

$$CIFC3 = \frac{\frac{实际成本+国内费用}{汇率}}{1-议付费率-利润率-佣金率-(1+投保加成)\times 保险费率} + 出口运费$$

$$\frac{\frac{110+2.28}{7}}{1-1‰-10\%-3\%-(1+10\%)\times 0.50\%} + 0.30 = 18.88(美元/双)$$

2.2.3 还价核算

在收到对方还价后,出口商应结合对方需求和市场竞争情况,正确合理地进行还价核算,还价核算与前述出口报价核算的原理相同,只是还价核算正好是报价核算的逆运算,前述报价核算是已知成本费用和利润,核算报价是多少,而还价核算是在报价改变后,核算构成价格的各要素将如何变化,从而作出自己的还价策略。通过还价核算,出口商应了解在价格降低后对预期利润的影响,或者分析一旦降价后,成本费用能否降低,以使利润不变。出口还价所采用的计算公式为

人民币总利润=人民币总收入-人民币总成本和费用支出

＝成交总金额－实际总成本－所有国内费用－出口总运费－总保险费－总佣金
＝(客户还价－运费－保险费－佣金)×汇率×数量－(商品进价＋国内费用－退税)×数量

例 2 - 5　某公司欲出口 500 台某机械产品至日本东京，1 台装 1 纸箱，尺码为 115 cm×68 cm×98 cm，毛重 510 千克，净重 480 千克，我方报出含 6% 利润率的 FOB 价，每台 USD303.00。对方还盘 USD324.00 CFR TOKYO。请问从上海到东京的每运费吨（重量吨或尺码吨）运费为多少美元时我方能保持 5% 的利润率？（运费按 W/M 计，结果保留 2 位小数）

解　出口实际外汇成本：$303×(1-6\%)=284.82$（美元）

每台机器运费：$324×(1-5\%)-284.82=22.98$（美元）

因为

$$1.15×0.68×0.98=0.766\ 36>0.51$$

所以按尺码计，能保持 5% 利润率所需的运费（折合为尺码吨）为

$$\frac{22.98}{0.766\ 36}=29.99（美元/FT）$$

【技能实训】

根据下列资料核算出口报价。

1. 宏远公司欲出口一 20'货柜不锈钢餐具至鹿特丹（ROTTERDAM），纸箱包装（2 套/箱，56 cm×32.5 cm×49 cm），国内含税购货成本为 180 元人民币/套。已知上海至鹿特丹 20'FCL 海洋运费为 2 200 美元，增值税税率为 17%，退税税率为 9%。加一成投保一切险加战争险，保险费率分别为 0.8% 和 0.2%。这批货的国内运杂费共 2 000 元，包装费每箱 2 元，出口商检费 100 元，报关费 150 元，港区港杂费 600 元，其他业务费用共 1 800 元。如果公司预期利润率为 6%，另外客户要求 3% 的佣金。

请计算 CIFC3 ROTTERDAM 价格（美元汇率为 7∶1）（计算过程保留 4 位小数，结果保留 2 位小数）。

2. 某公司向日本出口 2 500 件衬衣，海运运费共计 3 000 美元，按发票金额加成 10%，投保一切险和战争险，保险费率分别为 0.7%、0.3%，衬衣国内含税供货价格为每件 38 元人民币，公司出口费用定额率为供货成本的 5%，国内费用共计 5 000 元；增值税税率 17%，出口退税税率 5%；出口商进行此项交易需垫款 30 天，银行年利率为 8%（一年按 360 天计），当时人民币对美元汇率是 7.5∶1。

(1) 若客户还盘的价格为 CIFC3 OSAKA USD7.2/PC，请计算我方的利润率和总利润是多少？

(2) 若公司利润率保持 10%，请计算国内最低供货价格。

2.3　合同的履行

在实际业务中，买卖双方交易磋商，达成一致即意味着合同成立，双方一经签订书面合同，该合同就成为约束双方的法律文件。任何一方不得擅自变更或解除合同。合同一方当事人不履行合同或履行合同义务不符合约定条款，则必须承担法律责任。

进出口合同的履行要经过很多工作环节，这其中要办理很多手续，牵涉多种单据，

各种单据之间既相互独立,又相互联系。因此,在单据的流转中,要注意每个工作环节中所使用单据的种类、内容及相互之间的联系,以提高工作效率。

2.3.1 出口合同的履行

我国出口贸易中,除个别交易使用 FOB 术语外,多数采用 CIF 或 CFR 术语按信用证支付方式成交,合同履行主要包括备货、催证、审证、改证、租船订舱、报关、保险、制单、审单、结汇等。在这些工作环节中,以货(备货)、证(催证、审证和改证)、船(租船订舱)、款(交单结汇)4 个方面的工作最为重要。只有环环相扣,做好这 4 个主要环节的工作,才能避免出现"有货无证"、"有证无货"、"有货无船"、"有船无货"或者单证不符等现象,使合同履行顺利进行。

1. 备货

合同签订后,为了保证按时、按质、按量完成合同规定的交货任务,出口方必须根据合同认真备货,搞好备货工作,其主要内容包括向生产部门或供货部门安排或催交货物;做到货物质量、数量合格、包装完好并且符合合同及信用证的要求。备货的时间应根据合同和信用证的规定,并结合船期来安排,以利船货衔接,防止发生船货脱节现象。

凡属国家规定或合同规定必须经国家出入境检验检疫机构出证的商品,在货物备齐后,最迟应于报关或装运前 7 天向国家出入境检验检疫机构申请检验检疫,填写《中华人民共和国出入境检验检疫出境货物报验单》。只有取得国家出入境检验检疫机构发给的"出境货物通关单",海关才准放行。凡无此通关单者海关不予放行。

申请检验检疫时一般需提交下列单据:合同、信用证、商业发票、换证凭证、装箱单、厂检单、包装性能结果单、许可/审批文件等。

2. 催证、审证和改证

在按信用证支付方式成交时,催证、审证、改证是履行合同时很重要的一环。

1) 催证

在出口合同签订后,可以根据情况通过函电或其他途径催促国外商人及时开证。催开信用证的工作,应当根据合同的规定,并结合备货和船期情况进行。

2) 审证

国外开来的信用证内容必须与买卖合同的规定一致,在未征得我方同意之前,不得随意增减或改变其内容。但在实际业务中,由于种种原因,往往会出现信用证内容与合同规定不符的情况,为了保证安全收汇和出口合同的顺利履行,防止因信用证内容与合同规定不符而给我方造成经济损失,在收到国外来证后,必须对信用证的内容进行认真审核。

3) 改证

当发现信用证内容与合同规定不符,如非改不可的,应及时要求外商改证。对可改可不改的,可以酌情处理,例如,合同规定不准分批装运,而来证规定准许分批装运,可不改;反之,如果合同规定允许分批装运,而来证规定不准分批装运的,则一般要改;但是,在货物已经备妥,运输又无困难的情况下,不分批装运也无难处,则也可不改。对于同一张信用证中的问题,最好一次提出修改,以简化手续和节省费用。

3. 租船订舱

凡按 CIF 和 CFR 条件成交的出口货物应由我方安排运输。因此,各进出口公司在备货的同时，还必须做好租船订舱工作。

出口公司向运输公司或其代理办理托运时，需填写托运单（Booking Notes），亦称"订舱委托书"，作为订舱的依据。托运单是托运人（发货人）根据外销合同条款和信用证条款的内容填写并向承运人（船公司，一般为装货港的船方或其代理人）办理货物托运的单证。托运单的主要内容包括：货名、件数、包装式样、标志、重量、尺码、目的港、装船期限、结汇期限及能否分批、转船等。承运人根据上述内容，并结合船舶的航线、挂靠的港口、船期及舱位等考虑能否接受委托。托运时需提交的主要单据有出口货物明细单、商业发票、装箱单、报关单、出口收汇核销单、出库单、外贸合同（必要时）、出口许可证（必要时）等。

4. 报关

出口货物在装船之前，都要按规定手续办理报关，只有经海关检查放行以后，货物才能装船。

在此环节，需要缮制出口货物报关单。报关单加盖出口企业报关章及报关员印章后，作为向海关申报出口、凭以放行的单据。根据我国海关规定，一般货物除海关特准的外，需在装船 24 小时前办理出口报关手续。报关时，凭报关单向海关申报，海关验明货物无误后，在装货单上加盖放行章，这时货物才能装上运输工具出运。

报关时需提交的单据主要有 3 类。

(1) 基本单证：商业发票、装箱单或重量单、装货单（S/O）、外汇核销单。

(2) 特殊单证：配额许可证、特殊管理证件、减免税证明、加工贸易登记手册。

(3) 预备单证：合同、产地证、委托单位工商执照等。

5. 投保

凡是以 CIF 条件成交的货物，在货物装运前必须向保险公司办理投保手续。办理投保时，需缮制投保单。保险单上载有运输货物的船名，因此投保工作应在船只配妥后、装船前及时办理。保险单由保险公司负责缮制、签发，但由于保险单是议付单据之一，所以在缮制投保单时必须根据信用证条款或合同条款制作，其中被保险人、被保险货物、保险金额、保险险别等必须准确填制。出口公司需根据信用证条款或合同条款及时向保险公司提供上述投保所需资料。

6. 发出装船通知

货物装运完毕后，出口企业必须及时向买方发出装船通知（Shipping Advice）。特别是在 FOB 或 CFR 条件成交时应由买方投保，因而发出装船通知尤为重要。在 CIF 条件下，出口企业也应及时发出装船通知，便于买方掌握运输信息，做好接货、销售、转卖、加工等准备工作，有利于业务的进一步开展。有时信用证规定装船通知的电传或电报副本是议付的单据之一，这时必须按信用证要求提供上述副本。

7. 签证、认证

签证是指原产地证、GSP Form A 产地证等单证的签发，此类单证一般由出入境检验检疫机构按出口方的委托签发；认证是指由买方指定的机构（我政府机关或对方国家驻我国的机构）在我某些出口单据上作必要的证明，确认其为合法文件。签证、认证工作都必须在交单结汇前办妥。

8. 缮制结汇单据

出口货物装船之后，应按合同和信用证要求正确地缮制各种单据，制单时必须做到"单证相符"和"单单一致"。在备妥有关单据后，应及时向银行办理交单结汇手续。出口结汇所使用的单据一般有以下几种。

1) 商业发票

出口托运、报关、投保、结汇等环节都要用到商业发票（Commercial Invoice），出口企业在收到信用证并审核无误后即可根据信用证缮制商业发票，商业发票是全套出口单据的核心单据，其主要作用是供外商凭以收货、支付货款和报关纳税的依据。在商品发票中，主要包括编号、日期、合同号码、收货人名称、付款人名称、装运工具及起讫地点、商品名称、品质、规格、数量、唛头、价格及付款条件等内容。

2) 装箱单和重量单

装箱单（Packing List）和重量单（Weight List）是商业发票的补充文件，一般与商业发票一并缮制。其主要作用是便于国外买方在货物到达目的港后进行报关、查验和核对货物。

3) 提单

提单（Bill of Lading，B/L）是议付单据中必不可少的重要单据，提单上各项内容必须符合信用证条款及合同条款的内容。其主要作用是卖方凭以结汇，买方凭以提货和承托双方计收运费的依据。

4) 保险单

按 CIF 条件成交时，保险单（Insurance Policy or Insurance Certificate）是结汇中不可缺少的单据之一。其主要内容一般包括：被保险人、货物名称、数量、装卸港、载运工具、开航日期、保险险别、保险金额、保险费率、保费，以及保险公司所承担的责任和赔付地点、赔付方法与条款解释的依据等。

5) 检验证明

检验证明（Inspection Certificate）是出口货物经过商品检验机构检验或鉴定合格后，所取得的检验证书、品质证书、重量证书、检疫证明等证件。这些证件是证明商品的品质、重量或卫生状况的依据，也是处理有关品质和重量索赔和理赔的依据。

6) 汇票

汇票（Draft）是清算债务与支付货款的重要工具，也是议付货款中的主要单据之一，汇票应与其他单据一起送交银行结汇。在我国出口业务中，通常使用的是商业汇票，而绝大部分商业汇票是跟单汇票。汇票一般填制一式两份。

7) 其他单据

除上述一般经常使用的单据外，在出口业务中，有时根据进口国家的规定和买方的要求，还须填写其他单据，如海关发票和提供产地证书等。

9. 审核结汇单据

在制单环节，出口企业除严格按信用证要求缮制各种结汇单据外，还应在向银行交单前尽量将各种单证集合在一起，采用多种方法对单据进行全面审核，审查单单之间是否一致，各个单证的内容是否正确完整，单据的份数是否符合信用证的要求，单证上的签章或背书是否齐全等，从而确保信用证项下所要求的单据做到"单单一致"、"单证一致"。

10. 交单结汇

出口企业应在信用证规定的交单期及有效期内将符合信用证规定的单据交到指定的银行议付货款。

11. 业务善后

1) 遭到拒付

信用证结算方式是一种银行信用，开证行或付款行凭出口商提交的全套合格单据付款，但由于单据与信用证不符，出口商可采用"表提"（表盖提出）或"电提"等方法请求买方或银行付款，进口方开证行或付款行审单后，有可能拒付货款或退回单证，对此，出口方应查明原因及时解决，以避免损失。

2) 索赔和理赔

履行出口合同时，我方向外商索赔的情况较少，通常是我方对外商提出的索赔进行处理，即理赔。索赔和理赔是一项很重要的工作，必须弄清事实，分清责任，实事求是地予以妥善解决。

2.3.2 进口合同的履行

进口合同订立后，进口企业应当履行的主要义务是支付货款和收取货物。在我国进口业务中，大多采用 FOB 贸易术语、信用证支付方式成交。履行进口合同的程序一般包括开立信用证、催装、租船订舱、通知船期、派船去国外港口接运货物、投保、付款赎单、进口报关、接卸货物、进口报验、拨交、索赔等环节。

1. 开立信用证

信用证付款的进口货物，在签订合同后，进口商应按约定期限向银行办理开证手续。如合同规定需要外商先办理出口许可证或提供担保、在其未履行这些手续前，一般不宜轻易开证。信用证开出后，不论是由对方或我方提出修改，均需经双方商妥后才能办理。如外商要求改证的理由充分，可同意修改；否则，不应同意修改。

2. 派船接货

进口货物如按 FOB 条件成交，我方应负责租船订舱，为使船货衔接，要及时向船公司办理租船订舱手续，并及时将船名、船期通知对方，以便其准备装船。与此同时，我方还应随时了解和掌握外商备货和装船的情况，以便做好催装工作。

3. 投保

FOB 和 CFR 进口合同，由我方负责办理货物运输的保险。我方接到对方的装船通知后，应及时将船名、提单号、装运港、装船日期或开船日期、商品名称、数量、金额、目的港等有关内容通知保险公司，办理投保手续。

4. 审单付汇

国外出口商装运货物后，向当地银行议付货款。我国银行在收到国外银行寄来的汇票和单据后，根据信用证的规定，核对单据无误后，即向国外银行付款。如发现国外银行寄来的单据有单证不符现象时，应立即处理，要求国外有关当事人改正，或停止对外付款。

5. 报验、报关提货

国家规定需法定检验或受收货人委托检验的进口货物到港后，收货人必须向商检机构申报检验，并向商检机构提供进口合同、商业发票、提单、装箱单、到货通知及其他相关单证，报验的时间应在合同规定的索赔有效期内。

进口货物到港报验后，收货人或货代公司根据进口单据填制进口货物报关单，向海关申报，报关单要随附发票、提单、保险单、减免税或免验的证明文件及海关认为必要的签证和认证文件。海关以报关单、进口许可证等为依据，对进口货物进行实际的核对和查验，以确保货物的合法进口。

根据《中华人民共和国海关进出口税则》的规定，除少数进口商品免税外，对绝大多数进口商品都征收进口货物关税，进口货物的纳税人应从海关填发税款缴款书之日起15日内缴纳税款。进口货物在办完向海关申报、接受查验、缴纳关税等手续后，由海关在货物提货单据上签印放行，进口商或其代理人必须凭海关签印放行的货运单据才能提货。

6. 索赔

进口索赔并非是必要的环节。但当进口货物与合同规定不符，给进口商造成损失时，就要根据具体原因和责任归属，向出口商或承运方或保险公司提出索赔。在办理索赔时应向理赔方提供索赔清单、有关单证及由相关部门出具的损失检验证书、公证报告等。

2.4 业务善后

2.4.1 出口业务善后：接受单据与拒付

当出口方提交整套装运单据后，业务就进入了善后阶段。如果买方或开证行对单据没有提出异议，说明出口方已得到买方或开证行的付款保证。进口方在目的港接受货物后，本笔交易即为顺利完成。但如果买方或开证行认为货物与单证不一致，就会拒付。收到拒付通知后，出口方首先要确定拒付原因，与银行相互配合，做好应变工作，共同把无法正常收汇的风险和损失降至最低点。同时迅速与买方联络，寻求解决方法，尽量说服买方接受货物。

在善后阶段，业务员通常就本笔业务的相关情况与客户进行交流，这就是业务善后函。善后函的作用是总结经验、吸取教训、增进友谊，有利于今后的业务发展。根据业务发展情况的不同，善后函可分为以下两大类。

1. 开证行接受单据时的善后函

出口方可以感谢对方所做的努力，对增进双方的了解表示高兴；也可以展望未来，希望能继续扩大合作，收到更多的订单，或借此推荐新产品等。例如：

① We are glad to know that the issuing bank has honored our draft against L/C No. AB001234.

② We hope this deal will be the basis of the further development of our business relationships.

③ We can ensure that you will find the goods shipped to your entire satisfaction.

④ We are looking forward to your repeat orders.

2. 遭到开证行拒付时的善后函

在业务中，遭到买方或开证行拒付是经常遇到的事情。遇到此类问题，首先应与进口商联系，弄清每一笔拒付的背景情况，对症下药。

对于开证行的拒付（有理拒付和无理拒付），应具体分析，采取对策。例如，货物出现品质差异或单据出现不符点时，要针对问题，积极采取措施或配合银行修改单据，挽回损失。又如，买方或开证行为了拖延付款时间好进行验货或者为了要求降价而提出拒付，这时，一要据理力争，二要随时关注货物和进口商的动向。如拒付是由于进口商对货物不满意或出口方原因引起的，可适当让步；如拒付确属进口方损害了出口方的利益，除了与银行联系反驳事宜以外，还要向船公司了解进口商是否已借单提货。如果已经提货，收款就有可能了，因为，提单被拿去提货，开证行已无法退回全套单据，只能全额付款。对于一些明显超出处理时限的拒付可以不予理会，许多不符点都是拖延付款时间而已，所以遇到拒付时，不要先否定自己，更不要因为害怕收不到货款而草率同意降价要求。

业务中遭到拒付时，出口方处于极为不利的地位，这时，语气应当诚恳、委婉，并且具有说服力，以赢得买方的谅解，如回顾双方以往的愉快合作等。重要的是应当强调单证不符点是细微的，并不影响货物的品质，不会给进口方的利益造成损害。例如：

① We feel deeply sorry for the mistake in our negotiation documents, which is made as a result of our clerk's carelessness.

② We really hope this incident will not affect negatively our friendly cooperation.

③ We can guarantee that the quality of the goods is exactly in line with the stipulations of the relative contract.

④ Since our goods have been shipped on time, would you be kind to make the payment through your bank?

⑤ You may rest assured that such a mistake will never occur again.

当然，有时作出一些具体的让步，如适当减价，也是必要和明智的。

【案例】

1. 开证行接受单据时的善后函样信

==

To: A PRODUCTS PL (FAX: 001-45689999)   Attn: Peter
From: B TRADING CO., LTD. (FAX: 86-755-12345678)   Alice Wang
Date: Mar 9th, 2007

Dear Peter,

Per our Bank's notice, we have received USD10088 against L/C No. AB/ABCO1616LC under Contract No. AB123. You can be sure that the goods shipped will meet your needs just well. We believe the conclusion of this transaction will help to further our mutual understanding and pave the way for more business in the future.

In order to promote commercial intercourse with overseas business circle, we are pleased to take steps in world trade. Not only various terms of payment, but more forms of business cooperation can be adopted in the time to come. Needless to say, with the development of our trade relations. There will be more and more topics of interest to be discussed between us. We are expecting your advice.

As you might not be aware of the new development in our product range, we are airmailing to you a copy of our latest illustrated price list. If any item interests you, please let us know. We will give you a special discount of 1‰ for orders which qty more than 10 000 pcs in further one year.

We hope our handling of your first order will lead to further transactions between us and look forward to your favorable reply.

Yours truly,
Alice (Toy Department)
B Trading Co., Ltd.
Room 2601-2610 King Building, Shennan Road, Shenzhen. Guangdong, China
ZipCode: 312000, Tel: 0755-1234567, Fax: 0755-1234568, E-mail: AliceWang@BTC.com

2. 遭到开证行拒付时善后函样信

ABC Trading Co., Ltd.
18th Floor Kingstar Mansion, 676 Dongfang Road, Cfg, China
Tel: 0575-1234567, Fax: 0575-1234568
Zip Code: 312000
Purchasing Division
A V & G
♯888 Jalan Street, New York America
Tel: +01-57479298
Fax: +01-57472393
August 14, 2007
E-mail: yougli@jbs.com.cn
Dear Mr. John,

We are very concerned when yesterday we received the notification from American Development Bank complaining about the discrepancies on L/C No. 07/0814-GHR.

After investigation of the matter, we found it was a typing mistake made unknowingly by our new clerk. We are really sorry for all the inconvenience we have brought you and assure you that such a matter will never occur again.

However, for this time, could you kindly instruct your banker to accept the above-mentioned documents and reimburse the amount of the shipped goods to us on a collection basis. We can take our name to guarantee the high quality and sound state of the shipment. There's no miscarriage at all.

We would be greatly appreciated that you could help us in consideration of the long-term trade relations between us and thank you for your friendly cooperation.

We are looking forward to favorable reply.

Yours sincerely,
ABC Trading Co., Ltd.
Alice (Miss)
Daily Articles Division

2.4.2 进口业务善后:索赔与理赔

合同履行过程中,如果一方违反合同规定,直接或间接地给另一方造成损失,受损失的一方有权向违约方提出赔偿要求,以弥补其所受损失,这就是索赔;违反合同的一方对受损方提出的赔偿要求的处理,则称之为理赔。在外贸业务中,卖方向买方的索赔较少见,较多见的是买方向卖方提出索赔。

索赔时,买方必须查明造成损失的事实,分清索赔责任。根据不同情况,买方索赔的责任人主要是出口商、承运人和保险公司。因此索赔类型主要有以下3种。

1. 向出口商提出索赔

由出口商责任导致的索赔属于贸易索赔。主要包括:卖方拒不交货、逾期装运、短交货物、货物的品质规格与合同不符、错发错运、包装不妥、随船单证不全或漏填错发等致使买方遭受损失,这类责任保险公司不予赔偿而由出口商承担。

向出口商索赔,一般要求提供进口商品检验报告和索赔函。

2. 向承运人提出索赔

由于承运人的责任而导致的索赔叫运输索赔。主要包括如下内容。

(1) 短卸误卸:是指卸船交货数量少于提单所列数量。其原因可能是没有把全部货物卸完或误卸他港。

(2) 途中短损:承运人承担货物自装船起至离船前期间发生的整件缺失或装卸破损的责任。根据《统一提单的若干法律的国际公约》(以下简称《海牙规则》),承运人的责任范围以提单所注明的范围为限。

(3) 延迟交货:向承运人索赔应提供进口商品检验报告、索赔报告、承运人或港务管理机构出具的破损事故证明书或短卸证明书、提货单的正本或副本、商品发票的副本、品质证明文件或装箱单等。

3. 向保险公司索赔

保险公司主要承担保险责任范围内的,货物因自然灾害、意外事故或运输装卸过程中事故等受损情况,应向保险公司索赔。

向保险公司索赔应提供进口商品检验报告、海难证明书或事故证明书、索赔报告、保险单正本或副本、提货单、进口发票、出口品质、重要证明文件、装箱单、出口商品检验报告。

2.4.3 索赔理赔信函的主要内容

1. 索赔信函内容
(1) 说明写信原因。
(2) 说明索赔理由。
(3) 提出具体的索赔要求。
(4) 结束语。

2. 理赔信函内容
(1) 说明写信原因。
(2) 说明对事故的调查报告。

（3）提出具体的理赔方法。
（4）诚恳地向对方道歉。

【案例】

1. 索赔函范本

Dear Sir,

       Re：Contract No. 08A093 for Cashmere

We are writing to inform you that the cashmere under Contrace No. 08A093 discharged at Tianjin in such an unsatisfactory condition. The survey report from TIANJIN ENTRY-EXIT INSPECTION AND QUARANTINE (CIQ) evidence that there's short weight of 3 tons, obviously due to the improper packing. Therefore, we have to lodge a short weight claim against you for US $ 36 936.

We trust you can understand that we expect the compensation for our damaged goods and we look forward to your settlement at an early date.

Yours Sincerely

2. 理赔函范本

Dear Sir,

     Re：Claim on short weight of Contract No. 08A093 for Cashmere

We are receipt of your letter dated 16 March, 2007, claiming for short weight of cashmere.

After carefully looking into the matter, we have found that out cashmere was properly weighed at the time of loading. We really cannot account for the reason for your complaint. But since the goods were examined by TIANJIN ENTRY-EXIT INSPECTION AND QUARANTINE (CIQ) upon arrival at Tianjin, we have no choice but accept your claim immediately.

As you expect, we therefore settlement of claim for US $ 36 936 by T/T.

We sincerely apologized for the trouble and would like to assure you that all possible steps will be taken by us to avoid any recurrence of similar mistake in our future dealings.

Yours Faithfully

【技能实训】

1. 3月8日，我公司已经接到议付行的通知，信用证开证行已如数付清货款。至此，该笔交易顺利结汇。请向外方公司去函致谢，并邮寄新的商品价目表。为了双方的长远合作，我方承诺，如果在未来一年内，单笔订单数量超过1万件，我公司将在现有价格的基础上再给予1%的特别优惠以示我方的诚意。

2. 8月14日，议付行通知我方由于发票上显示的货号与信用证规定的不一致所以美国发展银行拒付。经查，系单证员误将货号 KTato-0180 打成了 KTato-0880。因此，请向外方公司致函解释并附寄更正后的发票，希望其尽快付款。

3. 天津光大进出口公司从美国进口 10 000 码尼龙布（Nylon cloth）。货物抵达天津新港，光大公司提货后发现有500码严重损伤和污损，无法销售。光大公司立即申请商检机构检验，并根据天津出入境检验检疫局的检验报告向美国公司提起索赔金额1 230美元。美国公司经调查发现损伤或脏污是由包装不良所致，同意赔偿。

请根据以上信息，撰写索赔函和理赔函。

第 3 章

【本章导读】
信用证概述
申请开立信用证
信用证的审核与修改

【学习目标和要点】
通过本章学习,学生应能够了解开立信用证的程序,了解信用证业务中,进出口双方各自应履行的义务及相关业务环节操作程序,熟知审证的要点和修改的规则,看懂信用证内容并根据合同指出信用证存在的问题,学会填制信用证申请书,撰写催证函和改证函。

信 用 证

如果进出口双方在洽谈交易时明确以信用证作为付款方式，则在买卖合同签订之后，出口商可能要进行的工作是催促进口商按合同规定按时开出信用证，而进口商则应根据合同的规定和要求向其所在地的银行提出开立信用证的申请。

3.1 信用证概述

信用证支付方式是随着国际贸易的发展，在银行及其他金融机构参与国际贸易结算的过程中逐步形成的。信用证支付方式规定由银行承担付款责任，较好地解决了买卖双方互不信任的矛盾，因此，这种支付方式发展很快，并在国际贸易中被广泛应用。

3.1.1 信用证定义

信用证（Letter of Credit，L/C）是指开证银行根据开证申请人的请求和指示，向受益人开立的在一定金额和一定期限内凭规定的单据承诺付款的凭证。简言之，信用证就是银行开立的一种有条件的承诺付款的书面文件。这里的条件是指受益人必须提交符合信用证规定的各种单据。

国际商会《跟单信用证统一惯例》（简称《UCP600》）第二条解释：就本惯例而言，信用证意指一项不可撤销的安排，无论其名称或描述如何，该项安排构成开证行对相符交单予以承付的确定承诺。

3.1.2 信用证的当事人

1. 开证申请人

开证申请人（Applicant）是指向银行申请开立信用证的人，在信用证中又称开证人（Opener），一般是进口方或实际买主。开证人应在合同规定的期限内开立信用证，并向开证行交付押金，在开证行对单据付款后，对开证行付款赎单。但若受益人提交的单据不符合信用证条款的规定，开证人有权拒绝付款。

2. 开证行

开证行（Opening Bank 或 Issuing Bank）是指接受开证申请人的委托，向出口方开立信用证并承担付款责任的银行，一般是进口方所在地银行，也可能是出口方所在地银行或第三国的银行。开证行一旦开出信用证，就必须对受益人提交的符合信用证规定的单据付款。若开证人不能付款赎单，开证行有权处理单据和货物，也有权向开证人追索垫款。

3. 通知行

通知行（Advising Bank 或 Notifying Bank）是指受开证银行委托，将信用证转交出口方的银行。它只证明信用证的表面真实性，帮助受益人澄清有关信用证的疑点，不承担其他义务。通知行一般是开证行在出口方所在地的代理行。

4. 受益人

受益人（Beneficiary）是指接受信用证并享受其利益的人，一般是出口方或实际供货人。如果受益人发现其收到的信用证条款与合同条款不符，应立即要求修改信用证或表示拒绝接受；受益人一旦接受了信用证，就要在信用证规定的期限内装运货物和向银行交单,若银行不能付款,则有权要求进口方履行付款义务。

5. 议付行

议付行(Negotiating Bank)是指根据开证行的授权买入或贴现受益人开立和提交的符合信用证规定的汇票或单据的银行。议付银行可以是指定的银行,也可以是非指定的银行,由信用证的条款来规定。大多数情况下,受益人愿意选择通知行作为议付行。

6. 付款行

付款行(Paying Bank)是指信用证上指定的付款银行。它一般是开证行,也可以是开证行指定的另一家银行,根据信用证的规定来决定。

7. 保兑行

保兑行(Confirming Bank)是指应开证行的请求在信用证上加具保兑的银行。保兑行具有与开证行相同的责任和地位,一般由通知行兼任。

8. 偿付行

偿付行(Reimbursing Bank)是指受开证行的委托,向议付行或其他垫款行偿还垫款的银行。偿付行的出现,往往是由于信用证上使用的是偿付行所在国家的货币。若偿付行不能及时偿付,开证行要负责赔偿有关垫款行的利息损失。

3.1.3 信用证的主要内容

信用证没有固定统一的格式,但基本内容大致相同,主要有以下几项。

(1) 对于信用证本身的说明,包括信用证的种类、编号、开证日期、金额、装运期、有效期、到期地点,以及信用证有关当事人的名称、地址等。

(2) 对汇票的规定,包括汇票出票人、受票人、种类、金额、汇票期限及付款人等。

(3) 对货物要求,包括货物名称、品质规格、数量(重量)、包装、价格等。

(4) 装运条款,包括运输方式、装运港(地)、目的港(地)、装运日期、是否分批装运或转运等。

(5) 对单据要求,规定应附哪些单据及对有关单据的具体要求和应出具的份数,这是信用证最重要的内容。单据主要包括 3 类:①货物单据(包括发票、装箱单、重量单、产地证、商检证明书等);②运输单据(包括提单以及对提单内容填写的要求);③保险单据。除这 3 类单据外,还可能要求提供其他单据或证明等。

(6) 特殊条款,一般书写在背面,根据进口国政治经济贸易情况的变化,或每一笔具体业务的需要作出的规定。例如,限制船舶国籍和船舶年龄、限制航线和港口等。

(7) 责任文句,开证行对受益人即汇票持有人保证付款的责任文句。

此外,由于各国银行普遍采用国际商会的《跟单信用证统一惯例》作为信用证业务的规范,所以信用证上一般都注明"本证按国际商会《跟单信用证统一惯例》办理"。

3.1.4 信用证方式支付的一般程序

使用信用证方式结算货款,从开证申请人向银行申请开立信用证到开证行付清货款,需要经过很多业务环节,并需办理各种手续。由于信用证种类不同,信用证条款有着不同的规定,其业务环节和手续也不尽相同。但是从信用证方式支付一般程序来看,主要有以下几个环节。

（1）进口方与出口方订立买卖合同，规定以信用证方式支付货款。

（2）开证申请人（进口方）向开证银行（当地银行）提出开证申请，按买卖合同内容填写开证申请书，缴纳押金或提供其他担保、手续费，请开证行开证。

（3）开证行接受开证申请后，按开证申请书的内容，开出信用证，将信用证正本寄给出口方所在地的分行或代理行（通知行），请其通知受益人。

（4）通知行接到信用证审查并核实印鉴、密押无误后，将信用证转给受益人。

（5）受益人接到信用证后，认真核对信用证与合同是否符合，如发现不符，可以要求开证申请人通过开证行修改，或根本拒收信用证。如信用证无误，按信用证规定装运货物，并缮制信用证要求的各种单据，开立汇票，在信用证有效期内向银行交单议付。

（6）议付行经过审核信用证与单据相符以后，按汇票金额，扣除利息和手续费，将余款垫付给受益人。如发现单证不符，则可拒收。

（7）议付行把受益人交来的单据寄交开证行或其指定的付款行要求偿付。

（8）开证行在审单无误后，向议付行付款。

（9）开证行办理转账或汇款给议付行的同时通知开证申请人付款赎单。

（10）开证申请人付款并取得装运单据，凭装运单据向承运人提货。

3.1.5 信用证的特点

1. 信用证付款是一种银行信用，开证行负有第一性付款责任

信用证支付方式是一种银行信用，开证行以自己的信用作出付款保证。《跟单信用证统一惯例》规定，开证行自开立信用证之时起即不可撤销地承担承付责任，只要受益人提交的单据符合信用证条款，开证行必须承付。因此，开证行承担第一性的付款责任。开证行对受益人的付款责任是独立的，受益人可持信用证向开证行凭单索汇，而无须先找进口方。即使作为开证人的进口方事后丧失偿付能力，只要受益人提交了符合信用证条款规定的单据，开证行都必须对受益人付款。

2. 信用证是一项自足的文件

信用证是依据买卖合同开立的，但一经开立，即成为独立于买卖合同之外的契约，不受买卖合同的约束。《UCP600》第4条规定："就性质而言，信用证与可能作为其开立基础的销售合同或其他合同是相互独立的交易，即使信用证中含有对此类合同的任何援引，银行亦与该合同完全无关，且不受其约束。因此，银行关于承付、议付或履行信用证下其他义务的承诺，不受申请人基于开证行或与受益人之间的关系而产生任何请求或抗辩的影响。"所以，信用证是一项独立自足的文件，信用证各当事人的权利和责任完全以信用证条款为依据，不受买卖合同的约束。

3. 信用证是一种单据的买卖

在信用证项下，实行的是凭单付款原则。银行以受益人提交的单据是否与信用证条款相符为依据，决定是否付款。《UCP600》第5条规定："银行处理的是单据，而不是单据可能涉及的货物、服务或履约行为"。所以，信用证业务是一种"单据业务。"《UCP600》第14条规定："按指定行事的指定银行、保兑行（如果有的话）及开证行须审核交单，并仅基于单据本身确定其是否在表面上构成相符交单。"第34条规定："银行对任何单据的形式、完整性、准确性、内容真实性、虚假性或法律效力。或对单据中规定或附加的一般或特殊条件，概不负责"。所以，在信用证项下，实行单据"严格符合的原则"，不仅要求单证一致，而且要求单单一致。

3.1.6 国际商会《跟单信用证统一惯例》

由于信用证的安全保证和资金融通的作用能在很大程度上缓解买卖双方互不信任的矛盾和满足进出口商都要求加速资金周转的愿望，第一份现代的银行信用证自19世纪80年代在英国伦敦出现以后，很快在全世界得到推广，到20世纪初，跟单信用证在国际贸易中已被广泛应用并已具有相当规模。但是，因为从事国际贸易的商人和有关的银行分处不同国家和地区，法律规则和业务操作习惯各不相同，加上使用的语言各异，特别是在国际上对跟单信用证有关当事人的权利、责任以及所用条款和术语的定义等缺乏统一的解释和公认的准则，各银行大都根据各自的操作习惯和利益自行其是、各持己见，因此，信用证的各有关当事人之间的争议和纠纷经常发生，甚至引起司法诉讼。因此，制定一套能够约束信用证有关当事人并能为各方共同遵守的统一、明确的规则，以便于国际结算的进行和国际贸易的顺利发展，就成为信用证业务有关各方的共同需要和迫切愿望。在这种情况下，国际商会根据美国代表的提议，由法国代表执笔编写了《商业跟单信用证统一规则》(Uniform Regulations for Commercial Documentary Credit)第一版本，于1929年在阿姆斯特丹大会上通过，1930年5月15日实施，称为ICC第74号出版物。它对跟单信用证的定义、有关名词和术语以及信用证业务的有关各方的权利和义务作了解释，还建议各国银行予以采用。但由于这个"规则"仅仅反映了个别国家银行的观点，只被法国和比利时两个国家的银行所采用。为此国际商会于1931年即着手修改，于1933年2月，作为第82号出版物颁布了第一个跟单信用证统一惯例，定名为《商业跟单信用证统一惯例》(Uniform Customs and Practice for Commercial Documentary Credits)。其后，随着国际贸易的不断发展，新的运输技术和运输方式的出现和广泛运用，以及在使用《商业跟单信用证统一惯例》过程中所暴露的问题，国际商会又对其作过多次修改，颁布过多种版本。首次修订本颁布于1951年6月，编号为151号，于1952年1月1日开始实施。自1962年颁布的第二次修订本并于1963年7月1日实施的第222号出版物起，改称为《跟单信用证统一惯例》(Uniform Customs and Practice for Documentary Credits，简称UCP)。以后又先后于1974年、1983年和1993年分别以第290号(1975年10月1日起实施)、第400号(1984年10月1日起实施)和第500号(1994年1月1日起实施)3个出版物颁布第三次、第四次和第五次修订本。跟单信用证的第六次修订本是2006年10月公布的ICC第600号出版物，于2007年7月1日正式实施。

《跟单信用证统一惯例》并不是国际性的法律，但它已被世界各国银行普遍接受和使用，至今已被170多个国家的银行所采用，并成为国际上处理信用证业务的惯例，各国法院几乎都把《跟单信用证统一惯例》作为裁决跨国的信用证纠纷的"法律准则"。但是，《跟单信用证统一惯例》毕竟只是一项国际贸易惯例，为了得到法律上的保护，必须在信用证上注明："本证根据国际商会2007年修订本第600号出版物《跟单信用证统一惯例》办理 (This credit is subject to the Uniform Customs and Practice for Documentary Credits UCP (2007 Revision) International Chamber of Commerce publication NO. 600)。"

3.2 催证

在正常情况下,买方最迟应在货物装运期 15 天(有时也规定为 30 天)前开立信用证并到达卖方,以便给卖方充足的时间办理装运,如准备货物、预订舱位等。但在实务中,由于市场变化、资金短缺或其他原因,买方不能在合同规定的时间及时开出信用证的事时有发生。

3.2.1 催促开立信用证

为使合同顺利履行,在下列情况下,卖方应注意催促对方开立信用证,以便如期装运。

(1) 签约日期和履约日期相隔较远,应在合同规定开证日之前,去信表示对该笔交易的重视。并提醒对方及时开证。

(2) 根据卖方备货和船舶情况,如果有可能提前装运时,也可与对方商量,要求其提前开证。

(3) 国外买方未在合同规定的期限内开证,卖方可催促对方开证;或延展开证期;或在催证同时保留索赔,要求损害赔偿。

(4) 开证期限未到,但发现客户资信不佳,或市场情况有变,也可催促对方开证。

3.2.2 撰写催证函

撰写催证函时,注意用词要得体,不要使用责怪和厌烦的口吻。应该有礼貌地说明所订货物已经备妥,但有关的信用证却没有收到。对催证函的写法并无统一规定和要求,但一般包含如下内容。

(1) 有关信用证还未收到。例如:

We repeatedly requested you by faxes to expedite the opening of the relative letter of credit so that we might effect shipment for the above mentioned order, but after the lapse of 3 months, we have not yet received the covering L/C.

The shipment time for your order is approaching, but we have not yet received the covering L/C.

(2) 要求迅速开立信用证。例如:

We wish you will rush the relevant L/C so that we can effect punctual shipment.

The 800 bicycles under Contract 268 have been ready for shipment for quite some time, but we have not yet received your covering L/C to date. Please open the L/C as soon as possible so that we may effect shipment.

(3) 开证注意事项。例如:

The stipulations of the relevant L/C should strictly conform to the terms specified in our contract.

(4) 陈述不及时开证的责任。例如:

We hope that you will take commercial reputation into account in all seriousness and open L/C at once, otherwise you will be responsible for all the losses arising therefrom.

【相关单证】

单证3-1　催证函

Dear sirs,

With reference to the 4 000 dozen shirts under our Sales Confirmation No. TE151, we wish to draw your attention to the fact that the date of delivery is approaching, but up to the present we have not received the covering Letter of Credit. Please do your utmost to expedite its establishment, so that we may execute the order with in the prescribed time.

In order to avoid subsequent amendment, please see to it that the L/C stipulations are in exact accordance with the terms of the contract.

We look forward to receiving your favorable response at an early date.

Yours faithfully

　　参考译文如下。

敬启者:

　　关于我方第TE151号售货确认书项下的4 000打衬衣,我们希望提请你方注意,交货日期日益临近,而有关信用证迄今仍未收到。请速开证,以便这笔订货得以顺利执行。为了避免日后修改,务请注意信用证规定事项与合同条款完全一致。

　　盼早复佳音。

【案例】

　　河北恒泰进出口贸易公司业务员杨光为保证在2008年8月交货,于2008年7月3日向美国PACIFIC INTERNATIONAL INC.发出催证文函。

HEBEI HENGTAI IMPORT & EXPORT CORPORATION

NO. 231 HEPING ROAD, SHIJIAZHUANG, HEBEI, CHINA

TEL: 86-0311-84576936　　FAX: 86-0311-84576937

TO: PACIFIC INTERNATIONAL INC.

FM: HEBEI HENGTAI IMPORT & EXPORT CORPORATION

DT: Jul 3, 2008

Dear Mr. Smith,

With reference to our Sales Contract No. 02AGI8185, we wish to draw your attention to the fact that the goods are ready for dispatch, but up to the present we have not received the covering L/C. Neither have we received any information from you about the above L/C.

To secure punctual fulfillment of the contract, please rush the L/C. We hope that the relevant L/C will reach us within 10 days, otherwise we shall not be able to deliver the goods on time.

We hope that you can understand our situation and give us close cooperation. We look forward to your early reply.

Yours faithfully,
HEBEI HENGTAI IMPORT & EXPORT CORPORATION
Yang Guang

【技能实训】

1. 假设你是龙华国际贸易公司（LONGHUA TRADING CO., LTD.）的业务员赵明，你收到了加拿大 ABC 公司（ABC GENERAL TRADING CO.）签返的编号为 DTC5210 的销售确认书，双方约定信用证不迟于 11 月 25 日前到达，但现在期限已到，却仍未收到信用证。因此，请你给 ABC 公司的业务员 Andy Burns 去函催证，并提醒对方我方通知行为"中国银行河北分行"，而非只是"中国银行"，以免寄错。写信时间为 2006 年 11 月 25 日。

2. 假设你是华润进出口有限公司（Huarun Import & Export Co., Ltd.）的业务员刘杰，加拿大 Carters Trading Company, LLC 的 Joe Brown 先生向你公司签返了编号为 CTC5682 的销售合同，但信用证迟迟未到，由于工厂的生产计划近两个月都排得很满，因此请你给 Joe Brown 先生去函催证，以免延误装运。写信时间为 2008 年 4 月 28 日。

3.3 申请开立信用证

如果进出口双方签订国际货物买卖合同并确立信用证为结算方式后，进口商则应按贸易合同规定向当地银行申请开立信用证。开证人申请开证时，应填写开证申请书。开证申请书是银行开具信用证的依据。银行按照开证申请书开立信用证后，在法律上就与进口商构成了开立信用证的权利与义务关系，双方的契约就是开证申请书。

3.3.1 申请开立信用证的程序

进口商在合同规定的时间向中国银行或其他经营外汇业务的银行办理申请开立信用证手续如下。

1. 递交有关合同的副本及附件

进口商在向银行申请开证时，要向银行递交进口合同的副本以及所需附件，如进口许可证、进口配额证、某些部门审批文件等。首次到银行办理进口开证手续应提交：营业执照副本、企业有权从事外贸经营活动的文件原件、法人代表授权书、被授权人的签样、外汇局备案表等。

2. 填写开证申请书

进口商向银行申请开立信用证以前，一般要填写开证申请书。开证申请书一般为一式三份，一份留业务部门；一份留财务部门；一份交银行。填写开证申请书时，必须按合同条款的具体规定，写明信用证的各项要求，内容要明确、完整，无词意不清的记载。

开证申请书是开证银行开立信用证的依据，由银行专门印发，包括正反面内容。正面内容是对信用证内容的要求，即开证人按合同要求开证行在信用证上列明的条款，也是开证行凭以向受益人或议付行付款的依据。包括受益人名称和地址、信用证及合同号码、信用证的有效期及到期地点、装运期、信用证的性质、货物的描述、对单据的要求、信用证的金额、种类、信用证中的特别条款及其他一些条款等。反面内容是开证人对开证行的声明或具结，用以明确双方责任，题目一般为开证申请人承诺书（开证人签字）。

3. 缴纳押金和开证手续费

按照国际贸易的习惯做法，进口商向银行开立信用证，应向银行缴付一定比例的押金或其他保证金，其金额一般为信用证金额的百分之几到百分之几十，具体由开证行根据申请人的资信和市场行情等规定。在我国的进口业务中，开证行根据不同企业和交易情况，要求开证申请人缴付一定比例的人民币保证金，然后银行才开证。同时，开证申请人还必须按规定向开证行缴纳一定比率的开证手续费（一般为 1.5‰）。

4. 开证行开立信用证

开证行收到进口商的开证申请后，应立即对开证申请书的内容及其与合同的关系、开证申请人的资信状况等进行审核，在确信可以接受开证申请人的申请并收取开证申请人提交的押金和开证手续费后，应严格按照开证申请书的指示拟订信用证条款，并将所开立的信用证由邮寄或电传或通过 SWIFT 电信网络送交出口地的联行或代理行（统称通知行），由他们代为通知或转交受益人。

3.3.2 申请开立信用证的注意事项

向银行申请开立信用证，具有很强技术性和专业性，稍有疏忽就有可能引起改证并付出不必要的费用，增加进口成本，因此在申请开立信用证时，应注意以下几个方面。

（1）申请开立信用证前，一定要落实进口批准手续及外汇来源。

（2）信用证的开证时间应按合同规定办理。如果买卖合同中规定有开证日期，进口商应在规定的期限内开立信用证；如果合同中只规定了装运期而未规定开证日期，进口商应在合理时间内开证，一般掌握在合同规定的装运期前 30~45 天左右申请开证，以便出口方收到信用证后在装运期内安排装运货物。

（3）开证要求"证同一致"，正本合同中规定要在信用证上明确的条款都必须列明，不能用"参阅××号合同"或"第××号合同项下货物"等条款，也不能将有关合同附件附在信用证后，因信用证是一个独立的文件，不依附于任何贸易合同。

（4）单据条款要明确。信用证的特点之一是单据买卖，因此进口商在申请开证时，必须列明需要出口人提供的各项单据的种类、份数及签发机构，明确规定各种单据的出单人，并对单据的内容提出具体要求。

（5）合同规定的条款应转化在相应的信用证条件里。如合同以 CFR/CIF 条件成交，信用证应要求受益人在提交的清洁已装船提单上注明"运费已付"字样等。信用证结算方式下，只要单据表面与信用证条款相符合，开证行就必须按规定付款。如信用证申请书中含有某些条件而未列明应提交与之相应的单据，银行将认为未列此条件，而不予理睬。

（6）特别条款的利用。若开证人有一些特别的指示，而该指示又不能以单据方式表现出来，则可利用特别条款来说明，如技术规格、质量的说明、包装的搭配以及迟期提单可以接受等。

（7）信用证中应明确规定是否允许分批装运、转运、是否接受第三者装运单据等条款。

（8）开证申请书文字应力求规范、完整、明确。进口商要求银行在信用证上载明的事项，必须完整、明确，不能使用含糊不清的文字。应避免使用"约"、"近似"等类似词语，这样一方面可使银行处理信用证或卖方履行信用证的条款时有所遵循，另一方面也可以此保护自己的权益。

（9）各银行事先印制的固定格式申请书中凡涉及选择的项目，一律在有关项目前打"×"表示选中。网上申请开证的客户必须注册企业网上银行证书版后才能办理相应业务。

3.3.3 信用证的开立形式

开证行应开证申请人的要求，可以用以下两种方式开立信用证。

1. 信开

信用证使用初期银行采用信开方式开立。信开（L/C opened by mail）是指银行以航空邮寄的方式将信用证送达通知行，邮寄方式有平邮、航空挂号及特快专递等。随着通信方式的发展，目前信开方式信用证已不多见。

2. 电开

电开（L/C opened by teletransmission）是指以电报、电传或 SWIFT 等电信方式开立信用证。开证行将信用证加注密押后以电信方式通知受益人所在地的代理行，即通知行，请其转知受益人。电开信用证在实际业务中使用十分广泛，尤其是用 SWIFT 方式开立的信用证。电开信用证又分"全电开证"和"简电开证"。"全电开证"是指将信用证的全部内容加注密押后发出，该电信文本为有效的信用证正本。"简电开证"是指将信用证主要内容发电预先通知受益人，银行承担必须使其生效的责任，但简电本身并非信用证的有效文本，不能凭以议付或付款，银行随后寄出的"证实书"才是正式的信用证。

3.3.4 信用证申请书的内容及其填制

信用证申请书（Irrevocable Documents Credit Application）的格式并不统一，各银行都有自己印制的格式，但其具体内容和项目基本相同。

（1）Date（申请开证日期）：在申请书右上角填写实际申请日期。

（2）To（致）：银行印制的申请书上事先都会印就开证银行的名称、地址，银行的 SWIFT CODE、TELEX NO. 等也可同时显示。

（3）Issue by air mail /With brief advice by teletransmission /Issue by express delivery/Issue by teletransmission（传递方式）：即信开、简电、快递、电开 4 种方式，需要哪一种方式，在其前面方框中打"×"。

（4）Irrevocable Documentary Credit（信用证性质）：不可撤销跟单信用证已印制好，不必重新填写，如要增加保兑或可转让等内容，可直接加上。

（5）Date and place of expiry（信用证的有效期和到期地点）：由申请人填写，有效期通常掌握在装运期后 15 天，到期地点一般在议付地。

（6）Number（信用证号码）：由开证行填写。

（7）Applicant（申请人）：填写合同买方即进口企业的全称，详细地址。

（8）Beneficiary（受益人）：填写合同卖方即出口企业的全称，详细地址。

(9) Advising Bank（通知行）：由开证行填写。

(10) Amount（信用证金额）：填写合同规定的总值。必须用数字和文字两种形式表示并需注明币别，如果有一定比例的上下浮动幅度，亦应明确表示出来。

(11) Partial shipments and transshipment（分批与转运）：应根据合同的规定明确表示"允许"或"不允许"，在选择的项目前方框中打"×"。

(12) Loading on board/dispatch/taking in charge at /from（装运条件）：应根据合同规定填写装运地（港）及目的地（港），最晚装运日期，如有转运地（港）也应写清楚。

(13) Trade Term（贸易条件）：有 CIF、FOB、CFR 及"其他条件"4 个备选项目，根据合同成交的贸易术语在该项前方框中打"×"，如是其他条件，则应先在"Other terms"前的方框中打"×"，然后再在该项目的空白处写明有关的贸易术语。

(14) Credit available with（付款方式）：有"即期付款"（by sight payment）、"承兑"（by acceptance）、"议付"（by negotiation）和"延期付款"（by deferred payment）等，申请书上已印有这 4 种付款方式，应根据合同的付款方式确定选项，并在其前面的方框中打"×"。如果是延期付款信用证，还应在该选项"at"之后加注延期付款的具体条件，如收到单据后若干天付款等。

(15) Beneficiary's draft（汇票要求）。应根据合同的规定，填写信用证项下应支付发票金额的一定百分比。如合同规定的所有货款都用信用证支付，则应填写信用证项下汇票金额是发票金额 100%；如合同规定该笔货款由信用证和托收两种方式支付，各支付 50%，则应填写信用证项下汇票金额是全部发票金额的 50%；以此类推。汇票的支付期限，可根据合同规定填写即期或远期，如是远期汇票，必须填写具体的天数。最后填写付款人，根据《UCP600》的规定，信用证项下汇票的付款人必须是开证行或指定付款行。

(16) Documents required（所需的单据）：各银行提供的申请书中已印就的单据条款通常为十几条，从上至下一般为发票、运输单据（提单、空运单、铁路运输单据及运输备忘录等）、保险单、装箱单、质量证书、装运通知和受益人证明等，最后一条是"其他单据"。填制单据条款时应注意事项如下。

① 在所需单据前的括号里打"×"，然后在该单据条款后填上具体的要求，如一式几份，应包括什么内容等，要求不完整的，可在该单据条款后面填写清楚。

② 有些单据本身又有一些选项可供选择，可在要选择项目前的括号中打"×"，如无括号，可以划掉非选项目。

③ 其他单据栏，可将本笔交易中所需的除上述所列范围外的其他单据列在此处。

(17) Covering（货物的描述）：填写合同项下的货物，包括品名、规格、数量、包装、单价条款、唛头等。所有内容必须与合同规定一致，价格条款里附带"As per INCOTERMS 2000"、数量条款中可规定"More or less"或"About"、使用某种特定包装物等特殊要求必须清楚列明，不得有误。

(18) Additional instructions（附加条款）：如需要已印就的条款，可在条款前打"×"，内容不完整的，可根据合同规定和买方的需要填写清楚，对合同涉及但未印就的条款可以作补充填写，有几条可顺序添加几条。

（19）申请书下面是有关申请人的开户银行（填银行名称）、账户号码、联系人、联系电话、申请人（法人代表）签字等内容。

申请人除了填写信用证申请书内容外，还应注意其背面条款。这些条款是开证申请人与开证行之间协议的组成部分，一般是由开证行在印制申请书时就已根据其习惯做法和国际惯例确定下来。

【相关单证】

单证3-2　信用证开证申请人承诺书

信用证开证申请人承诺书

中国银行：

　　我公司已办妥一切进口手续，现请贵行按我公司开证申请书内容（见背面英文）开出不可撤销跟单信用证，为此我公司愿不可撤销地承担有关责任如下。

　　一、我公司同意贵行依照国际商会第600号出版物《跟单信用证统一惯例》办理该信用证项下一切事宜，并同意承担由此产生的一切责任。

　　二、我公司保证按时向贵行支付该证项下的货款、手续费、利息及一切费用等（包括国外受益人拒绝承担的有关银行费用）所需的外汇和人民币资金。

　　三、我公司保证在贵行收到通知书中规定的期限之内通知贵行办理对外付款/承兑，否则贵行可认为我公司已接受单据，同意付款/承兑。

　　四、我公司保证在单证相符的条件下办理有关付款/承兑手续。如因单证有不符之处而拒绝付款/承兑，我公司保证在贵行收到通知书中规定的日期之前将全套单据如数退还贵行并附书面拒付理由，由贵行按国际惯例确定能否对外拒付。如贵行确定我公司所提拒付理由不成立，或虽然拒付理由成立，但我公司未能退回全套单据，或拒付单据退到贵行已超过收到通知书中规定的期限，贵行有权主动办理对外付款/承兑，并从我公司账户中扣款。

　　五、该信用证及其项下业务往来函电及单据如因邮、电或其他方式传递过程中发生遗失、延误、错漏，贵行当不负责。

　　六、该信用证如需修改，由我公司向贵行提出书面申请，由贵行根据具体情况确定能否办理修改。我公司确认所有修改当由信用证受益人接受时才能生效。

　　七、我公司在收到贵行开出的信用证、修改书副本后，保证及时与原申请书核对，如有不符之处，保证在接到副本之日起，两个工作日内通知贵行。如未通知，当视为正确无误。

　　八、如因申请书字迹不清或词意含混而引起的一切后果由我公司负责。

开证申请人
（签字盖章）
　年　月　日

第 3 章 信 用 证

【相关单证】

单证 3-3 信用证申请书

IRREVOCABLE DOCUMENTARY CREDIT APPLICATION

To: BANK OF CHINA   Date:

☐Issue by airmail ☐With brief advice by teletransmission ☐Issue by express delivery ☐Issue by teletransmission（which shall be the operative instrument）	Irrevocable Documentary Credit Number Date and place of expiry
Applicant	Beneficiary
Advising Bank	Amount
Partial shipments Transshipment ☐Allowed ☐not allowed ☐Allowed ☐not allowed	Credit available with ☐by sight payment ☐by acceptance ☐by negotiation ☐by deferred payment at against the documents detailed herein ☐and beneficiary's draft for ____% of invoice value at on
Loading on board/dispatch/taking in charge at/from not later than for transportation to:	
☐FOB ☐CFR ☐CIF ☐or other terms	

Documents required: (marked with ×)
1. (　) Manually Signed Commercial Invoice in copies indicating this L/C No. and Contract No.
2. (　) Full set (included original and non-negotiable copies) of Clean On Board "Freight" Ocean Bills of Lading made out to [ ] to order/[ ] to the order of and blank endorsed, marked "freight [ ] prepaid/[ ] to collect showing freight amount" notifying [ ] the applicant/[ ]
3. (　) Air Waybills showing "Freight" and consigned to
4. (　) RailWay Bills showing "Freight" and consigned to
5. (　) Memorandum issued by　　　consigned to
6. (　) Full set (included original and copies) of Insurance Policy/Certificate for 110% of the invoice value, showing claims payable in China, in currency of the draft blank endorsed, covering ([ ] ocean marine transportation \ [ ] air transportation \ [ ] over, land transportation) All Risks and War Risks.
7. (　) Packing List/Weight Memo in copies indicating quantity/gross and net weights of each package and packing conditions as called for by the L/C.
8. (　) Certificate of Quantity/Weight in copies issued by [ ] manufaiture/[ ] seller/[ ] independent surreyor at the loading port, indicating the actual surveyed quantity/Weight of shipped goods as well as the packing condition.
9. (　) Certificate of Quality in ____ copies issued by
10. (　) Beneficiary's certified copy of cable/telex dispatched to the applicant within ____ hours after shipment advising [ ] name of vessel/[ ] flight No. /[ ] wagon No. date, quantity, weight and value of shipment.
11. (　) Beneficiary's Certificate certifying that extra copies of documents have been dispatched according to the contract terms,
12. (　) Shipping Co's Certificate attesting that the carrying vessel is chartered or booked by Applicant or their shipping agents:
13. (　) Other documents, if any:

Covering:

Additional instructions:
1. (　) All banking charges outside the opening bank are for beneficiary's account.
2. (　) Documents must be presented within ____ days after the date of issuance of the transport documents but within the validity of this credit.
3. (　) Third party as shipper is not acceptable. Short Form/bank Back B/L is not acceptable.
4. (　) Both quantity and amount ____% more or less are allowed.
5. (　) Prepaid freight drawn in excess of L/C amount is acceptable against presentation of original charges voucher issued by shipping Co. /Air. Line/or it's agent.
6. (　) All documents to be forwarded in one cover, unless otherwise stated above.
7. (　) Other terms, if any:

Account No.:   with _____ (name of bank)
Transacted by: (Applicant: name, signature of authorized person)
Telephone No.:   (with seal)

【案例】

美国 PACIFIC INTERNATIONAL INC. 的 Paul Smith 先生收到杨光的催证函后，于 2008 年 7 月 5 日向当地的 CATHAY BANK, LOS ANGELES 申请开证，开证申请书如下。

IRREVOCABLE DOCUMENTARY CREDIT APPLICATION

TO: CATHAY BANK, LOS ANGELES   Date: JUL. 5, 2008

☐Issue by airmail ☐With brief advice by teletransmission ☐Issue by express delivery ☒Issue by teletransmission (which shall be the operative instrument)	Irrevocable Documentary Credit Number Date and place of expiry SEP 15, 2008 CHINA

Applicant   PACIFIC INTERNATIONAL INC.
       129 HAYWARD WAY STREET
       MONTE, CA 91513
	Beneficiary
	HEBEI HENGTAI IMPORT & EXPORT CORPORATION
	NO. 231 HEPING ROAD, SHIJIAZHUANG
	P. R CHINA

Advising Bank	
Partial shipments Transshipment ☒Allowed ☐not allowed ☒Allowed ☐not allowed	Amount (in words) USD 22,050.00 (in figure) SAY U.S DOLLARS TWENTY TWO THOUSAND AND FIFTY ONLY
Loading on board/dispatch/taking in charge at/from CHINESE PORT not later than AUG. 31, 2008 for transportation to: LOS ANGELES PORT, USA	Credit available with ☒by sight payment ☐by acceptance ☒by negotiation ☐by deferred payment at against the documents detailed herein
☐FOB ☒CFR ☐CIF ☐or other terms	☐and beneficiary's draft for 100% of invoice value at sight on issuing bank

Documents required: (marked with ×)
1. (×) Manually Signed Commercial Invoice in __3__ copies indicating this L/C No. and Contract No.
2. (×) Full set (included original and non-negotiable copies) of Clean On Board Ocean Bills of Lading made out to [×] to order/[ ] to the order of and blank endorsed, marked " freight [×] prepaid/[ ] to collect showing freight amount" notifying [×] the applicant/[ ] SHOWING CONTRACT NO. AND THIS CREDIT NO.
3. ( ) Air Waybills showing "Freight" and consigned to
4. ( ) RailWay Bills showing "Freight" and consigned to
5. ( ) Memorandum issued by _____ consigned to
6. ( ) Full set (included original and copies) of Insurance Policy/Certificate for 110% of the invoice value, showing claims payable in China, in, currency of the draft blank endorsed, covering ([ ] ocean marine transportation\[ ] air transportation \ [ ] over, land transportation) All Risks and war Risks.
7. (×) Packing List/Weight Memo in __3__ copies indicating quantity/gross and net weights of each package and packing conditions as called for by the L/C.
8. ( ) Certificate of Quantity/Weight in copies issued by [ ] manufacturer/[ ] Seller/[ ] independent surveyor at the loading port, indicating the actual surveyed quantity/Weight of shipped goods as well as the packing condition.
9. (×) Certificate of Quality in __3__ copies issued by AUTHORITY INSTITUTION.
10. (×) Beneficiary's certified copy of cable/telex dispatched to the applicant within __72__ hours after shipment advising [×] name of vessel/[ ] flight No. /[ ] wagon No. date, quantity, weight and value of shipment.
11. (×) Beneficiary's Certificate certifying that extra copies of documents have been dispatched according to the contract terms.
12. ( ) Shipping Co's Certificate attesting that the carrying vessel is chartered or booked by Applicant or their shipping agents;
13. ( ) Other documents, if any:
Covering: 4500 DOZEN 100% COTTON STRIPE TOWEL, ART NO. ABC69, SIZE: 30″×60″
         WEIGHT: 175GMS PER PIECE AT USD4.90 PER DOZEN
         PACKING: ONE DOZEN IN A POLYBAG, 20DOZENS IN A BALE
         TRADE TERMS: CFR LOS ANGELES

Additional instructions:
1. (×) All banking charges outside the opening bank are for beneficiary's account.
2. (×) Documents must be presented within __15__ days after the date of issuance of the transport documents but within the validity of this credit.
3. ( ) Third party as shipper is not acceptable. Short Form/bank Back B/L is not acceptable.
4. ( ) Both quantity and amount—% more or less are allowed.
5. ( ) Prepaid freight drawn in excess of L/C amount is acceptable against presentation of original charges voucher issued by shipping Co./Air. Line/or it's agent.
6. (×) All documents to be forwarded in one cover, unless otherwise stated above.
7. ( ) Other terms, if any:

Account No.:   with _____ (name of bank)
Transacted by: (Applicant: name, signature of authorized person)
Telephone No.:   (with seal)

【技能实训】

1. 根据下列销售确认书及实际需要填写开证申请书

销售确认书
SALES CONFIRMATION

卖方:
SELLERS: SHEMSY NEGOCE ID CORP.

编号:
NO: HT2006X06

地址:
ADDRESS: 75 ROUTE 96570 DARDILLY, FRANCE

日期:
DATE: APR 22, 2006

买方:
BUYERS: HEBEI TAIHUA IMP. & EXP. CO.

签约地点:
SIGNED AT: SHIJIAZHUANG

地址:
ADDRESS: 365 YUHUA ROAD, SHIJIAZHUANG, CHINA

传真:
FAX:

兹经买卖双方同意按下列条款成交:
THE UNDERSIGNED SELLERS AND BUYERS HAVE AGREED TO CLOSE THE FOLLOWING TRANSACTIONS ACCORDING TO THE TERMS AND CONDITIONS STIPULATED BELOW:

品名及规格 NAME OF GOODS AND SPECIFICATIONS	数量 QUANTITY	单价 UNIT PRICE	总值 AMOUNT
LEATHER BAGS			CIF XINGANG
ITEM NO. SL100	100PCS	USD20.00/PC	USD2 000.00
ITEM NO. SG120	200PCS	USD15.00/PC	USD3 000.00
ITEM NO. SF200	300PCS	USD30.00/PC	USD9 000.00
合同总额 TOTAL VALUE	6 000PCS		USD14 000.00

SAY US DALLARS FOURTEEN THOUSAND ONLY

1. 数量及总值均有5%的增减,由卖方决定。
WITH 5% MORE OR LESS BOTH IN AMOUNT AND QUANTITY ALLOWED AT THE SELLERS OPTION.

2. 包装:
PACKING: CARTON

3. 装运唛头:
SHIPPING MARKS: AS PER BUYER'S DEMANDS

4. 装运期:
TIME OF SHIPMENT: WITHIN 30 DAYS AFTER RECEIPT OF L/C, ALLOWING PARTIAL SHIPMENTS AND TRANSHIPMENT.

5. 装运口岸和目的地:
LOADING & DESTINATION: DELIVERY FROM MARSEILLES TO XINGANG

6. 保险:
INSURANCE: TO BE EFFECTED BY THE SELLER FOR 110% OF INVOICE VALUE TO COVER INSTITUTE CARGO CLAUSE (A), INSTITUTE WAR CLAUSE UP TO XINGANG CHINA

INCLUING WAREHOUSE TO WAREHOUSE.

7. 付款条件：

PAYMENT: BY COFIRMED, IRREVOCABLE L/C TO BE AVAILABLE BY SIGHT DRAFT TO REACH THE SELLERS BEFORE MAY 1, 2006 AND TO REMAIN VALID FOR NEGOTIATION IN CHINA UNTIL 15 DAYS AFTER THE AFORESAID TIME OF SHIPMENT. THE L/C MUST SPECIFY THAT TRANSIPMENT AND PARTIAL SHIPMENTS ARE ALLOWED.

8. 仲裁条款：

ARBITRATE CLAUSES: ANY DISPUTE ARISING OUT OF IN CONNECTION WITH THIS CONTRACT SHALL BE REFERRED TO CHINA INTERNATIONAL ECONOMIC AND TRADE ARBITRATION COMMISSION FOR ARBITRATION IN ACCORDANCE WITH ITS EXISTING RULES OF ARBITRATION. THE PLACE OF ARBITRATION SHALL BE BEIJING, THE ARBITRAL AWARD IS FINAL AND BINDING UPON THE TWO PARTIES.

备注：
REMARK：

买方	卖方
THE BUYERS	THE SELLERS
HEBEI TAIHUA IMP. & EXP. CO.	SHEMSY NEGOCE ID CORP.

2. 根据下面提供的合同填写信用证申请书

CONTRACT
Original

No. N8TB336
Date: JUNE 15, 2005

The buyers: ZHENGDA PACKING CO. LTD.
95 HONGGUANG ROAD, SHIJIAZHUANG, CHINA
Telex: Fax:
The sellers: HANSOL CORPORATION
9TH FL, KWANGHWAMUN BLDG, 211 SEJONE-RO, CHONGRO-KU, SEOUL, KOREA
Telex: Fax:

1. COMMODITY：   DUPLEX BOARD WITH GREY BACK
2. BRAND：   HANSOL HI-Q
3. SPECIFICATIONS：   250GSM, 31″×47″L.G.
4. QUANTIY：   100.0MTS
(2% MORE OR LESS IN QUANTITY AND AMOUNT IS ALLOWED)
5. PACKING：   STANDARD PACKING IN CONTAINER.
6. UNIT PRICE：   USD 415/MT CFR XINGANG, CHINA
7. TATOL VALUE：   USD41 500.00
8. TIME OF SHIPMENT：   BEFORE THE END OF JULY
9. PORT OF SHIPMENT：   KOREA MAIN PORT
10. PORT OF DESTINATION： XINGANG, CHINA
11. INSURANCE：   TO BE EFFECTED BY THE BUYER

12. PAYMENT: The Buyers, upon receipt from the Sellers of the delivery advice, shall, in 15~20 days prior to the date of delivery, open an irrevocable Letter of Credit with the Bank of China, in favour of the Sellers, for an amount equivalent to the value of the shipment. The Credit shall be payable against the presentation of draft drawn on the opening bank and the shipping documents. The Letter of Credit shall be valid until the 15th day after the date of shipment is effected. By L/C at 90 days after date of B/L.

REMARKS:

1. PACKING: To be packed in strong wooden case (s) or in carton (s), suitable for long distance ocean marine transportation and to change of climate, well protected against moisture and shocks.

The Sellers shall be liable for any damage of the commodity and expenses incurred on account of improper packing or inadequate and improper protective measures taken by the Sellers in regard to the packing.

2. SHIPPING MARK: The Sellers shall mark on each package with fadeless paint the package number, gross weight, net weight, measurement and the wordings: "KEEP AWAY FROM MOISTURE", "HANDLE WITH CARE" etc. And

the shipping mark:　　　N8TB336
　　　　　　　　　　XINGANG CHINA
　　SELLERS　　　　　　　BUYERS
HANSOL CORPORATION　　ZHENGDA PACKING CO. LTD.

3.4 信用证的审核

信用证是依据买卖双方签订的合同开出的，其条款也应与合同条款相符合。但在实际业务中，由于多种原因，国外开来的信用证与合同规定、贸易惯例或外贸政策不符的情况时有发生。因此，为了顺利完成出口和收汇工作，出口商在收到信用证后，必须依据销售合同和《跟单信用证统一惯例》对信用证内容逐项进行认真审核。

3.4.1 信用证审核的要点

审核信用证是银行和出口企业共同承担的责任，但审核内容各有侧重。实际业务中银行主要负责鉴别信用证的真伪，出口企业则着重审核信用证的内容与买卖合同条款是否一致。

1. 银行审证的要点

银行主要从三方面审核信用证。一是审核信用证各项内容是否符合我国的方针政策以及是否有歧视性内容。来证如载有歧视性或错误或政治性条款，应要求改正。二是审核开证行的政治背景、资信能力等方面的内容，对于资信不佳的银行应酌情采取适当的保全措施。三是审核信用证的真实性、开证行的付款责任和索汇路线等问题。

2. 出口方审证的要点

出口方一般主要审核以下几点。

(1) 审核开证申请人和受益人。对照买卖合同条款，审核开证申请人、受益人名称和地址是否正确，以防错发错运，影响收汇。

(2) 审核信用证的金额及货币。信用证的金额应与合同金额一致，大写和小写金额一致；如合同订有溢短装条款，信用证金额还应包括溢短装部分的金额；信用证采用的支付货币应与合同规定的支付货币一致。

(3) 审核信用证的有效期和到期地点。有效期和到期地点关系到出口商能否及时交单，有效期应与运输相协调。到期地点若在国外，则有关单据必须在到期日前寄达开证银行或指定付款银行，对出口商来说，由于寄单费时且有可能延误，因而风险较大。为此，出口商应争取在出口地到期，否则，应注意提前交单，以防逾期。

(4) 审核运输条款。审核信用证对运输路线、分批装运和转运以及运输工具的要求、装运期限的规定是否与合同一致；来证中指定船龄、船籍、船公司或不准在某港口转船等条款能否办到等。来证中的装运港（地）和目的港（地），应与合同相符，交货地点也必须与价格条款相一致，如不符则应修改；装运期原则上必须与合同规定一致。如信用证到达过迟，不能按期装运，应及时电请国外买方展期。信用证的有效期与装运期应有一定的合理间隔，以便在货物装运后有足够的时间进行制单、交单等工作。如为"双到期"，受益人可视具体情况提请对方修改。

(5) 审核汇票条款。来证规定开立汇票的内容如即期、远期等应与合同中支付条款的规定相符。

(6) 审核货物描述。来证中有关品名、品质、规格、数量、包装、唛头、单价、佣金等是否与合同规定一致。如不一致，一般不应轻易接受，原则上应要求改证。

(7) 审核单据条款。审核信用证所要求单据的种类、份数及填制要求是否能够办到。一些需要认证的单据特别是使馆认证等能否及时办理和提供；由其他机构或部门出具的有关文件如出口许可证、运费收据、检验证明等能否提供或及时提供。如发现有不适当的要求和规定，应酌情作出适当处理。

(8) 审核有关保险的规定。审核来证要求的保险险别或投保金额是否超出了合同的规定，在以 FOB、CFR 条件成交时，若来证要求由出口商办理保险，审核来证金额中是否已包括保险费。

(9) 其他条款的合理性。如银行费用的支付，有无软条款、信用证中有无矛盾之处，如 FOB 条件下要求提供保险单等。若发现有不利的条款，一般不应接受。如该条款没有对出口商不利之处，而且也能办到，则可灵活掌握。

经过对信用证全面和仔细的审核以后，如果发现问题，需要出口商对外交涉修改或澄清的，应当参照国际上的习惯做法办理。对于出口方今后制单不会产生不符点的问题，尽量不修改信用证。如果认真仔细地逐条审核来证条款之后，仍有把握不住的内容，一定要向经验丰富的业务人员及有关方面的专家咨询。

3.4.2 信用证审核中常见问题

实务中，信用证审核中常出现问题的地方需特别注意。

(1) 信用证的性质。有下列情况之一的，不是一项有效的付款保证或该项付款保证是存在缺陷问题的：信用证内容不完整；信用证未生效或有限制性生效的条款；信用证为可撤销的；信开信用证中没有保证付款的责任文句；信用证内未加列受《UCP600》约束的条款；信用证未按合同要求加保兑；由开证人直接寄送的信用证。

（2）信用证当事人。受益人的名称或地址有误；开证申请人的名称或地址有误。

（3）金额货币。信用证金额不够（不符合合同、未达到溢短装要求）；金额大小写不一致；信用证货币币种与合同规定不符。

（4）信用证有关期限。信用证中没有规定到期日（有效期）；到期地点在国外；信用证的到期日和装运期有矛盾；装运期、到期日或交单期规定与合同不符；装运期或有效期的规定与交单期矛盾；交单期时间过短。

（5）运输、保险条款。装运港（地）或目的港（地）与合同规定或成交条件不符；分批或转运规定与合同规定不符；转运地与合同规定或成交条件不符；转运期限与合同规定不符；保险险别、保险金额与合同规定不符等。

（6）货物描述。品名、规格等与合同不一致；数量与合同规定不符；包装的数量、种类或方式等与合同规定不符；唛头与已刷唛头不一致；商品的单价与合同不符；使用的贸易术语与合同不一致；货物的单价、数量与总金额不吻合；援引合同号码有误等。

（7）单据条款。汇票的付款期限与合同规定不符；在信用证方式下，汇票的付款人为开证申请人；发票种类不当；商业发票要求领事签证；提单收货人一栏的填制要求不当；提单抬头和背书要求有矛盾；提单运费条款规定与成交条件矛盾；要求提单的出单日期比装运期早；正本提单全部或部分直寄客户；对运输工具、方式或路线的限制无法接受；原产地证书出具机构有误，如为国外机构或无授权机构；漏列必须提交的单据，如 CIF 成交条件下的保险单；费用条款规定不合理；运输工具限制过严；要求提交的检验证书种类与实际不符；保险单种类不对；保险险别范围与合同规定不一致；投保金额未按合同规定。

（8）常见的影响安全收汇的软条款。信用证暂不生效条款；信用证规定必须由开证申请人或其指定的人签署有关单据的条款；信用证对银行的付款、承兑行为规定了若干前提条件，如货物清关后才付款或信用证前后条款相互矛盾等。

【案例】

河北恒泰公司业务员杨光收到 CATHAY BANK, LOS ANGELES 开来的信用证后，随即对信用证进行了审核。

销 售 合 同
SALES CONTRACT

合同号码：
Contract No.：02AG18185
日期：
Date：JUN. 20, 2008

卖方：
The Sellers：HEBEI HENGTAI IMPORT&EXPORT CORPORATION

电话：
TEL：86-0311-84576936

地址：
Address：NO. 231 HEPING ROAD, SHIJIAZHUANG, HEBEI, CHINA

传真：
FAX：86-0311-84576937

买方：
The Buyers：PACIFIC INTERNATIONAL INC.

电话：
TEL：1-213-2891024

地址：
Address：129 HAYWARD WAY STREET, MONTE, CA 91513

传真：
FAX：1-213-2891025

兹经买卖双方同意，由买方购进，卖方出售下列货物，并按下列条款签订本合同：
This Contract is made by and between the Buyers and the Sellers; whereby the Buyers agree to buy and the Sellers agree to sell the undermentioned goods on the terms and conditions stated below：

(1) 货物名称、规格 Name of Commodity, Specifications	(2) 数量 Quantity	(3) 单价 Unit Price	(4) 总值 Amount
100% COTTON STRIPE TOWEL ART NO. ABC69 SIZE：30″×60″	4 500 DOZS	CIF LOS ANGELES USD 4.90/DOZ	USD22 050.00
5% more or less both in amount and quantity allowed		Total Amount	USD22 050.00

合同总额 Total Contract Value：
SAY U.S. DOLLARS TWENTY TWO THOUSAND AND FIFTY ONLY

(5) 包装：
Packing Terms：To be packed in bale. One dozen to a polybag, 20 dozens in a bale

(6) 装运口岸：
Port of Loading：CHINESE PORT

(7) 目的口岸：
Port of Destination：LOS ANGELES PORT, USA

(8) 唛头：
Shipping Marks：PACIFIC
　　　　　　　　18185
　　　　　　　　LOS ANGELES
　　　　　　　　1-225

(9) 装运期限：
Time of Shipment：Not later than AUG. 31, 2008, allowing transshipment and partial shipment

(10) 付款条件：
Terms of Payment：The Buyer shall open through a bank acceptable to the seller an irrevocable Letter of Credit at sight to reach the seller 20 days before the month of shipment valid for negotiation in China until the 15th day after the date of shipment.

(11) 保险：
Insurance：The Seller shall cover insurance against All Risks and War Risk for 110% of invoice value as per Ocean Marine Cargo Clause of the People's Insurance Company of China dated 1/1/1981.

(12) 单据：

Documents:

议付时卖方应提交如下单据:

The Seller shall present the following documents to the bank for negotiation:

① Manually signed commercial invoice in triplicate certifying the origin of goods and contents to be true and correct.

② Full set of clean on board ocean bills of lading made out to order and blank endorsed and marked "Freight Prepaid" and notify applicant showing contract No. and this credit No. .

③ Packing list in triplicate indicating quantity/gross and net weight of each package and packing conditions as called for by the L/C.

④ Manually signed certificate of China origin in triplicate issued by authority institution.

(13) 装运通知

Advice of Shipment: The Sellers shall upon competition of loading, advise immediately the Buyers by cable of the contract number, name of commodity, number of packages, gross and net weights, invoice value, name of vessel and loading date.

(14) 品质/数量异议：如买方提出索赔，凡属品质异议须于货到目的口岸之日起30天内提出，凡属数量异议须于货到目的口岸之日起15天内提出，对所装货物所提任何异议于保险公司、轮船公司、其他有关运输机构或邮递机构所负责者，卖方不负任何责任。

Quality/Quantity Discrepancy: In case of quality discrepancy, claim should be filed by the Buyer within 30 days after the arrival of the goods at port of destination, while for quantity discrepancy, claim should be filed by the Buyer within 15 days after the arrival of the goods at port of destination. It is understood that the Seller shall not be liable for any discrepancy of the goods shipped due to causes for which the Insurance Company, Shipping Company, other Transportation Organization /or Post Office are liable.

(15) 不可抗力：由于人力不可抗拒事故，使卖方不能在合同规定期限内交货或者不能交货，卖方不负责任。但卖方必须立即通知买方，并以挂号函向买方提出有关政府机关或者商会所出具的证明，以证明事故的存在。由于人力不可抗拒事故致使交货期限延期一个月以上时，买方有权撤销合同。卖方不能取得出口许可证不得作为不可抗力。

Force Majeure: In case of Force Majeure the Sellers shall not held responsible for delay in delivery or non-delivery of the goods but shall notify immediately the Buyers and deliver to the Buyers by registered mail a certificate issued by government authorities or Chamber of Commerce as evidence thereof. If the shipment is delayed over one month as the consequence of the said Force Majeure, the Buyers shall have the right to cancel this Contract. Sellers' inability in obtaining export licence shall not be considered as Force Majeure.

(16) 延期交货及罚款：除本合同第 (15) 条人力不可抗拒原因外，如卖方不能如期交货，买方有权撤销该部分的合同，或经买方同意在卖方缴纳罚款的条件下延期交货。买方可同意给予卖方15天优惠期，罚款率为每10天按货款总额的1%，不足10天者按10天计算。罚款自第16天起计算。最多不超过延期货款总额的5%。

Delayed Delivery and Penalty: Should the Sellers fail to effect delivery on time as stipulated in this Contract owing to causes other than Force Majeure as provided for in Clause (15) of this Contract, the Buyers shall have the right to cancel the relative quantity of the contract, or alternatively, the Sellers may, with the Buyers' consent, postpone delivery on payment of penalty to the Buyers. The Buyers may agree to grant the Sellers a grace period of 15 days. Penalty shall be charged at the rate of 1% of the total value for every 10 days, odd days less than 10 days should be counted 10 days. The total penalty shall be calculated from the 16th day and shall not exceed 5% of the total value of the goods involved.

(17) 仲裁：一切因执行本合同或与本合同有关的争执，应由双方通过友好方式协商解决。如经协商不能得到解决时，应提交北京中国国际贸易促进委员会对外经济贸易仲裁委员会。按照中国国际贸易促进委员会对外经济贸易仲裁委员会仲裁程序暂行规定进行仲裁。仲裁委员会的裁决为终局裁决，对双方均有约束力。仲裁费用除非仲裁委员会另有决定外，由败诉一方负担。

Arbitration：All disputes in connection with this Contract or the execution thereof shall be friendly negotiation. If no settlement can be reached, the case in dispute shall then be submitted for arbitration to the Foreign Economic and Trade Arbitration Commission of the China Council for the Promotion of International Trade in accordance with the Provisional Rules of Procedure of the Foreign Economic and Trade Arbitration Commission of the China Council for the Promotion of International Trade. The Award made by the Commission shall be accepted as final and binding upon both parties. The fees for arbitration shall be borne by the losing party unless otherwise awarded by the Commission.

买方　　　　　　　　　　卖方
The Buyers　　　　　　　The Sellers

信用证
LETTER OF CREDIT

```
BASIC HEADER      F 01 BKCHCNBJA5×× 9828 707873
APPL. HEADER      O 700 1630000731 CATHUS6LA××× 1809 042841 0708010730 N
                                  +CATHAY BANK, LOS ANGELES, USA
(BANK NO.: 2504307)               +LOS ANGELES, USA
MT700             ISSUE OF A DOCUMENTARY CREDIT
SEQUENCE OF TOTAL       27: 1/1
FORM OF DOC. CREDIT     40A: IRREVOCABLE
DOCUMENTARY CREDIT NUMBER     20: LC-710-076405
DATE OF ISSUE     31C: 080706
DATE AND PLACE OF EXPIRY    31 D: 080915 USA
APPLICANT    50: PACIFIC INTERNATIONAL INC.
                 128 HAYWARD WAY STREET
                 MONTE, CA 91513
BENIFICIARY  59: HEBEI HENGTAI IMPORT & EXPORT CORPORATION
                 NO. 231 HEPING ROAD,
                 SHIJIAZHUANG, HEBEI, CHINA
CURRENCY CODE, AMOUNT     32B: USD 22 050.00
PERCENTAGE CREDIT AMOUNT TOLERANCE     39A: 5/5
AVAILABLE WITH/BY    41D: ANY BANK BY NEGOTIATION
DRAFT AT...       42C: SIGHT
DRAWEE            42A: CATHAY BANK, LOS ANGELES, CA
PARTIAL SHIPMENTS       43P: NOT ALLOWED
TRANSSHIPMENT     43T: ALLOWED
LOADING /DISPATCH/TAKING /FORM     44A: CHINESE PORT
FOR TRANSPORTATION TO...     44B: LOS ANGELES PORT, USA
LATEST DATE OF SHIPMENT     44C: 080831
DESCRIPTION OF GOODS AND/OR SERVICES       45A:
```

                          4 500 DOZEN 100% COTTON STRIPE TOWEL, ART NO. ABC69, SIZE: 30″×60″
                          WEIGHT: 175 GMS PER PIECE AT USD4.90 PER DOZEN
                          PACKING: ONE DOZEN IN A POLYBAG, 20 DOZENS IN A CARTON
                          TRADE TERMS: CIF LOS ANGELES
DOCUMENTS REQUIRED   46A:
         +MANUALLY SIGNED COMMERCIAL INVOICE IN TRIPLICATE CERTIFYING
          THE ORIGIN OF GOODS AND CONTENTS TO BE TRUE AND CORRECT.
         +2/3 SET OF CLEAN ON BOARD OCEAN BILLS OF LADING MADE OUT TO
          ORDER AND BLANK ENDORSED AND MARKED "FREIGHT COLLECT" AND
          NOTIFY APPLICANT SHOWING CONTRACT NO. AND THIS CREDIT NO..
         +INSURANCE POLICIES/CERTIFICATE IN DUPLICATE ENDORSED IN
          BLANK FOR 110% OF INVOICE VALUE COVERING ALL RISKS AND
          WAR RISK AS PER PEOPLE'S INSURANCE COMPANY OF CHINA DAT-
          ED 1/1/1981. WITH CLAIMS PAYABLE AT LOS ANGELES PORT IN
          THE CURRANCY OF DRAFT.
         +PACKING LIST IN TRIPLICATE INDICATING QUANTITY/GROSS AND
          NET WEIGHTS OF EACH PACKAGE AND PACKING CONDITIONS AS
          CALLED FOR BY THE L/C.
         +MANUALLY SIGNED CERTIFICATE OF CHINA ORIGIN IN TRIPLICATE
          ISSUED BY AUTHORITY INSTITUTION.
         +SHIPPING ADVICE GIVING FULL DETAILS OF SHIPMENT MUST BE
          SENT TO APPLICANT BY FAX WITHIN 3 DAYS FROM THE DATE OF
          SHIPMENT SHOWING THE NAME OF CARRYING VESSEL, DATE OF
          SHIPMENT, SHIPPING MARKS, AMOUNT AND L/C NO. AND A COPY
          OF SUCH FAX ADVICE TOGETHER WITH A COPY OF FAX TRANSMIS-
          SION REPORT MUST ACCOMPANY THE DOCUMENTS.
         +BENEFICIARY'S CERTIFICATE STATING THAT ONE COMPLETE SET
          OF NON-NEGOTIABLE SHIPPING DOCUMENTS TO BE SENT TO APPLI-
          CANT BY DHL WITHIN 2 DAYS AFTER SHIPMENT.
ADDITIONAL CONDITIONS.   47A:
         +INSURANCE TO BE EFFECTED BY BUYER.
         +A DISCREPANCY FEE OF USD50 WILL BE DEDUCTED FROM PROCEEDS
          ON EACH SET OF DISCREPANT DOCUMENTS PRESENTED UNDER
          THIS CREDIT. AMOUNT AND QNTY 5PCT MORE OR LESS ALLOWED.
DETAILS OF CHARGES   71B: ALL BANKING CHARGES OUTSIDE OF OUR COUNT-
                          ER ARE FOR ACCOUNT OF BENEFICIARY.
PRESENTATION PERIOD   48: DOCUMENTS MUST BE PRESENTED WITHIN 3 DAYS
                          AFTER THE DATE OF SHIPMENT, BUT WITHIN THE
                          VALIDITY OF THE CREDIT.
CONFIRMATION   49: WITHOUT
INSTRUCTIONS   78: +ALL DOCUMENTS MUST BE FORWARDED TO US IN ONE COVER
                          BY COURIER SERVICE, UNLESS OTHERWISE STATED ABOVE.

　　　　　　　　　　　　　　＋WE HEREBY UNDERTAKE THAT UPON RECEIPT OF THE
　　　　　　　　　　　　　　ORIGINAL DOCUMENTS IN COMPLIANCE WITH THE TERMS
　　　　　　　　　　　　　　OF THIS CREDIT. THE DRAFTS DRAWN UNDER WILL BE DU-
　　　　　　　　　　　　　　LY HONORED.
"ADVISE THROUGH"　　　57A：BANK OF CHINA, HEBEI BRANCH
SENDER TO RECEIVER INFORMATION　　72：THIS CREDIT IS SUBJECT TO THE UNI-
　　　　　　　　　　　　　　FORM CUSTOMS AND PRACTICE FOR DOCUMENTARY CRED-
　　　　　　　　　　　　　　ITS, 2007 REVISION, I.C.C. PUBLICATIONS NO. 600.
TRAILER　　　　　　　MAC：A75A8689 CHK：39D0ADB5BC9A

经审核杨光发现如下错误：

(1) 信用证规定交单地点在美国，非常不利；

(2) 信用证中开证申请人地址"128 HAYWARD WAY STREET"错误，正确的是"129"；

(3) 信用证中分批装运"NOT ALLOWED"错误，正确的是"ALLOWED"；

(4) 信用证中包装条款"IN A CARTON"错误，正确的是"IN A BALE"；

(5) 信用证海运提单条款中提单份数"2/3 SET OF CLEAN ON BOARD OCEAN BILLS OF LADING"对受益人非常不利，应该为"3/3"；

(6) 信用证海运提单条款中"FREIGHT COLLECT"错误，正确的是"FREIGHT PRE-PAID"；

(7) 信用证交单期"WITHIN 3 DAYS AFTER THE DATE OF SHIPMENT"错误，根据合同，应该为"WITHIN 15 DAYS AFTER THE DATE OF SHIPMENT"。

信用证审核记录

证号	LC-710-076405	合同号		02AG18185	
开证行	CATHAY BANK, LOS ANGELES, USA				
开证申请人	PACIFIC INTERNATIONAL INC.				
货物名称	100% COTTON STRIPE TOWEL	数量	4 500 DOZS	金额	USD22 050.00
价格条件	CFR LOS ANGELES	装运期	AUG. 31, 2008	有效期	SEP. 15, 2008
存在问题及处理意见 1. 信用证规定交单地点在美国，非常不利，修改； 2. 信用证中开证申请人地址"128 HAYWARD WAY STREET"错误，修改； 3. 信用证中分批装运"NOT ALLOWED"错误，修改； 4. 信用证中包装条款"IN A CARTON"错误，修改； 5. 信用证海运提单条款中提单份数"2/3 SET OF CLEAN ON BOARD OCEAN BILLS OF LADING"对受益人非常不利，修改； 6. 信用证海运提单条款中"FREIGHT COLLECT"错误，修改； 7. 信用证交单期"WITHIN 3 DAYS AFTER THE DATE OF SHIPMENT"错误，修改。				修改记录 —	
注意事项				议付情况	

【技能实训】

1. 根据下列合同审核信用证,找出信用证内容的不符点
1) 合同资料

SALES CONTRACT

NO.: JY04125
DATE: NOV. 6, 2004

THE SELLER: ZHEJIANG JINYUAN TEA FOODSTUFF CO. LTD.
118 LONGJING STREET, HANGZHOU,
P. R. CHINA

THE BUYER: WENSCO FOODS LTD.
1191 GREEN LAND STREET, WELL D. COQUITLAM, B. C.,
CANADA

This Contract is made by and between the Buyer and Seller, whereby the Buyer agree to buy and the Seller agree to sell the under-mentioned commodity according to the terms and conditions stipulated below:

Commodity & Specification	Unit	Quantity	Unit Price	Amount
CHINESE TEA			CIF COQUITLAM	
T16 HEALTH TEA	CARTONS	150	USD110	USD16 500.00
T17 WEN JING TEA	CARTONS	200	USD120	USD24 000.00
T18 FAT REDUING TEA	CARTONS	300	USD130	USD39 000.00
TOTAL		650 CARTONS		USD79 500.00

More or less 5% of the quantity and the amount are allowed
TOTAL CONTRACT VALUE: SAY U. S. DOLLARS SEVENTY NINE THOUSAND FIVE HUNDRED ONLY

PACKING: To be packed in carton.

MARKS:
Shipping marks includes WFL, S/C No., port of destination and carton No.

TIME OF SHIPMENT:
Within 60 days upon receipt of the L/C which accord with relevant clauses of this Contract.

PORT OF LOADING AND DESTINATION:
From Shanghai, China to Coquitlam, Canada
Transshipment is allowed and partial shipment is prohibited.

INSURANCE: To be effected by the seller for 110% of invoice value covering All Risks and War Risks as per CIC of PICC dated 01/01/1981.

TERMS OF PAYMENT: By irrevocable Letter of Credit at 60 days after sight, reaching the seller not later than Nov. 30, 2004 and remaining valid for negotiation in China for further 15 days after the effected shipment. In case of late arrival of the L/C, the seller shall not be liable for any delay in shipment and shall have the right to rescind the contract and/or claim for damages.

DOCUMENTS:
+ Signed Invoice in triplicate, one original of which should be certified by Chamber of Commerce or CCPIT and legalized by UAE embassy/consulate in seller's country.
+ Full set (3/3) of clean on board ocean Bills of Lading marked "freight prepaid" made out to order blank endorsed notifying the applicant.
+ Insurance Policy in duplicate endorsed in blank.
+ Packing List in triplicate.
+ Certificate of Origin certified by Chamber of Commerce or CCPIT and legalized by UAE embassy/consulate in seller's country.

INSPECTION:
The certificate of Quality issued by the China Entry-Exit Inspection and Quarantine Bureau shall be taken as the basis of delivery.

CLAIMS:
In case discrepancy on the quality or quantity (weight) of the goods is found by the buyer, after arrival of the goods at the port of destination, the buyer may, within 30 days and 15 days respectively after arrival of the goods at the port of destination, lodge with the seller a claim which should be supported by an Inspection Certificate issued by a public surveyor approved by the seller. The seller shall, on the merits of the claim, either make good the loss sustained by the buyer or reject their claim, it being agreed that the seller shall not be held responsible for any loss or losses due to natural cause failing within the responsibility of Shipowners of the Underwriters. The seller shall reply to the buyer within 30 days after receipt of the claim.

LATE DELIVERY AND PENALTY:
In case of late delivery, the Buyer shall have the right to cancel this Contract, reject the goods and lodge a claim against the Seller. Except for Force Majeure, if late delivery occurs, the Seller must pay a penalty, and the Buyer shall have the right to lodge a claim against the Seller. The rate of penalty is charged at 0.5% for every 7 days, odd days less than 7 days should be counted as 7 days. The total penalty amount will not exceed 5% of the shipment value. The penalty shall be deducted by the paying bank or the Buyer from the payment.

FORCE MAJEURE:
The seller shall not held responsible if they, owing to Force Majeure cause or causes, fail to make delivery within the time stipulated in the Contract or cannot deliver the goods. However, in such a case, the seller shall inform the buyer immediately by cable and if it is requested by the buyer, the seller shall also deliver to buyer by registered letter, a certificate attesting the existence of such a cause or causes.

ARBITRATION:
All disputes in connection with this contract or the execution thereof shall be settled amicably by

negotiation. In case no settlement can be reached, the case shall then be submitted to the China International Economic Trade Arbitration Commission for settlement by arbitration in accordance with the Commission's arbitration rules. The award rendered by the commission shall be final and binding on both parties. The fees for arbitration shall be borne by the losing party unless otherwise awarded.

THE SELLER	THE BUYER
ZHEJIANG JINYUAN TEA FOODSTUFF CO. LTD.	WENSCO FOODS LTD.

2) 信用证资料

MT 700 ISSUE OF A DOCUMENTARY CREDIT
SENDER   BANK OF NOVA SCOTIA, TORONTO, CANADA
RECEIVER   HANGZHOU CITY COMMERCIAL BANK, HANGZHOU, CHINA
SEQUENCE OF TOTAL: 27: 1/1
FORM OF DOC. CREDIT: 40A: IRREVOCABLE
DOC. CREDIT NUMBER: 20: KKK061888
DATE OF ISSUE: 31C: 041115
APPLICABLE RULES: 40E: UCP LATEST VERSION
DATE AND PLACE OF EXPIRY: 31D: DATE 050130 PLACE IN CANADA
APPLICANT: 50: WENSCO FOODS LTD.
        1191 GREEN LAND STREET, WELL D. COQUITLAM, B. C., CANADA
BENEFICIARY: 59: ZHEJIANG JINYUAN TEA FOODSTUFF CO. LTD.
        118 LONGJING STREET, HANGZHOU, P. R. CHINA
AMOUNT: 32B: CURRENCY USD AMOUNT 79 500.00
AVAILABLE WITH/BY: 41D: ANY BANK IN CHINA, BY NEGOTIATION
DRAFTS AT…: 42C: 120 DAYS AFTER SIGHT
DRAWEE: 42A: BANK OF NOVA SCOTIA, TORONTO, CANADA
PARTIAL SHIPMTS: 43P: PROHIBITED
TRANSSHIPMENT: 43T: ALLOWED
PORT OF LOADING/AIRPORT OF DEPARTURE: 44E: CHIENESE MAIN PORT
PORT OF DISCHARGE: 44F: COQUITLAM, CANADA
LATEST DATE OF SHIPMENT: 44C: 050101
DESCRIPTION OF GOODS AND/OR SERVICE: 45A:
3 ITEMS OF CHINESE TEA INCLUDING:
T16 HEALTH TEA   150 CARTONS
T17 WEN JING TEA   200 CANTONS
T18 FAT REDUING TEA   300 CARTONS
AS PER S/C JY04125 DATED NOV. 6, 2004
PRICE TERM: CIF COQUITLAM
DOCUMENTS REQUIRED: 46A:
    +SIGNED INVOICE IN TRIPLICATE, ONE ORIGINAL OF WHICH SHOULD BE
     CERTIFIED BY CHAMBER OF COMMERCE OR CCPIT AND LEGALIZED BY UAE
     EMBASSY/CONSULATE IN SELLER'S COUNTRY.

+PACKING LIST IN TRIPLICATE.
+CERTIFICATE OF CHINESE ORIGIN CERTIFIED BY CHAMBER OF COMMERCE OR CCPIT AND LEGALIZED BY UAE EMBASSY/CONSULATE IN SELLER'S COUNTRY.
+NSURANCE POLICY/CERTIFICATE IN DUPLICATE ENDORSED IN BLANK FOR 120% INVOICE VALUE, COVERING ALL RISKS AND WAR RISK OF CIC OF PICC (1/1/1981) INCL. WAREHOUSE TO WAREHOUSE AND I. O. P AND SHOWING THE CLAIMING CURRENCY IS THE SAME AS THE CURRENCY OF CREDIT.
+FULL SET (3/3) OF CLEAN ON BOARD OCEAN BILLS OF LADING MADE OUT TO APPLICANT MARKED FREIGHT PREPAID AND NOTIFY APPLICANT.
+SHIPMENT ADVICE SHOWING THE NAME OF THE CARRYING VESSEL, DATE OF SHIPMENT, MARKS, QUANTITY, NET WEIGHT AND GROSS WEIGHT OF THE SHIPMENT TO APPLICANT WITHIN 3 DAYS AFTER THE DATE OF BILL OF LADING.

ADDITIONAL CONDITION: 47A:
+DOCUMENTS DATED PRIOR TO THE DATE OF THIS CREDIT ARE NOT ACCEPTABLE.
+THE NUMBER AND THE DATE OF THIS CREDIT AND THE NAME OF ISSUING BANK MUST BE QUOTED ON ALL DOCUMENTS.
+TRANSSHIPMENT ALLOWED AT HONGKONG ONLY.
+SHORT FORM/CHARTER PARTY/THIRD PARTY BILL OF LADING ARE NOT ACCEPTABLE.
+SHIPMENT MUST BE EFFECTED BY 1×20' FULL CONTAINER LOAD. B/L TO SHOW EVIDENCE OF THIS EFFECT IS REQUIRED.
+THE GOODS SHIPPED ARE NEITHER ISRAELI ORIGIN NOR DO THEY CONTAIN ISRAELI MATERIALS NOR ARE THEY EXPORTED FROM ISRAEL, BENEFICIARY'S CERTIFICATE TO THIS EFFECT IS REQUIRED.
+ALL PRESENTATIONS CONTAINING DISCREPANCIES WILL ATTRACT A DISCREPANCY FEE OF GBP40.00 PLUS TELEX COSTS OR ORTHER CURRENCY EQUIVALENT. THIS CHARGE WILL BE DEDUCTED FROM THE BILL AMOUNT WHETHER OR NOT WE ELECT TO CONSULT THE APPLICANT FOR A WAIVER.

CHARGES: 71B: ALL CHARGES AND COMMISSIONS ARE FOR ACCOUNT OF BENEFICIARY.

PERIOD FOR PRESENTATION: 48: WITHIN 5 DAYS AFTER THE DATE OF SHIPMENT, BUT WITHIN THE VALIDITY OF THIS CREDIT.

CONFIRMATION INSTRUCTION: 49: WITHOUT

INFORMATION TO PRESENTING BANK: 78: ALL DOCUMENTS ARE TO BE REMITTED IN ONE LOT BY COURIER TO BANK OF NOVA SCOTIA, VANCOUVER INTERNATIONAL TRADE SERVICES MALL LEVEL, 650 WEST GEORGIA STREET, VANCOUVER, B. C., CANADA V6B-4P6.

2. 根据下述销售合同资料审核信用证内容，找出信用证内容的不符点
1) 合同资料

销 售 合 同
SALES CONTRACT

Contract NO.: RT05342
Date: Mar. 20, 2005
Signed at: SHANGHAI

Sellers: SHANGHAI TOOL IMPORT & EXPORT CO., LTD.　　　Tel: 021-65756156
Address: 31, GANXIANG ROAD SHANGHAI, CHINA　　　Fax: 021-65756155

Buyers: MAMUT ENTERPRISESAV　　　Tel: 024-4536-2453
Address: TARRAGONA75-3ER, BARCELONA, SPAIN　　　Fax: 024-4536-2452

This contract is made by and between the Sellers and Buyers, whereby the Sellers agree to sell and the Buyers agree to buy the under-mentioned goods according to the conditions stipulated below:

(1) 货号、品名及规格 Name of commodity and specifications	(2) 数量 Quantity	(3) 单价 Unit Price	(4) 金额 Amount
HAND TOOLS		FOB SHANGHAI	
① 9pc Extra Long Hex Key Set	1 200 SETS	USD 1.76	USD 2 112.00
② 8pc Double Offset Ring Spanner	1 200 SETS	USD 3.10	USD 3 720.00
③ 12pc Double Offset Ring Spanner	800 SETS	USD 7.50	USD 6 000.00
④ 12pc Combination Spanner	1 200 SETS	USD 3.55	USD 4 260.00
⑤ 10pc Combination Spanner	1 000 SETS	USD 5.80	USD 5 800.00
AS PER PROFORMA INVOICE NO. 20050329 DATED MARCH 10, 2005			
Total Amount	5 400 SETS		USD 21 892.00

(5) Packing: 8pc Double Offset Ring Spanner
　　　　　　Packed in 1 plastic carton of 16 sets each;
　　　　　　9pc Extra Long Hex Key Set, 12pc Combination Spanner, 10pc Combination Spanner
　　　　　　Packed in 1 plastic carton of 10 sets each;
　　　　　　12pc Double Offset Ring Spanner
　　　　　　Packed in 1 plastic carton of 8 sets each;
　　　　　　Packed in THREE 40'CONTAINER
(6) Delivery from SHANGHAI, CHINA to BARCELONA, SPAIN

(7) Shipping Marks: M. E
　　　　　　　　　BARCELONA
　　　　　　　　　C/NO. 1-UP
(8) Time of Shipment: Last Date Of May 10, 2005
(9) Partial Shipment: Not Allowed
(10) Transshipment: Allowed

(11) Term of Payment: By 100% Confirmed Irrevocable Letter of Credit to be available at 30 days after sight draft to be opened by the sellers.

L/C must mention this contract number L/C advised by BANK OF CHINA SHANGHAI BRANCH. All banking charges outside China (the mainland of China) are for account Drawee.

(12) Arbitration: Any dispute arising from the execution of or in connection with this contract shall be settled amicably through negotiation. In case no settlement can be reached through negotiation, the case shall then submitted to China International Economic & Trade Arbitration Commission in Shanghai (or in Beijing) for arbitration in accordance with its arbitration rules. The arbitration award is final and binding upon both parties. The fee for arbitration shall be borne by losing party unless otherwise award.

                        The Seller   The Buyer
SHANGHAI TOOL IMPORT & EXPORT CO., LTD.   MAMUT ENTER PRISESAV

                          LILI   JUN

2) 信用证资料

DOCUMENTARY CREDIT

SEPUENCE OF TOTAL	*27: 1/1
FORM OF DOC. CREDIT	*40A: REVOCABLE
DOC. CREDIT NUMBER	*20: 31173
DATE OF ISSUE	31C: 050401
DATE AND PLACE OF EXPIRY	*31D: DATE 050531
APPLICANT	*50: MAMUT ENTERPRISESAV
	TARRAGONA75-3ER
	BARCELONA, SPAIN
ISSUING BANK	52A: CREDIT ANDORRA
	ANDORRA LA VELLA, ANDORRA
BENEFICIARY	*59: SHANGHAI TOOL IMPORT & EXPORT CO., LTD
	31, GANXIANG ROAD SHANGHAI, CHINA
AMOUNT	*32B: RURRENCY EUR AMOUNT 21 892.00
AVAILABLE WITH /BY	*41D: ANY BANK IN CHINA BY NEGOTIATION
DRAFTS AT…	42C: AT SIGHT
DRAWEE	41A: CREDIT ANDORRA
	ANDORRA LA VELLA, ANDORRA
PARTIAL SHIPMENTS	43P: ALLOWED
TRANSSHIPMENT	43T: NOT ALLOWED
LOADING ON BOARD	44A: SHANGHAI
FOR TRANSPORTATION TO	44B: BARCELONA (SPAIN)
LATEST DATE OF SHIPMENT	44C: 050510

DESCRIPT OF GOODS	45A: HAND TOOLS AS PER PROFORMA INVOICE NO. 20050339 DATED MARCH 10, 2005 FOB BARCHLONA
DOCUMENTS REQUIRED	46A:

　　　　　　　　　　+SIGHED COMMERCIAL INVOICE, 1 ORIGINAL AND 4 COPIES.
　　　　　　　　　　+PACKING LIST, 1 ORIGINAL AND 4 COPIES.
　　　　　　　　　　+CERTIFICATE OF ORIGIN GSP CHINA FORM A, ISSUED BY THE CHAMBER OF COMMERCE OR OTHER ARTHOUITY DULY ENTITLED FOR THIS PURPOSE.
　　　　　　　　　　+FULL SET OF B/L, (2 ORIGINAL AND 5 COPIES) CLEAN ON BAORD, MARKED "FREIGHT COLLECT", CONSIGNED TO: MAMUT ENTERPRISESAV, TARRAGONA75-3ER BARCELONA, SPAIN, TEL+376 823 323 FAX+376 860 914-860 807, NOTIFY: BLUE WATER SHIPPING ESPANA, ER2NA, A, 08003 BARCELONA (SPAIN)
　　　　　　　TEL: 34-93-2954848 FAX: 34-93-2681681.

CHARGES	71B: ALL BANKING CHARGES OUTSIDE SPAIN ARE FOR ACCOUNT OF BENEFICIARY.
PERIOD FOR PRESENTATION	48: DOCUMENTS MUST BE PRESENTED WITHIN 15 DAYS AFTER THE DATE OF SHIPMENT BUT WITHIN THE VALIDITY OF THE CREDIT.

3. 指出下述合同和信用证存在的问题
1) 合同资料

销 售 合 同
SALES CONTRACT

编号：
NO.: 2006026
日期：
DATE: Feb. 28, 2006

卖方：
SELLER: HUARUN TRADING CO., LTD.
地址：
ADDRESS: 350 JIANSHE STREET, SHIJIAZHUANG P. R. CHINA

买方：
BUYER: SAKAI TRADING CO., LTD.
地址：
ADDRESS: SANWA BLDG1-1 KAWARAMACH 2-CHOME CHUO-KU OSAKA 541, JAPAN

买卖双方同意按以下条款达成交易：
This contract is made by and agreed between the buyer and seller, in accordance with the terms and conditions stipulated below:

品名及规格 Commodity & Specifications	数量 Quantity	单价及价格条款 Unit Price & Trade Terms	金额 Amount
\multicolumn{4}{c}{CFR YOKOHAMA}			
FROZEN CHICKEN BREAST MEAT, A GRADE	24MTS	USD1 945.00 /MT	USD46 680.00

允许溢短装，由卖方决定
With More or less of shipment allowed at the sellers' option

总值
Total Value   USD FOURTY SIX THOUSAND SIX HUNDRED AND EIGHTY ONLY.

包装
Packing   Each pieces 1 KG, 1 piece into a packet, 12 packets into one carton, 24MTS into 2 000 cartons.

唛头
Shipping Marks   SAK
                            2006026
                           YOKOHAMA
                            1-2000

装运期及运输方式
Time of Shipment & means of Transportation   Not Later Than Apr. 30, 2006 BY VESSEL

装运港及目的地
Port of Loading & Destination   From Xingang, China to Yokohama, Japan
                                allowing transshipment and partial shipment

保险
Insurance   To be covered be the buyer.

付款方式
Terms of Payment   The Buyers shall open through a bank acceptable to the seller an Irrevocable Letter of Credit payable at sight of reach the seller 30 days before the month of shipment, valid for negotiation in China until the 15th day after the date of shipment.

备注
Remarks

The Buyer   The Seller

2）信用证资料
HUARUN TRADING CO. LTD.   SAKAI TRADING CO. LTD.
MT700 .... ISSUE OF A DOCUMENTARY CREDIT ....

SEQUENCE OF TOTAL   27: 1/1
FORM OF DOCUMENTARY CREDIT   40A: IRREVOCABLE
DOCUMENTARY CREDIT NUMBER   20: LCG7687GU6788
DATE OF ISSUE   31C: 060325
DATE AND PLACE OF EXPIRY   31D: 060515 CHINA

APPLICANT	50:	SAKAI TRADING CO., LTD.
		SANWA BLDG1-1 KAWARAMACH 2-CHOME CHUO-KU OSAKA 561, JAPAN
BENEFICIARY	59:	HUARUN TRADING CO., LTD.
		350 JIANSHE STREET, SHIJIAZHUANG
		P. R CHINA
CURRENCY CODE, AMOUNT	32B:	USD46 680.00
PERCENTAGE CREDIT AMT TOL.	39A:	05/05
AVAILABLE WITH... BY...	41D:	ANY BANK IN CHINA BY NEGOTIATION
DRAFTS AT...	42C:	AT SIGHT FOR 100 PCT OF THE INVOICE VALUE
DRAWEE	42D:	THE SUMITOMO BANK LTD OSAKA JAPAN
PARTIAL SHIPMENT	43P:	NOT ALLOWED
TRANSSHIPMENT	43T:	ALLOWED
LOADING/DISPATCH/TAKING IN CHARGE/FM	44A:	ANY CHINESE PORT
FOR TRANSPORTATION TO...	44B:	YOKOHAMA, JAPAN
LATEST DATE OF SHIPMENT	44C:	060420
DESCRIPTION OF GOODS/SERVICES	45A:	

    FROZEN CHICKEN BREAST MEAT, A GRADE,
    PACKING: 1KG×12/CARTON,
    UNIT PRICE: USD1 945.00/MT CFR YOKOHAMA
    QUANTITY: 2 000CARTONS/24MTS

DOCUMENTS REQUIRED: 46A:
1. MANUALLY SIGNED COMMERCIAL INVOICE IN 5 COPIES.
2. FULL SET INCLUDING 2 NON-NEGOTIABLE COPIES OF CLEAN ON BOARD OCEAN BILLS OF LADING MADE OUT TO ORDER AND BLANK ENDORSED, MARKED "FREIGHT PREPAID" NOTIFYING APPLICANT.
3. PACKING LIST IN 3 COPIES.
4. CERTIFICATE OF QUALITY ISSUED BY CIQ, STATING THAT THE GOODS ARE UP TO EU STANDARDS.
5. CERTIFICATE OF ORIGIN FORM A ISSUED BY CIQ.
6. ONE COPY OF FAX SENT TO THE APPLICANT ADVISING SHIPMENT IN DETAILS WITHIN 5 WORKING DAYS OF SHIPMENT IS MADE.

ADDITIONAL CONTITIONS 47A:
1. A DISCREPANCY FEE OF USD54.00 OR ITS EQUIVALLENT WILL BE DEDUCTED FROM THE PROCEEDS IF DOCUMENTS ARE PRESENTED WITH DISCREPANCY (IES).
2. INSURANCE COVERED BY THE APPLICANT.
3. QUANTITY 5 PCT MORE OR LESS ARE ALLOWED.

```
            CHARGES                         71B: ALL BANKING CHARGES OUTSIDE THE O-
                                                 PENING BANK ARE FOR BENEFICIARY'S
                                                 ACCOUNT.
            PERIOD FOR PRESENTATIONS        48: DOCUMENTS MUST BE PRESENTED FOR NE-
                                                GOTIATION WITHIN 21 DAYS AFTER BILL
                                                OF LADING DATE.
            CONFIRMATION INSTRUCTION        49: WITHOUT
            ADVISE THROUGH BANK             57A: BANK OF CHINA, HEBEI BR.
            INSTR. TO PAY/ACPT/NGG BANK     78:
                1. ALL DOCUMENTS ARE TO BE FORWARDED TO THE OPENING
                   OFFICE BY REGISTERED IN TWO CONSECUTIVE LOTS.
                2. UPON RECEIPT OF ALL DOCUEMNTS IN ORDER, WE WILL DU-
                   LY HONOUR/ACCEPT THE DRAFTS AND EFFECT THE PAY-
                   MENT AS INSTRUCTED AT MATURITY.
            SENDER TO RECEIVER INFO         72: THIS LC IS SUBJECT TO UCP 1993 ICC PUB.
                                                NO. 500.
```

3.5 信用证的修改

对信用证进行全面细致的审核以后,如果没有任何问题,出口商即可按信用证条款发货、装运、制单结汇。如发现有不符买卖合同或不利于出口方安全收汇的条款,应及时处理。对于影响安全收汇,难以接受或做到的信用证条款,必须要求国外客户通过开证行进行修改;凡不违反政策原则,经过努力可以做到而又不增加太多费用的条款,可以不做修改,按信用证规定发货。由于修改信用证的条款涉及各当事人的权利和义务,因而不可撤销的信用证在其有效期内的任何修改,都必须征得各有关当事人的同意。

3.5.1 信用证的修改流程

信用证的修改流程如图 3-1 所示。

1. 出口商提出要求修改信用证

出口商(受益人)在审核信用证后,如果发现有不符合合同或有不利于出口商安全收汇的条款,应及时联系进口商通过开证行对信用证进行修改,撰写改证函。改证函的写法并无统一规定和要求,但一般包含如下内容。

(1) 感谢对方开来的信用证。例如:

① Thank you for your L/C No. LC-710-076405 issued by Cathay Bank, Los Angeles dated Jul. 6, 2007.

② We are very pleased to receive your L/C No. LC-710-076405 issued by Cathay Bank, Los Angeles dated Jul. 6, 2007

(2) 列明不符点并说明如何修改。例如:

① However, we are sorry to find it contains the following discrepancies.

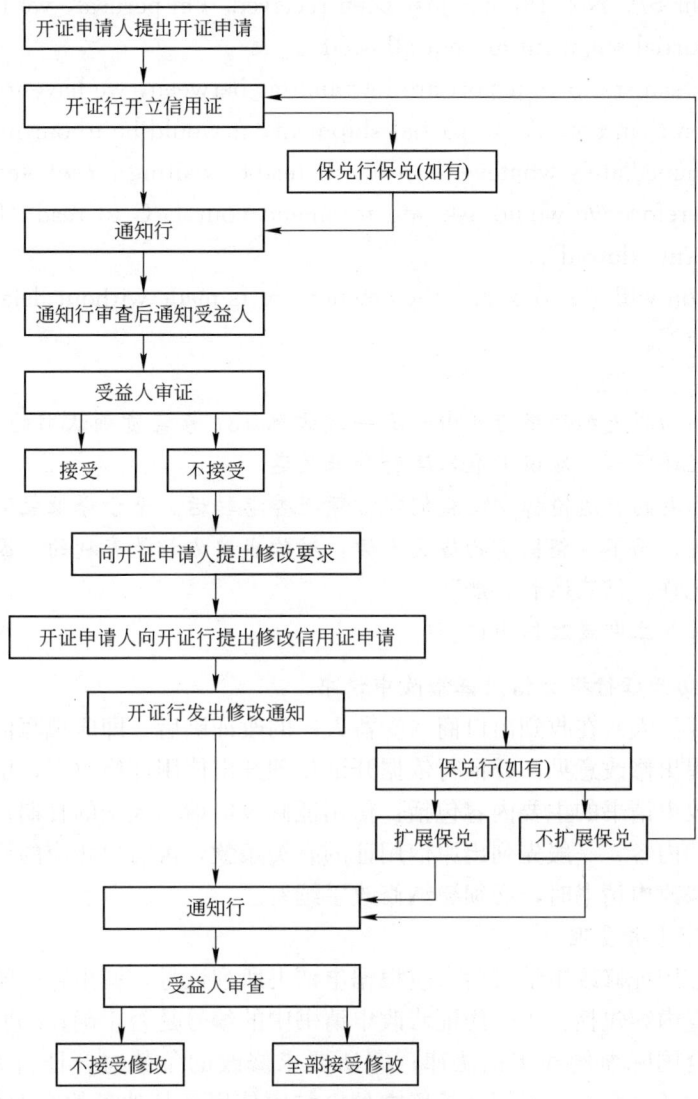

图 3-1 信用证的修改流程

② But the following points are in discrepancies with the stipulations of our S/C No. 02AG18185.

③ The expiry date should be July 25, 2005 instead of July 15, 2005.

(3) 感谢对方合作，并希望信用证修改书早日开到。例如：

Thank you for your kind cooperation. Please see to it that the L/C amendment reach us within next week. Otherwise we cannot effect punctual shipment.

【相关单证】

单证 3-4　信函范例

Dear Sirs,

　　We are pleased to inform you that L/C No. H-15 issued by the Chartered Bank of

Liverpool for our S/C No. 187 has just been received. On perusal, we find that transshipment and partial shipment are not allowed.

As direct steamers to your port are few and far between, we have to ship via Hong Kong more often than not. As to partial shipment, it would be to our mutual benefit if we could ship immediately whatever is ready instead of waiting for whole shipment to be completed. Therefore we would ask you to amend your L/C to read "Part shipments and transshipment allowed".

We hope you will see to it that the amendment is made without delay.

参考译文如下：

敬启者：

你方通过利物浦麦加利银行开出的有关我方第187号售货确认书的信用证第H-15号刚刚收到。经详阅后，发现不准转运和分批装运。

由于驶往你港的直达轮稀少，我们常常须经香港转运。至于分批装运，如能将备妥的货物立即装运，而不等整批货物备妥再运，对你我双方都是有利的。因此请你方将信用证修改为"允许分批装运和转船"。

希望你方注意立即修改信用证。

2. 进口商向开证行提交信用证修改申请书

进口商（开证人）在收到出口商（受益人）的改证函后，即应填写信用证修改申请书，向开证行提出修改意见。开证行依据开证步骤开出信用证修改书，由通知行交受益人。信用证修改申请书的主要内容包括：信用证修改申请书提交的日期；修改的原信用证编号；修改的内容，一般先列出原信用证的有关条款，再写出相应的修改条款，申请人提交信用证修改申请书时，必须缴纳修改手续费。

3. 开证行审查并受理

银行接到信用证修改申请书后，应根据申请书所列证号，调出存档的原信用证副本对照审核。审查内容包括：①信用证修改申请书中的编号是否正确；②所要求修改的条款内容是否符合国际惯例和本国法律；③所要求修改的条款对开证行有无不利之处；④所要求修改的条款之间有无相互矛盾之处，与原信用证其他条款有无相互矛盾之处；⑤如果是提出增加信用证金额，则要增收保证金。

4. 开证行向通知行发出信用证修改通知书

开证行审核无误后，根据修改申请书的要求，以迅速的方式按原来的传递路线向各有关当事人发出信用证修改通知书。然后将修改通知书副本按修改日期依次附贴于信用证留底备查，同时，将另一副本送交申请人。

5. 通知行将信用证修改通知书送达受益人确认

受益人收到修改通知书后，如果同意接受，则信用证项下的修改自此生效。如果受益人拒绝接受修改，将修改通知书退回通知行，并附表示拒绝接受修改的书面文件，则信用证项下的修改视为无效。

3.5.2 改证中的注意事项

受益人在审核信用证时，如发现信用证条款或要求违背国家政策、与合同规定不相符或不能接受时,应及时向对方提出修改要求。修改信用证,应持慎重态度,须权衡轻重灵活掌握。

(1) 同一张信用证中,如有多处需要修改的,原则上非修改不可的,应坚决要求修改;可改可不改的,应视具体情况可不做修改。凡需修改的各项内容应一次向国外客户提出,避免由于疏忽或考虑不周而多次提出修改要求。

(2) 对于开证行根据客户申请发出的修改通知书,认真审核信用证修改通知书的内容,根据《UCP600》的规定,对同一修改通知书中的修改内容不允许部分接受。因此,如发现修改后的内容仍不符或部分不符也要全部退回并再次提请修改,部分接受将会被视为拒绝修改的通知。

(3) 受益人应对开证申请人提出的修改发出接受或拒绝的通知。根据《UCP600》的规定,在受益人告知通知修改的银行其接受该修改之前,原信用证(或含有先前被接受的修改的信用证)的条款对受益人仍然有效。受益人应提供接受或拒绝修改的通知。如受益人未能给予通知,当交单与信用证以及尚未表示接受的修改的要求一致时,即视为受益人已经作出接受修改的通知,并且从此时起,该信用证被修改。

(4) 进口商来证后,又主动要求修改来证内容,受益人若对修改内容不接受,可以拒绝,但应立即发出拒绝接受修改的通知。在该通知发出后,即可按原证各项条款和内容办理出运。

(5) 保兑行有权对修改不保兑,但它必须不延误地将该情况通知开证行及受益人。

(6) 有关信用证修改必须通过原信用证通知行传递方为有效,不能由开证行直接通知或由开证申请人径自寄予受益人。

【相关单证】

单证 3-5 信用证修改申请书

APPLICATION FOR AMENDMENT TO LETTER OF CREDIT
信用证修改申请书

No. of Credit Facility:　　　　　　　　Date:
授信额度编号:　　　　　　　　　　　　日期:
To: Bank of China　　　　　　Branch (Sub-Branch)
致:中国银行　　　　　　　　分(支)行
L/C No.: _____　　Amount: _____
信用证号码:_____　　金　额:_____
Amendment No.:
修改次数(银行填写):

Please amend the above L/C by Swift/Telex as follows (marked with "×"):
请以 SWIFT/电传方式修改上述信用证如下(注有"×"部分):

(　　) Shipment date is extended to _____
(　　) Expiry date is extended to _____
(　　) Increasing credit amount by _____ to _____

Others：
（　　）＿＿＿＿＿＿＿＿＿＿＿＿＿＿＿＿＿

All other terms and conditions remain unchanged.
其余条款不变。
Charges and fees if any, are for our A/C No. ＿＿＿＿＿＿
修改之手续费及电信费用请从我司＿＿＿＿＿＿账号扣付。

　　　　　　　　Stamp and signature（s）of the applicant
　　　　　　　　　　　　　申请人签章

银行审查意见：
经办：
复核：　　　　　　授权：

【案例】

河北恒泰公司业务员杨光对信用证审核后，7月10日发函要求美国PACIFIC INTERNATIONAL INC. 的Paul Smith先生通过开证行修改信用证。

HEBEI HENGTAI IMPORT & EXPORT CORPORATION
NO. 231 HEPING ROAD, SHIJIAZHUANG, HEBEI, CHINA
TEL：86-0311-84576936　　FAX：86-0311-84576937

TO：PACIFIC INTERNATIONAL INC.
FM：HEBEI HENGTAI IMPORT & EXPORT CORPORATION
DT：Jul. 10, 2008
Dear Sir,
Thank you very much for your Letter of Credit No. LC-710-086405. However, upon checking, we have found the following discrepancies and would appreciate it very much if you will make the necessary amendments as early as possible so as to facilitate our shipping arrangement.
(1) The address of the applicant should be 128 HAYWARD WAY STREET instead of 129 HAYWARD WAY STREET.
(2) The credit should expire on Sep. 15, 2008 for negotiation in China instead of Sep. 15, 2008 for negotiation in USA.
(3) Partial shipment should be allowed.
(4) The goods are to be packed in bale instead of carton.
(5) The Bill of Lading should be 3/3.
(6) The Bill of Lading should be marked "freight prepaid".
(7) Document should be presented within 15 days after the date of shipment.
We await your early amendments.

Yours sincerely
HEBEI HENGTAI IMPORT & EXPORT CORPORATION
Yang Guang

【技能实训】

1. 请根据河北粮油进出口公司审单的意见，给国外进口方 TOMOS Company Ltd. 35～36 Street London U. K. 拟写一份改证函

HEBEI CEREALS AND OILS IMP. & EXP. CORP.
18th FLR. Liangyou Building,
120 Heping West Road, Shijiazhuang, China
Tel：86-0311-58818850，Fax：86-0311-58899655

审证意见
信用证号码：H982/M056378
合同号码：HY 88CLM 98
开证行：英国米兰银行（MIDLAND BANK LTD.）
申请人：TOMOS Company Ltd.
审证结果：
（1）信用证大小写金额不一致，大写金额错误，合同金额是 USD15 000.00。
（2）汇票付款期限为见票后60天内付款，与合同规定的即期付款不符合。
（3）合同规定允许分批装运和转船，而信用证中却禁止分批装运和转船。
（4）保险加成率合同规定110％，而信用证中却规定150％。
（5）信用证中要求运输单据签发后5天内交单议付，交单日太紧，建议改为15天。
（6）信用证中没有写明受《UCP600》条款约束的字句，建议加上。

2. 结合下列合同和信用证的相关资料，拟写改证函
（1）合同条款如下。
卖方：河北华润食品公司
买方：温哥华加拿大食品公司
商品名称：梅林牌草莓酱（Strawberry Jam）
规格：350克听装
数量：1 000箱（每箱50听）
单价：CIF温哥华，每箱30加元
总值：30 000加元
包装：纸板箱装
保险：由卖方按发票金额110％投保一切险
装运期：2008年5月
装运港：中国港口
目的港：温哥华
唛头：由卖方选定
支付条款：凭不可撤销、可转让即期信用证付款。信用证须不迟于装运月份前30天到达卖方。有效期应为最后装运期后15天在中国到期。
签订日期、地点：2008年3月4日于石家庄
合同号码：SC-3
（2）信用证内容如下。

Date: Apr. 1, 2008

To: Bank of China, Shijiazhuang

We hereby open our Irrevocable Letter of Credit No. 9876543 in favour of Hebei Huarun Food Corp., Vancouver for account of China National Cereals, Oils & Foodstuffs Corp. up to an amount of CA＄3 000.00 CIF Vancouver (Say Canadian Dollars Three Thousand Only), for 110% of the invoice value relative to the shipment of: Canned Strawberry Jam 1 000 cartons (each 50 cans). As per Contract SC-3, from Vancouver, Canada to China port Drafts to be drawn at sight on our bank and accompanied by the following documents, marked "×":...

Partial shipments permitted.

Transshipment permitted.

Shipment must be effected not later than May 31, 2008.

This L/C is valid at our counter until Jun. 15, 2008.

For Bank ABC

  3. 结合下列合同和信用证的相关资料, 拟写改证函

  (1) 合同条款如下。

  卖方: 河北纺织品进出口公司 (Hebei Textiles Import & Export Corporation, Beijing)

  买方: 新加坡通用贸易公司 (General Trading Company, Singapore)

  商品名称: "玫瑰"牌印花细布 ("Rose" Brand Printed Shirting)

  规格: 30×36 72×69 35/6″×42 码

  数量: 28 100 码

  单价: HKD3.00/YARD CIF SINGAPORE, 含佣金3%

  总值: HKD84 300.00

  装运期: 2006年1月31日前自中国港口至新加坡, 允许分装运和转船。

  付款条件: 凭不可撤销即期信用证付款, 于装运期前30天开到卖方, 并于上述装运期后15天内在中国议付有效。

  保险: 由卖方根据中国人民保险公司1981年1月1日中国保险条款按发票金额的110%投保一切险和战争险。

  签订日期、地点: 2005年10月11日于石家庄

  合同号码: PS-1234

  (2) 开来信用证如下。

ABC BANK

Date: Nov. 1, 2005

To: Bank of China Shijiazhuang

We hereby open our Irrevocable Letter of Credit No. L-1234 in favor of Hebei Textiles Import & Export Corp. for account of General Trading Company, Singapore, up to an aggregate amount of HK＄84 300.00 (Say US Dollars Two Hundred and One Thousand Six Hundred Only) CIFC 2% Singapore for 100% of the invoice value relative to the shipment of:

28 100 pieces of Rose Brand Printed Shirting 30×36 72×69 35/6″×42 yards as per Contract No. PS-1234 dated October 11, 2005.

From China port to Singapore.

Drafts to be drawn at 30 days after sight on our bank and accompanied by the following documents marked "×":...

(×) Signed Commercial Invoice in triplicate.
(×) Full set of Clean on Board Bills of Lading made out to our order quoting L/C NO. L-1234. marked Freight Paid.
(×) One original Marine Insurance Policy or Certificate for 150% full invoice value covering All Risks and War Risks, and TPND with claims payable in Singapore in the currency of draft (s).
Partial shipments are permitted.
Transshipment is prohibited.
Shipment must be effected not later than January 31, 2006, Draft (s) drawn under this credit must be negotiated in Singapore on or before January 31, 2006.

第4章

【本章导读】
进出口货物托运工作概述
海洋运输托运流程及托运单缮制
航空运输托运流程及托运单缮制

【学习目的和要点】
通过本章学习，学生应能够了解在国际货物买卖中，采用CIF、CFR术语成交时，出口方必须自付费用同承运人订立运输合同，了解运输的操作方式和订舱的基本程序，掌握出口货物托运单的填制要求，学会填制出口货物明细单和集装箱海运出口货物托运单，掌握杂货班轮和集装箱运输出口托运的有关做法。

进出口货物运输

4.1 进出口货物托运工作概述

4.1.1 进出口货物托运工作简介

进出口货物托运是指出口单位通过外运公司或其他有权受理对外货物运输业务的单位办理海、陆、空等出口货物的运输事宜。不同的运输方式办理不同的运输手续,出口货物托运单就是出口企业在报关前向运输公司申请租船、订舱的依据,是日后制作提单和相关运单的主要背景材料。尽管它不直接影响收汇,但是若缮制错漏、延误等,就会影响结汇单据的正确缮制和快速流转,从而影响卖方安全收汇。

4.1.2 运输方式的选择

1. 海洋运输

海洋运输是国际贸易运输中使用最广泛的运输方式。目前,其运量在国际货运总量中占80%以上。海洋运输之所以被如此广泛使用,主要是因为与其他运输方式相比,它有以下几个明显的优点。

(1) 通过能力大。海洋运输可以利用四通八达的天然运输航道,它不像火车、汽车受轨道和道路的限制,故其通过能力大。

(2) 运量大。海洋运输船舶的运载能力,远远大于铁路运输车辆和公路运输车辆。如一艘万吨船舶的载重量一般相当于250~300个车皮的载重量。

(3) 运费低。按照规模经济的观点,因为运量大、航程远、分摊于每吨货运的运输成本就少,因此运费相对低廉。

海洋运输虽具有上述优点,但也存在不足之处。例如,海洋运输受气候和自然条件的影响较大,航期准确度差,而且风险较大。此外,海洋运输的速度也相对较低。

2. 航空运输

航空运输是一种现代化的运输方式,它与海洋运输和铁路运输相比,具有运输速度快、货运质量高且不受地面条件的限制等优点。因此,它最适宜运送急需物资、鲜活商品、精密仪器和贵重物品。近年来,随着国际贸易的发展以及国际货物运输技术的不断现代化,空运方式也日益普遍。目前,我国的进出口业务中,进口采用空运的有计算机、成套设备中的精密部件、电子产品等;出口商品中主要有丝绸、纺织品、海产品、水果和蔬菜等。这些进出口商品根据不同需要,可分为以下几种方式:①班机运输,是指固定时间、固定航线、固定始发站和目的站的飞机运输,适用于运送急需货物、鲜活商品以及节令性商品;②包机运输,是指包租整架飞机来运送货物;③集中托运,是指航空货运公司把若干单独货运的货物组成一整批货物,用一份总运单整批发送到预定目的地,由航空货运公司在那里的代理人收货、报关、分拨后交给实际收货人。

3. 铁路运输

在国际货物运输中,铁路运输是一种仅次于海洋运输的主要运输方式,海洋运输的进出口货物，一般也是通过铁路运输进行货物的集中和分散。

铁路运输有许多优点，如一般不受气候条件的影响，可保障全年的正常运输，而且运量较大，速度较快，有高度的连续性运转的可能，受风险影响较小。办理铁路货物运输手续比海洋运输简单，而且收货人和发货人可以在就近的始发站和目的站办理托运和提货手续。铁路运输可分为国际货物铁路联运和国内货物铁路运输两种。国际货物铁路联运是指使用一份统一的货物联运单据，由铁路负责经过两国或两国以上的铁路全程运输，并由一国铁路向另一国铁路移交货物时，不需要发货人和收货人参加的货物运输；国内货物铁路运输是指仅在本国范围内按《国内铁路货物运输规程》的规定办理的货物运输。

4. 集装箱运输和国际多式联运

集装箱运输是一种以集装箱为运输单位进行货物运输的一种现代化的运输方式，与传统货运方式相比，它具有以下优点。

(1) 提高了装卸效率，加速了船舶的周转。

(2) 有利于提高运输质量，减少货损货差。

(3) 节省各项费用，降低运货成本。

(4) 简化货运手续，便利货物运输。

(5) 把传统单一运输串联成连贯的成组运输，从而促进了国际多式联运的发展。

国际多式联运则是在集装箱运输的基础上产生和发展起来的一种综合性的连贯运输的方式，它一般以集装箱为媒介，把海、陆、空等单一的传统运输方式有机地结合起来，组成一种国际的连贯的运输，它是实现"门到门"运输的有效途径，既简化了手续，减少了中间环节，又加快了货运速度，降低了运输成本，并提高了货运质量。

综上可见，在选择运输方式时，应综合考虑货物的特点、对运输方式的要求和各种运输方式的特点，并从中加以比较，作出最佳选择。

4.2 海洋运输托运流程及托运单缮制

4.2.1 杂货班轮出口托运一般流程

杂货班轮出口托运一般流程如图 4-1 所示。

(1) 托运人在装货港向船公司或船舶代理人（简称船代）提出货物装运申请，递交托运单（B/N），填写装货联单。

(2) 船公司同意承运后，其代理人指定船名，核对装货单（S/O）与托运单（B/N）上的内容无误后，将托运单留底联留下，签发装货单（S/O）给托运人，要求托运人将货物及时送至指定的码头仓库。

(3) 托运人持装货单（S/O）及有关单证向海关办理货物出口报关、验货放行手续，海关在装货单（S/O）上加盖放行图章后，货物准予装船出口。

(4) 装货港的船舶代理人根据留底联编制装货清单（L/L）送船舶及理货公司、装卸公司。

(5) 大副根据装货清单（L/L）编制货物积载计划（stowage plan），交代理人分送

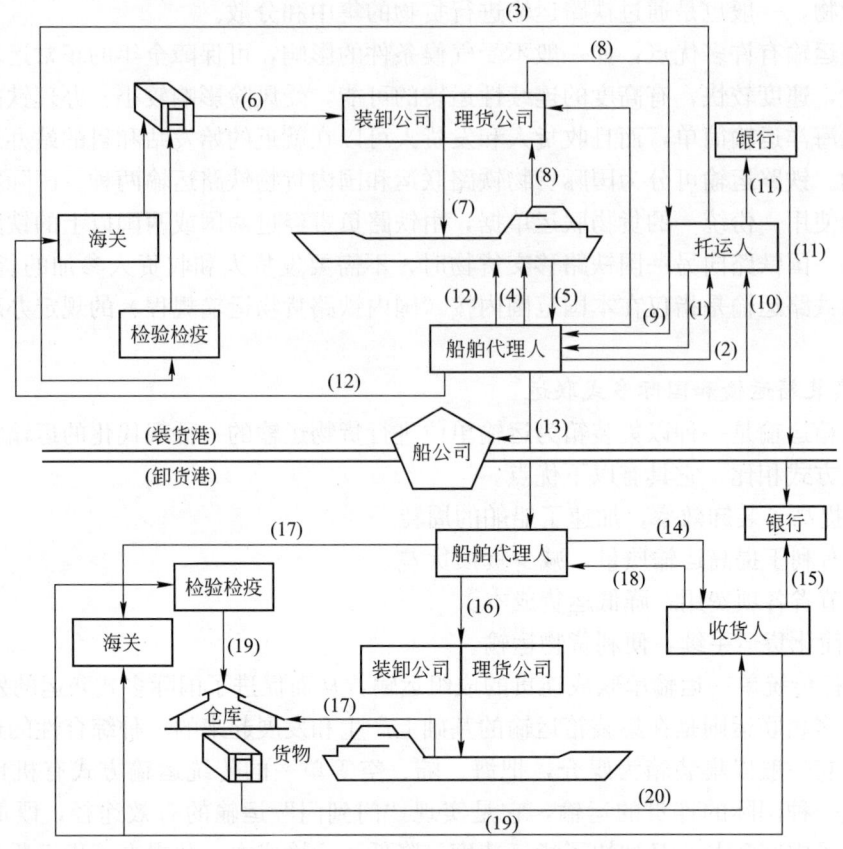

图 4-1 杂货班轮出口托运一般流程

理货、装卸公司等按计划装船。

（6）托运人将经过检验验关的货物送至指定的码头仓库准备装船。

（7）货物装船后，理货长将装货单（S/O）交大副，大副核实无误后留下装货单（S/O）并签发收货单（M/R）。

（8）理货长将大副签发的收货单（M/R）转交给托运人。

（9）托运人持收货单（M/R）到装货港的船舶代理人处付清运费（预付运费情况下）换取正本已装船提单（B/L）。

（10）装货港的船舶代理人审核无误后，留下收货单（M/R）、签发已装船提单（B/L）给托运人。

（11）托运人持已装船提单（B/L）及有关单证到议付银行结汇（在信用证支付方式下），取得货款，议付银行将已装船提单（B/L）及有关单证邮寄开证行。

（12）货物装船完毕后，装货港的船舶代理人编制出口载货清单（M/F）送船长签字后向海关办理船舶出口手续，并将载货清单（M/F）交船随带，船舶起航。

（13）装货港的船舶代理人根据已装船提单（B/L）副本或收货单（M/R）编制出口载货运费清单（F/M）连同已装船提单（B/L）副本或收货单（M/R）送交船公司结算代收运费，并将卸货港所需单证寄给卸货港的船舶代理人。

（14）卸货港的船舶代理人接到船舶抵港电报后，通知收货人船舶到港日期，做好提货准备。

（15）收货人到开证行付清货款取回已装船提单（B/L）（在信用证支付方式下）。

（16）卸货港的船舶代理人根据装货港的船舶代理人寄来的货运单证，编进口载货清单（M/F）及有关船舶进口报关和卸货所需的单证，约定装卸公司、理货公司、联系安排泊位，做好接船及卸货准备工作。

（17）船舶抵港后，卸货港的船舶代理人随即办理船舶进口手续，船舶靠泊后即开始卸货。

（18）收货人持正本已装船提单（B/L）向卸货港的船舶代理人办理提货手续，付清应付的费用后，换取代理人签发的提货单（D/O）。

（19）收货人办理货物进口手续，支付进口关税。

（20）收货人持提货单（D/O）到码头仓库或船边提取货物。

4.2.2 杂货班轮托运单的内容及其填制

在杂货班轮运输方式下，托运单（Booking Note）是指由托运人根据买卖合同和信用证的有关内容向承运人或其代理人办理货物运输的书面凭证。经承运人或其代理人对该单据签认，表示其已接受托运，承运人和托运人运输合同关系即告建立。托运单虽然不是出口结汇的正式单据，但由于它是日后制作提单的主要资料，因此比较重要。

1. 收货人

在信用证支付的条件下，对收货人（Consignee）的规定常用以下两种表示方法。

（1）记名收货人。记名收货人是直接将收货人的名称、地址完整地表示出来的方法。这一方法简单明了，收货人就是合同的买方。

（2）指示收货人。指示收货人常用空白指示和记名指示两种表示法。指示收货人掩饰了具体的收货人的名称和地址，使单据可以转让。在空白指示情况下，单据的持有人可自由转让单据。在记名指示情况下，记名人有权控制和转让单据。

2. 被通知人

被通知人（Notify）一栏中应填写接受船方发出货到通知的人的名称与地址。

被通知人的选择与确定的权利是合同的买方或买方代理人的。有时买方确定本人为通知人，有时将自己的代理人或其他与买方联系较密切的人确定为被通知人。被通知人的职责是及时地接受船方发出的到货通知并将该通知转告真正的收货人。

在极少数的交易中，可能出现要求空白收货人栏目和被通知人栏目。这是因为提出要求的一方准备买卖在途货物。制作单据时要在副本单据的被通知人栏中填写买方或开证申请人的名称与地址。

3. 唛头

一般而言，买卖合同或者信用证均规定了唛头（Shipping Marks）。填写这一栏时，要求填写内容和形式与所规定的完全一致。有时买卖合同和信用证中没有规定唛头，这时，卖方可以自行选择一个合适的唛头。在选择唛头时，要充分考虑买方提货方便、买方利益和买方所在国的特别要求。也可以不制作唛头，此时在该栏打印 N/M。

4. 数量

托运单中的数量（Quantity）是指最大包装的件数。例如，出口10万码花布，装在100个纸箱内,这个栏应填写100 CARTONS而不是100 000 YARDS。

5. 货物说明

货物说明（Description of Goods）一栏的填写允许只写统称。例如，出口各种用途的化工颜料。无须逐一列出颜料的规格、成分、用途，而只写"化工原料"。但是，如果同时出口化工颜料和瓷器产品，则应分别填写"化工颜料"、"瓷器"，而不允许只填写其中一种数量较多或金额较大的商品。

6. 重量

重量应分别计算毛重（Gross Weight）和净重（Net Weight）。

如果一次装运的货物中有几种不同的包装材料或完全不同的货物，那么在填写这一栏时，应先分别计算并填写每一种包装材料或每一种货物毛重和净重，然后合计全部的毛重和净重。在计算重量时，要求使用统一的计量单位。一般使用千克。

7. 尺码

在尺码（Measurement）栏中填写一批货的尺码总数。一般使用立方米。总尺码不仅包括各件货物尺码之和，还应包括件与件之间堆放时的合理空隙所占的体积。因此总尺码都略大于货物的尺码数。在货物说明类中，毛重、净重和尺码三栏将作为填写装箱单（Packing List）或重量单（Weight Note）的重要依据，因此要认真核查。

8. 分批装运

分批装运（Partial Shipment）的内容应严格按照合同或信用证条款填写。如果合同或信用证规定分若干批装运或对分批装运有进一步说明，不要将这些说明填入本栏，而应将这些说明填入"特别条款类"栏中。该栏主要填写允许或不允许分批转运。

9. 转船

转船（Transshipment）栏的填写要求与"分批"一致。只能填写"允许"或"不允许"。如果合同和信用证中对这一内容有其他说明，应在特别条款栏目中作出补充说明。

10. 装运期

在信用证支付条件下，装运期（Time of Shipment）是最重要的期限之一。要求严格遵守。装运期的表达可以全部使用阿拉伯数字，也可以使用英文与阿拉伯数字一起表示。例如，2004年5月6日可表示为05/06/2004，但最好用May 6th, 2004。

装运期还可以表示为一段时间。如2004年5—6月。有时表示为：不早于×月×日，不迟于×月×日（NOT EARLIER..., NOT LATER THAN...），装运期不迟于……（SHIPMENT NOT LATER THAN...），最迟装运期为×年×月×日（LATEST SHIPMENT...）。

11. 到期日

到期日（Expiry Date）即信用证的有效期。在信用证支付条件下，有效期和装运期有着较密切的关系，因此这两个项目往往先后出现在同一张单据中。这一栏的填写一般按信用证规定，但如果装运期空白不填的话，这一栏也可相应空白。空白的原因主要是托运时间距离装运期限、信用证到期日很长。

12. 运费

这一栏托运人不填，留给船公司或其他代理人填写。船公司或船代理是在计算运费之后，将应收运费总额填入这一栏。

13. 提单正本份数

信用证中一般都会用各种方式表示对提单正本份数的要求。例如：

来证要求："3 original Bills of Lading"是指 3 份正本提单；

来证要求："Full Set of Bills of Lading"是指全套提单。

14. 提单副本份数

提单副本究竟应提供多少份，一般在信用证中有明确规定。寄单所需份数在信用证中，一般也都要作出明确规定。

15. 存货地点

这一栏内容用中文填写。填写将出口的货物出口前最后一个存放仓库的名称和地点。

16. 运费缴付方式

运费缴付方式栏应填写"运费到付"或"运费预付"。填写两者中的哪一个取决于买卖合同中价格术语，常见的有 FOB、CFR 和 CIF，按 FOB 成交的买卖合同，该栏应该填写"运费到付"，而按 CFR 或 CIF 成交的买卖合同则应该填写"运费预付"。

17. 提单号码

这一栏内容仍然留给船方或其代理人填写。提单是由承运人签发的与托运人之间的契约证明文件。当提单号码和船名被填写在托运单上后，承运人、托运人之间的法律关系即被确定。同时更进一步证明船方或其代理人经办的配船工作完成。

一旦出现原定配载船舶无法适航、适货，需要更换配载船舶时，船方或其代理人应及时通知托运人。托运人将根据通知修改托运单中的有关栏目，包括船名和提单号码。但有时更换配载船舶后，船方或其代理人只通知托运人修改船名。

正是由于托运单上反映了提单号码，载明了承运人和托运人之间工作往来的原始记录，出口企业不仅应认真填写，而且还应保存好托运单，直至货款安全收回、货物如数到达、法定索赔期限结束。

18. 船名

这一栏内容由船方或其代理人填写。填写运载承运货物的船舶名称。当船方或其代理人将填有船名的托运单退还出口企业时，证明配船工作完成。

19. 托运单号码

填写托运单一般要填写与发票号码一致的内容。这样做一是为了使发票填写的内容与实际装货的情况完全一致，二是为了便于查寻、核对。

20. 运单日期

与托运单号码处理方法一样，运单日期填写与发票日期一样的内容，即开立发票的日期。但也可以早于发票日期，实务中，应按实际开立托运单的日期填写。

21. 起运地和目的地

这一栏内容由出口企业按信用证规定的要求填写。填写时应注意港口重名现象，如果有重名，往往要求在港口后写明国名。

22. 签字

在托运单的右下角由经办人签字，出口企业盖章。

23. 买方提出的特别条款

买方提出的特别条款来源于信用证有关装运的内容。例如，允许分两批装运（partial shipments allowed in two lots），装运由上海经香港至伦敦（shipment from Shanghai to London via Hong Kong）。像这类的由买方提出的特别条款应该一字不漏地填在托运单的此栏中，其目的是要求承运人严格履行。

24．卖方提出的特别条款

卖方提出的特别条款针对的是船方或其代理人的装运行为，旨在保护受载货物。因此，这些特别条款无须征得买方同意或确认。这类特别条款的内容包括：要求用集装箱装运；要求不与其他货物混杂；要求不被其他重物挤压；要求货物的装卸和放置不倒置等。

4.2.3 集装箱货物出口托运程序

1．FOB条件下的业务流程

FOB条件下整箱货进口货运代理业务流程如图4-2所示。

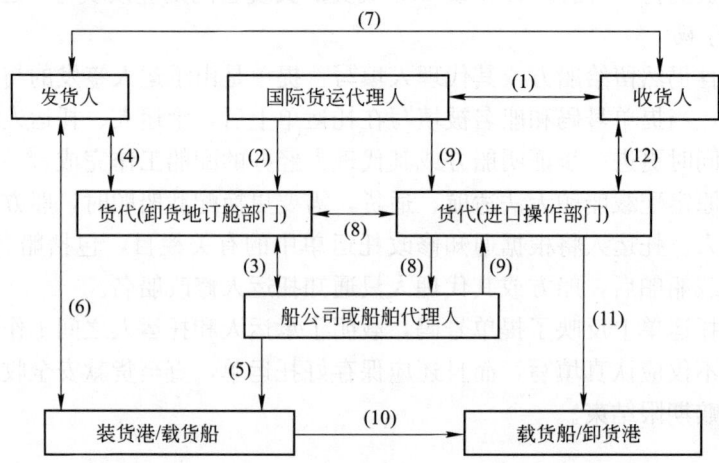

图4-2 FOB条件下整箱货进口货运代理业务流程

（1）收货人与国际货运代理人（简称货代）建立货运代理关系。
（2）货代办理卸货地订舱（home booking）业务前要落实货单齐备。
（3）货代缮制货物清单后，向船公司办理订舱手续，船公司进行订舱确认。
（4）货代通知发货人及装货港代理人。
（5）船公司安排载货船舶抵装货港。
（6）发货人将货物交给船公司，货物装船后发货人取得有关运输单证。
（7）发货人与收货人之间办理交易手续及单证。
（8）货代需掌握船舶动态，收集、保管好有关单证。
（9）货代及时办理进口货物的单证及相关手续。
（10）船舶抵卸货港卸货，货物入库、进场。
（11）办理货物进口报关等手续后凭提货单到现场提货（特殊情况下可在船边提货）。
（12）货代将货物交接给收货人，并办理空箱回运到空箱堆场等事宜。

2．CFR、CIF条件下的业务流程

CFR、CIF条件下整箱货进口货运代理业务流程如图4-3所示。

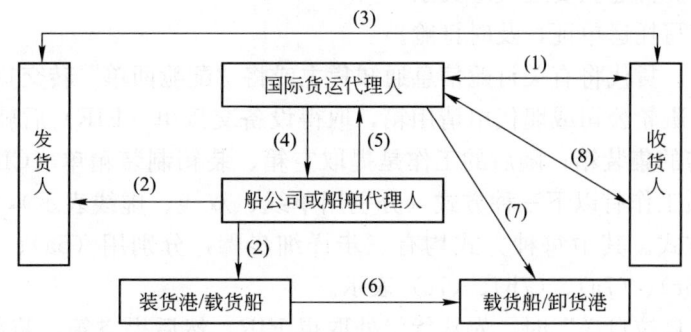

图 4-3 CFR、CIF 条件下整箱货进口货运代理业务流程

(1) 收货人与货代建立货运代理关系。
(2) 船公司装船,装船后签发提单给发货人。
(3) 发货人向收货人发出装船通知(尤其在 CFR 条件下,因为收货人要办理保险业务)。
(4) 货代需掌握船舶动态,收集、保管好有关单证。
(5) 货代及时办理进口货物的单证及相关手续。
(6) 船舶抵卸货港卸货,货物入库、进场。
(7) 办理货物进口报关等手续后凭提货单到现场提货(特殊情况下可在船边提货)。
(8) 货代将货物交接给收货人,并办理空箱回运到空箱堆场等事宜。

3. 集装箱整箱货出口货运代理业务流程

集装箱整箱货出口货运代理业务流程如图 4-4 所示。

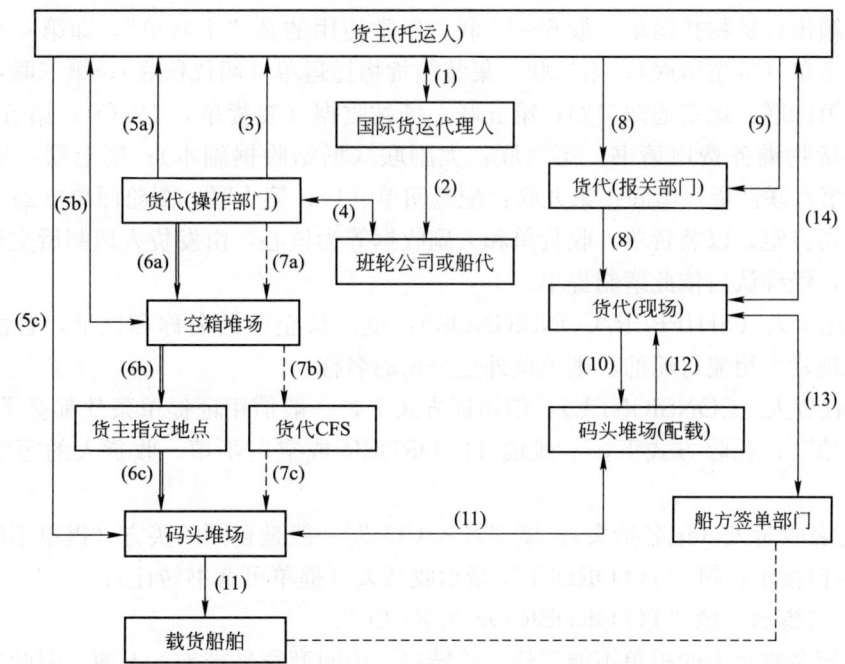

图 4-4 集装箱整箱货出口货运代理业务流程

（1）货主与货代建立货运代理关系。

（2）货主填写托运单证，及时订舱。

（3）订舱后，货代将有关订舱信息通知货主或将"配舱回单"转交货主。

（4）货代向班轮公司或船代申请用箱，取得设备交接单（EIR）后就可以凭以到空箱堆场提取所需的集装箱；随后的工作是提取空箱、装箱制装箱单（CLP）、交装有货物的重箱，该项工作有以下三种方式（分别用单线、双线、虚线表示），在实践中只选其中一种操作方式。其中每种方式均有三步详细步骤，分别用（5a）、（5b）、（5c）、（6a）、（6b）、（6c）、（7a）、（7b）、（7c）表示。

（5）货主"自拉自送"时，先从货代处取得 EIR，然后提空箱，装箱后制作 CLP，并按要求及时将重箱送码头堆场，即集中到港区等待装船。

（6）货代提空箱至货主指定地点装箱，制作 CLP，然后将重箱"集港"。

（7）货主将货物送到货代 CFS，货代提空箱，并在 CFS 装箱，制作 CLP，然后"集港"。

（8）货主委托货代报关、报检，办妥有关手续后将单证交货代（现场）。

（9）货主也可自行报关，并将单证交货代现场。

（10）货代（现场）将办妥手续后的单证交码头堆场（配载）。

（11）配载部门制订装船计划，经船公司确认后实施装船作业。

（12）实践中，在货物装船后可以取得场站收据（D/R）正本。

（13）货代可凭 D/R 正本到船方签单部门换取 B/L 或其他单据。

（14）货代将 B/L 等单据交货主。

4.2.4 集装箱托运单的内容及其填制

集装箱出口货物托运单一般 6~12 联，经常使用的是"十联单"，即第一联：集装箱货物托运单（货主留底）；第二联：集装箱货物托运单（船代留底）；第三联：运费通知（1）；第四联：运费通知（2）；第五联：场站收据（装货单）（S/O）；第五联副本：缴纳出口货物港务费申请书；第六联：大副联（场站收据副本）；第七联：场站收据（D/R）；第八联：货代留底；第九联：配舱回单（1）；第十联：配舱回单（2）。格式由各运输公司自定，以装货单、收货单和大副收据等为核心，由发货人填制后交给船公司进行配舱，经确认后依此缮制提单。

（1）托运人（SHIPPER/CONSIGNOR）：填出口企业的名称和地址，若由外贸运输公司代理货主租船订舱的，则填该外运公司的名称。

（2）收货人（CONSIGNEE）：信用证方式下，一般信用证提单条款都会予以规定，应按规定填写；托收方式下，一般填 TO ORDER 或空白不填。收货人的写法有以下几种：

① 记名收货人（记名抬头）：填"××CO."一般是合同的买方（提单不能转让）；

② 空白指示：填"TO ORDER"指示收货人（提单可背书转让）；

③ 记名指示：填"TO ORDER OF ××CO."。

由于记名收货人的提单不能转让，给转口、中间商贸易带来了不便，因此出现了指示收货人的填法，其补充了记名收货人的缺陷，却又给船方通知货方提货带来了不便，对此,由被通知人栏作补充。

(3) 被通知人(NOTIFY PARTY):一般由买方或其代理人指定,其职责是及时接受船方发出的到货通知并将之转告真实收货人,故要求填写详细名称和地址,但他不能提货。

信用证方式下,按规定填写;其他方式下,填写买方名称和地址。

(4) 编号(NO.):一般填写发票号码,信用证若有规定,则按信用证的规定填写。

(5) 装运港、目的港(PORT OF LODING、PORT OF DESTINATION/DISCHARGE):装运港即船方收货的港口,目的港即货物最终送达的港口,一般按信用证的规定填写,注意不能用国名或地名代替,若遇重名港口,应加注国名或地名。

(6) 标记及号码(MARKS & NO.):若信用证已规定,则按规定填写;若信用证未规定,一般由卖方自行设计;若无唛头,则应注明"N/M"。

(7) 货物说明(DESCRIPTION OF GOODS):填写货物的大类名称或统称,若同时出口不同的商品,则应分别填写。

(8) 数量(QUANTITY):按最大包装的实际件数填写,如10万码花布,分别用粗坯布捆成100捆,则填"100捆",若出口货物有多件,包装方式和材料都不同,则填每种货物的最大包装件数,如20个托盘,10个集装袋,25个捆包布匹,合计55件。

(9) 毛重(GROSS WEIGHT):计量单位为千克(KGS)。若一次装运的货物有几种不同的包装材料或者是完全不同的货物,则应分别填写,然后合计。

(10) 尺码(MEASUREMENT):整批货的体积总数,计量单位为立方米(m^3或CBM)。重量和尺码是船公司计算运费的基础,应如实填写。

(11) 运费付款方式:根据合同中的价格术语填写"运费到付(FREIGHT COLLECT)"或"运费预付(FREIGHT PREPAID/PAID)" CIF、CFR 术语填 FREIGHT PREPAID/PAID, FOB 术语填 FREIGHT COLLECT。若填了 FREIGHT PREPAID/PAID,则在 PREPAID AT 一栏内填写装运港的名称,若填了 FREIGHT COLLECT,则在 COLLECT AT 一栏内填目的港的名称。

(12) 分批装运、转船(PARTIAL SHIPMENT, TRANSSHIPMENT):严格按信用证的规定,填写允许或不允许。

(13) 装运期、有效期(DATE OF SHIPMENT,DATE OF EXPIRY):按信用证规定的最迟装运期和议付有效期分别填写,一般装运期比有效期早。若装运期空白,有效期也可空白,原因是:若托运期距装运期、信用证有效期较长,填写了,船方可能认为可以不立即安排装运,从而使托运人原订及早装运的目的落空。

(14) 制单日期:与发票日期一致。

(15) 提单正本份数(NO. S OF ORIGINAL B (S)/L):用阿拉伯数字表示,一般为"3"。

(16) 货物的交接方式(集装箱运输时):FCL-FULL CONTAINER LOAD,LCL—LESS THAN CONTAINER LOAD, CY—CONTAINER YARD, CFS—CONTAINER FREIGHT STATION。

整箱交接——FCL/FCL;整箱接、拼箱交——FCL/LCL;拼箱接、整箱交——LCL/FCL;拼箱交接——LCL/LCL。

整箱货是在海关监督下由货主在自己仓库或工厂自行将货物装箱并加铅封，然后运交承运人，一般都送到堆场（CY）。拼箱货适用于小票货物，货主将货交承运人，由承运人或其代理人根据货物的流向、性质和重量将分属于不同货主的货物拼装在一个集装箱内而发运，一般送到集散站（CFS）。

（17）货物种类（TYPE OF GOODS）：有普通货、冷藏货、液体、散货等。

（18）特殊条款：主要为运输方面的特殊要求，如货物不能倒置等配货要求、立即装运等。

（19）其他：由船方填写。

（20）签字：出口企业盖章，经办人签字。

【相关单证】

单证 4-1 海运出口货物托运单

海运出口货物托运单（散货）

托运人 Shipper _____ 船名 起运港 目的港 S/S _____ from _____ to _____					
标志及号码 Marks & No. s	数量 Quantity	货名 Description of Goods	重量千克 Weight Kilos		
			净 Net	毛 Gross	
共计件数（大写）Total Number of Packages（In Writing）			运费付款方式		
运费计算		尺码 Measurement			
备注					
抬头		可否转船	可否分批		
通知人		装运期	有效期	提单张数	
		银行编号	信用证号		

托运人签名盖章、日期

续表

SHIPPER（发货人）		
CONSIGNEE（收货人）		D/R NO.（编号）
NOTIFY PARTY（通知人）		集装箱货物托运单 货主留底　第一联
PRE-CARRIAGE BY（前程运输）	PLACE OF RECEIPT（收货地点）	
OCEAN VESSEL（船名）VOY NO.（航次）	PORT OF LOADING（装货港）	FINAL DESTINATION FOR THE MERCHANT'S REFERENCE（目的地）
PORT OF DISCHARGE（卸货港）	PLACE OF DELIVERY（交货地点）	

Container No. （集装箱号）	Seal No. （封志号）	Marks & No.s （唛头）	Kind of Packages Description of Goods （包装种类与货名）	No. of Containers or Packages （箱数或件数）	Gross Weight （毛重/千克）	Measurement （尺码/立方米）

TOTAL 合计（大写）					
Freight & Charges （运费与附加费）	Revenue Tons （运费吨）	Rate （运费率）	Per （每）	Prepaid （运费预付）	Collect （运费到付）
Ex. Rate （兑换率）	Prepaid at（预付地点）		Payable at（到付地点）	Place of Issue（签发地点）	
	Total Prepaid（预付总额）		No.s of Original B（s)/L（正本提单份数）		

Service Type on Receiving □-CY □-CFS □-DOOR	Service Type on Delivery □-CY □-CFS □-DOOR	Reefer-Temperature required （冷藏温度）	F	℃

TYPE OF GOODS （种类）	□Ordinary 普通　□Reefer 冷藏　□Dangerous 危险品　□Auto 裸装车辆 □Liquid 液体　□Live Animal 活动物　□Bulk 散货　□_____	危险品	Class: Property: IMD GCode Page: UN No.:

可否转船：	可否分批：	托运人签字盖章
装期：	效期：	
金额：		
制单日期：		

【案例】

河北恒泰进出口贸易公司业务员杨光为货物办理托运,货物将于天津港出口,承载船舶为QINLUN,编号:1502。

海运出口货物托运单(散货)

托运人 Shipper	HEBEI HENGTAI IMPORT & EXPORT CORPORATION NO. 231 HEPING ROAD, SHIJIAZHUANG, HEBEI, CHINA				
船名 起运港 的港 S/S	QINLUN V. 1502 From XINGANG to LOS ANGELES				目

标志及号码 Marks & No. s	数量 Quantity	货名 Description of Goods	重量千克 Weight Kilos	
			净 Net	毛 Gross
PACIFIC 18185 LOS ANGELES 1-225	4 500 DOZS 20 DOZS IN A BALE	100% COTTON STRIPE TOWEL ART NO. ABC69 SIZE:30″×60″	9450 KGS	10125 KGS
共计件数(大写)Total Number of Packages (In Writing)		TWO HUNDRED AND FIFITY BALES ONLY	运费付款方式	FREIGHT PREPAID

运费计算	尺码 Measurement 54 m³
备注	提单上需注明合同号码和信用证号码

抬头	To order	可否转船	ALLOWED	可否分批	ALLOWED
通知人	PACIFIC INTERNATIONAL INC. 129 HAYWARD WAY STREET MONTE, CA 91513	装运期	NOT LATER THAN AUG. 31, 2008	有效期	提单张数 3
		银行编号		信用证号	LC-710-076405

河北恒泰进出口贸易公司
2008年8月1日

【技能实训】

1. 根据以下发票填写托运单

MASON METAL INDUSTRY CO., LTD.
NO. 13, Wu-chun 2nd, Wu-ku Ind, Park, Taipei Hsien, Taiwan

COMMERCIAL INVOICE

FOR ACCOUNT AND RISK OF　　　INVOICE NO.: EX0362T/2
SUZHOU LIYAN MACHINERY CO., LTD.　DATE: MAR. 30, 2005
　　　　　　　　　　　　　　　SHIPPER BY: WING CHEONG V. WN095
　　　　　　　　　　　　　　　FROM: KEELUNG, TAIWAN
　　　　　　　　　　　　　　　TO: SHANGHAI

NO.	FULL DESCRIPTION OF GOODS	QUANTITY	UNIT PRICE	TOTAL AMOUNT FOB TAIWAN
	HOT ROLLED STEEL SHEET IN COIL			
1	SPHL-P/O 1.50 mm×120.0 mm×Coil	34 COIL 14 144 KGS	USD 0.5050/KG	USD 7 142.72
2	SPHL-P/O 2.00 mm×420.0 mm×Coil	10 COIL 20 780 KGS	USD 0.5050/KG	USD 10 493.90
3	SPHL-P/O 2.60 mm×140.0 mm×Coil	6 COIL 6 006 KGS	USD 0.5050/KG	USD 3 033.03
	TOTAL:	50 COIL 40 930 KGS		USD 20 669.65

MASON METAL INDUSTRY CO.,

E. & O. E.

2. 根据以下销售确认书填写托运单

SALES CONFIRMATION

S/C NO.: XL-MONSC10
DATE: APRIL 1ST, 2003

THE SELLER: GUANGZHOU XINCHUANG IMP. & EXP. CO., LTD.
ADDRESS: NO. 1100 SIPING ROAD GUANGZHOU, CHINA
THE BUYER: MONARCH TRADING S. A.
ADDRESS: PASEO DELA CASTELLANA 178 BARCELONA, SPAIN

Item No.	Commodity & Specifications	Unit	Quantity	Unit Price/ US $	Amount/ US $
	Daily Brand Tumblers			CIF C 5% BARCELONA	
1	71H5	SET	2 300	6.18	14 214.00
2	71H5B	SET	2 300	7.39	16 997.00
3	71H5F	SET	2 300	8.36	19 228.00
4	71H5F	SET	3 150	4.75	14 962.50
				TOTAL	65 401.50
TOTAL CONTRACT VALUE	SAY US DOLLARS SIXTY FIVE THOUSAND FOUR HUNDRED AND ONE AND CENTS FIFTY ONLY				

PACKING:　71H5, 71HB, 71H5F To be packed in gift box of 6 pieces each. 10 boxes to one export carton. Meas. 40 cm×25.5 cm×35.5 cm.
　　　　　71H10 To be packed in gift box of 12 pieces each. 6 boxes to one export carton. Meas. 40 cm×34 cm×35 cm

TERMS OF SHIPMENT:　DURING MAY 2003 PARTIAL SHIPMENT NOT ALLOWED, TRANSSHIPMNET

	ALLOWED
PORT OF LOADING & DESTINATION:	FROM GUANGZHOU, CHINA TO BARCELONA, SPAIN
PAYMENT:	BY IRREVOCABLE SIGHT LETTER OF CREDIT OPENED BY THE BUYER THROUGH A BANK ACCEPTABLE TO THE SELLER NOT LATER THAN APRIL 25TH 2003 AND REMAIN VALID FOR NEGOTIATION IN GUANGZHOU UNTIL 15TH DAY AFTER THE AFORESAID TIME OF SHIPMENT.
INSURANCE:	TO BE COVERED BY THE SELLER FOR 110% OF TOTAL INVOICE VALUE AGAINST ALL RISKS AND WAR RISKS AS PER AND SUBJECT TO CIC OF PICC.
THE SELLER: GUANGZHOU XINCHUANG IMP. & EXP. CO., LTD.	THE BUYER: MONARCH TRADING S. A.

4.3 航空运输托运流程及托运单缮制

4.3.1 航空运输托运流程

(1) 委托运输。由托运人自己填写货运托运书。托运书应包括下列内容栏：托运人、收货人、始发站机场、目的地机场、要求的路线/申请订舱、供运输用的声明价值、供海关用的声明价值、保险金额、处理事项、货运单所附文件、实际毛重、运价类别、计费重量、费率、货物的品名及数量、托运人签字、日期等。

(2) 审核单证。单证应包括：发票、装箱单、托运书、报送单项式、外汇核销单、许可证、商检证、进料/来料加工核销本、索赔/返修协议、到会保函、关封。

(3) 预配舱。代理人汇总所接受的委托和客户的预报，并输入计算机，计算出各航线的件数、重量、体积，按照客户的要求和货物重、泡情况，根据各航空公司不同机型对不同板箱的重量和高度要求，制订预配舱方案，并为每票货配上运单号。

(4) 预订舱。代理人根据所指定的预配舱方案，按航班、日期打印出总运单号、件数、重量、体积，向航空公司预订舱。

(5) 接受单证。接受托运人或其代理人送交的已经审核确认的托运书及报送单证和收货凭证。将收货记录与收货凭证核对，制作操作交接单，填上所收到的各种报关单证份数，给每份交接单配一份总运单或分运单。将制作好的交接单、配好的总运单或分运单、报关单证移交制单。

(6) 填制货运单。航空货运单包括总运单和分运单，填制航空货运单的主要依据是发货提供的国际货物委托书，委托书上的各项内容都应体现在货运单项式上，一般用英文填写。

(7) 接收货物。接收货物是指航空货运代理公司把即将发运的货物从发货人手中接过来并运送到自己的仓库。接收货物一般与接单同时进行。对于通过空运或铁路从内地运往出境地的出口货物，货运代理按照发货人提供的运单号、航班号及接货地点、日期，代其提取货物。如货物已在始发地办理了出口海关手续，发货人应同时提供始发地海关的关封。

接货时应对货物进行过磅和丈量，并根据发票、装箱或送货单清点货物，核对货物的数量、品名、合同号或唛头等是否与货运单上所列一致。

（8）标记和标签。

标记：包括托运人、收货人的姓名、地址、联系电话、传真；合同号等；操作（运输）注意事项；单件超过 150 千克的货物。

标签：航空公司标签上前三位阿拉伯数字代表所承运航空公司的代号，后八位数字是总运单号码。分标签是代理公司对出具分标签的标识，分标签上应有分运单号码和货物到达城市或机场的三字代码。一件货物贴一张航空公司标签，有分运单的货物，再贴一张分标签。

（9）配舱。核对货物的实际件数、重量、体积与托运书上预报数量的差别。对预订舱位、板箱的有效利用、合理搭配，按照各航班机型、板箱型号、高度、数量进行配载。

（10）订舱。接到发货人的发货预报后，向航空公司吨控部门领取并填写订舱单，同时提供相应的信息；货物的名称、体积、重量、件数、目的地；要求出运的时间等。航空公司根据实际情况安排舱位和航班。货运代理订舱时，可依照发货人的要求选择最佳的航线和承运人，同时为发货人争取最低、最合理的运价。订舱后，航空公司签发舱位确认书（舱单），同时给予装货集装器领取凭证，以表示舱位订妥。

（11）出口报关。将报关单与有关的发票、装箱单和货运单综合在一起，并根据需要随附有关的证明文件；以上报关单证齐全后，由持有报关证的报关员正式向海关申报；海关审核无误后，海关官员即在用于发运的运单正本上加盖放行章，同时在出口收汇核销单和出口报关单上加盖放行章，在发货人用于产品退税的单证上加盖验讫章，粘上防伪标志；完成出口报关手续。

（12）出仓单。配舱方案制订后就可着手编制出仓单：出仓单的日期、承运航班的日期、装载板箱形式及数量、货物进仓顺序编号、总运单号、件数、重量、体积、目的地三字代码和备注。

（13）提板箱。向航空公司申领板、箱并办理相应的手续。提板、箱时，应领取相应的塑料薄膜和网。对所使用的板、箱要登记、消号。

（14）货物装箱装板。注意事项：不要用错集装箱、集装板；不要用错板型、箱型；不要超装箱板尺寸；要垫衬。封盖好塑料纸，防潮、防雨淋；集装箱、板内货物尽可能配装整齐，结构稳定，并接紧网索，防止运输途中倒塌；对于大宗货物、集中托运货物，尽可能将整票货物装一个或几个板、箱内运输。

（15）签单。货运单在盖好海关放行章后还需要到航空公司签单，只有签单确认后才允许将单、货交给航空公司。

（16）交接发运。交接是向航空公司交单交货，由航空公司安排航空运输。

（17）航班跟踪。需要联程中转的货物，在货物运出后，要求航空公司提供二程、三程航班中转信息，确认中转情况。及时将上述信息反馈给客户，以便遇到不正常情况时及时处理。

(18) 费用结算。

4.3.2　航空托运书的内容及其填制

根据《统一国际航空运输某些规则的公约》（以下简称《华沙公约》）第 5 条第（1）和第（5）款规定，货运单应由托运人填写，也可由承运人或其代理人代为填写。实际上，目前货运单均由承运人或其代理人代为填制。为此，作为填开货运单的依据——托运书，应由托运人自己填写，而且托运人必须在上面签字或盖章。

托运书（Shippers Letter of Instruction，SLI），是指托运人用于委托承运人或其代理人填开航空货运单的一种表单，表单上列有填制货运单所需各项内容，并应有授权于承运人或其代理人代其在货运单上签字的文字说明。托运书包括下列内容栏。

1. 托运人

该栏填列托运人（SHIPPERS' NAME AND ADDRESS）的全称、街名、城市名称、国家名称及便于联系的电话、电传或传真号码。托运人可以是货主，也可以是货运代理人，有时承运人要求托运人提供托运人账号，以便承运人在收货人拒付运费时，向托运人索赔。

2. 收货人

填列收货人（CONSIGNEES' NAME AND ADDRESS）的全称、街名、城市名称、国家名称（特别是在不同国家内有相同城市名称时，更应注意填上国名）以及电话号、电传号或传真号，本栏内不得填写"to order"或"to order of the shipper"（按托运人的指示）等字样，因为航空货运单不能转让。收货人可以是实际收货人，也可以是货运代理人。收货人账号仅供承运人使用，一般不需要填写，除非承运人需要。

3. 始发站机场

填始发站机场（AIRPORT OF DEPARTURE）的全称，可填城市名称。但相同城市的不同国家，需要填写国际名称。

4. 目的地机场

填目的地机场（AIRPORT OF DESTINATION）名称或三字代码，例如，上海浦东国际机场的代码为"PVG"。如果机场名称不明确时，可填城市名称。如果某一城市名称用于一个以上国家时，应加上国名。例如，LONDON UK（伦敦，英国）；LONDON KY US（伦敦，肯塔基州，美国）；LONDON CA（伦敦，安大略省，加拿大）。

5. 要求的路线/申请订舱

要求的路线/申请订舱（REQUESTED ROUTING/REQUESED BOOKING）栏用于航空公司安排运输路线时使用，但如果托运人有特别要求时，也可填入本栏。

6. 供运输用的声明价值

供运输运的声明价值（DECLARED VALUE FOR CARRIAGE）栏填列供运输用的声明价值金额，该价值即为承运人赔偿责任的限额。承运人按有关规定向托运人收取声明价值费。但如果所交运的货物毛重每千克不超过 20 美元（或等值货币），无须填写声明价值金额，可在本栏内填入"NVD"（No Value Declared）（未声明价值），如本栏空着未填写时，承运人或其代理人可视为货物未声明价值。

7. 供海关用的声明价值

供海关用的声明价值（DECLARED VALUE FOR CUSTOMS）栏填写托运人向海关申报的货物价值，国际货物通常要受到目的站海关的检查，海关根据此栏所填数额征税。如果托运人不办理此项申明价值，必须打印上"NCV"（No Customs Value）字样。

8. 保险金额

中国民航各空运企业暂未开展国际航空运输代理保险业务，保险金额（INSURANCE AMOUNT REQUESTED）栏可以空白不填。

9. 处理事项

处理事项（HANDLING INFORMATION）栏填列附加的处理要求。例如，另请通知（ALSO NOTIFY），除填收货人之外，如托运人还希望在货物到达的同时通知他人，请另填写通知人的全名和地址；外包装上的标记；操作要求，如易碎、向上等。

10. 货运单所附文件

货运单所附文件（DOCUMENTATION TO ACCOMPANY AIR WAYBILL）栏填列随附在货运单上运往目的地的文件，应填上所附文件的名称。例如，托运人所托运的动物证明书（SHIPPER'S CERTIFICATION FOR LIVE ANIMALS）。

11. 件数和包装方式

件数和包装方式（NUMBER AND KIND OF PACKAGES）栏填列该批货物的总件数，并注明其包装方法。例如，包裹（Package）、纸版盒（Carton）、盒（Case）、板条箱（Crate）、袋（Bag）、卷（Roll）等。如货物没有包装时，就注明为散装（Loose）。

12. 实际毛重

实际毛重（ACTUAL GROSS WEIGHT）栏内的重量应由承运人或其代理人在称重后填入。如托运人已填上重量，承运人或其代理人必须进行复核。

13. 运价类别

运价类别（RATE CLASS）包括所适用的运价、协议价、杂费、服务费。

14. 计费重量（千克）

本栏内的计费重量（CHARGEABLE WEIGHT）应由承运人或其代理人在量过货物的尺寸（以厘米为单位）后，由承运人或其代理人算出计费重量后填入，如托运人已经填上，承运人或其代理人必须复核。

15. 费率

费率（RATE/CHARGE）栏可空着不填。

16. 货物的品名及数量（包括体积及尺寸）

填列货物的品名和数量（包括尺寸或体积）[NATURE AND QUANTITY OF GOODS (INCL. DIMENSIONS OR VOLUME)]。

若一票货物包括多种物品时，托运人应分别申报货物的品名，填写品名时不能使用"样品"、"部件"等这类比较笼统的名称。货物中的每一项均须分开填写，并尽量填写详细，如"9筒35毫米的曝光动画胶片"、"新闻短片（美国制）"等，本栏所填写内容应与出口报关发票、进出口许可证上列明的货物相符。

危险品应填写适用的准确名称及标贴的级别。

17. 托运人签字

托运人必须在托运人签字（SIGNATURE OF SHIPPER）栏内签字。

18. 日期

日期（DATE）栏填托运人或其代理人交货的日期。

4.3.3 航空运单的内容及其填制

航空运单（Air Waybill，AWB），是承运人签发给发货人表示已收妥货物接受托运的货运单据，不是货物的物权凭证，而仅是一种收据，是不可转让的运输单据，所以在运单上亦可表示："Not negotiable"（不可转让）。

我国国际航空货运单由一式十二联组成，包括三联正本、六联副本和三联额外副本。货运单要求用英文打印，现将航空运单各项栏目的填写说明如下。

1. 航空运单号码

航空运单号码（The Air Waybill Number）应清楚地印在货运单的左右上角以及右下角，航空运单的编号由航空公司编制，所以从航空运单号可以看出是哪一国的航空公司，例如，编号前三位数"781"是中国东方航空公司的代号，"999"是中国国际航空公司的代号。

2. 始发站机场（1）

填制始发站机场（Airport of Departure）的 IATA 三字代号（如果始发地机场名称不明确，可填制机场所在地城市的 IATA 三字代号）。

3. 货运单所属承运人的名称及地址（1C）

货运单所属承运人的名称及地址（Issuing Carries Name and Address）处一般印有航空公司的标志、名称和地址。例如，中国国际航空公司，则在本栏表明 AIR CHINA 作为承运人的名称；中国东方航空公司，则在本栏表明 CHINA EASTERN AIRLINES 作为承运人的名称。

4. 正本联说明（1D）

正本联说明（1D）（Reference To Originals）无须填写。

5. 契约条件（1E）

契约条件（Reference To Conditions of Contract）一般情况下无须填写，除非承运人需要。

6. 托运人

托运人（Shipper）栏包括如下内容。

（1）托运人姓名和地址（Shipper's Name and Address）（2）。

填制托运人姓名（全称）、地址、国家（或国家两字代号）以及托运人的电话、传真、电传号码。

（2）托运人账号（Shipper's Account Number）（3）。

此栏不需填写，除非托运人需要。

7. 收货人

收货人（Consignee）栏包括如下内容。

（1）收货人姓名和地址（Consignee's Name and Address）（4）。

填制收货人姓名（全称）、地址、国家（或国家两字代号）以及托运人的电话、传真、电传号码。

（2）Consignee's Account Number 收货人账号（5）。

此栏仅供承运人使用，一般不需填写，除非最后的承运人需要。

8. 填开货运单的承运人的代理人栏

承运人代理人（Issuing Carrier's Agent）栏内容如下。

（1）名称和城市（Name and City）（6）。

① 填制向承运人收取佣金的国际航协代理人的名称和所在机场或城市。

② 根据货物代理机构管理规则，该佣金必须支付给目的站国家的一个国际航协代理人，则该国际航协代理人的名称和所在地机场或城市必须填入本栏。填入"收取佣金代理人"（Commissionable Agent）字样。

（2）国际航协代号（Agent's IATA code）（7）。

① 代理人在非货账结算区（Non-CASS Areas），打印国际航协 7 位数字代号，例 14-30288。

② 代理人在货账结算区（CASS Areas），打印国际航协 7 位数字代号，后面是三位 CASS 地址代号，和一个冠以 10 位的 7 位数字代号检验位。如 34-41234/5671。

③ 货物财务结算系统（Cargo Accounts Settlement System，CASS）。一些航空公司为便于内部系统管理，要求其代理人在此处填制相应的代码。

（3）账号（Account No.）（3）。

本栏一般不需填写，除非承运人需要。

9. 运输路线

运输路线（Routing）栏包括如下内容。

（1）始发站机场

第一承运人地址和所要求的运输路线（Airport of Departure and Requested Routing）（9）。

此栏填制与栏中一致的始发站机场名称，以及所要求的运输路线。

（2）运输路线和目的站（Routing and Destination）。

① 至（第一承运人）［To（by First Carrier）］（11A）。填制目的站机场或第一个转运点的 IATA 三字代号（当该城市有多个机场，不知道机场全称时，可用城市代号）。

② 由第一承运人 By First Carrier（11B）。填制第一承运人的名称（全称与 IATA 两字代号皆可）。

③ 至（第二承运人）［To（by Second Carrier）］（11C）。填制目的站机场或第二个转运点的 IATA 三字代号（当该城市有多个机场，不知道机场全称时，可用城市代号）。

④ 由（第二承运人）［By（Second Carrier）］（11D）。填制第二承运人的 IATA 两字代号。

⑤ 至（第三承运人）［To（by Third Carrier）］（11E）。填制目的站机场或第三个转运点的 IATA 三字代号（当该城市有多个机场，不知道机场全称时，可用城市代号）。

⑥ 由（第三承运人）［By（Third Carrier）］（11F）。填制第三承运人的 IATA 两字代号。

（3）目的地机场（Airport of Destination）（18）。

填制最后承运人的目的地机场全称。（如果该城市有多个机场，不知道机场全称时，可用城市代号）

（4）航班/日期（Flight/Date）——仅供承运人用（19A）（19B）。

本栏一般不需填写，除非参加运输各有关承运人需要。

10. 财务说明（10）。

财务说明（Accounting Information）栏填制有关财务说明事项，如运费预付、到付或发货人结算使用信用卡号以及其他必要的情况。

11. 货币（12）

货币（Currency）栏①填制始发国的 ISO（国际标准组织）的货币代号；②除目的站"国家收费栏"（33A）～（33D）内的款项货运单上所列明的金额均按上述货币支付。

12. 运费代号（仅供承运人用）（13）

运费代号（CHGS Code）栏一般不需填写，仅供电子传送货运单信息时使用。

13. 运费

运费（Charges）栏包括如下内容。

（1）WT/VAL 航空运费（根据货物计算重量乘以适用的运价收取的运费）和声明的价值附加费的预付和到付（14A）（14B）。

货运单上（24A）、（25A）或（24B）、（25B）两项费用必须全部预付或全部到付。

（2）在始发站的其他费用预付和到付［Other（Charges at Origin）］（24A）（25A）。

货运单上（27A）、（28A）或（27B）、（28B）两项费用必须全部预付或全部到付；在（15A）中打"×"表示预付，在（15B）中打"×"表示到付。

14. 供运输用声明价值（16）

供运输用声明价值（Declared Value for Carriage）打印托运人向货物运输声明的价值金额；如果托运人没有声明价值，此栏必须打印"NVD"字样。

注：NVD——NO VALUE DECLARED（没有声明价值）

15. 供海关用声明价值（17）

供海关用声明价值（Declared Value for customs）打印货物及通过时所需的商业价值金额；如果货物没有商业价值，此栏必须打印"NCV"字样。

注：NCV——NO COMMERCIAL VALUE（没有商业价值）

16. 保险的金额（20）

保险的金额（Amount of Insurance）如果承运人向托运人提供代办货物保险业务时，此栏打印托运人货物投保的金额；如果承运人不提供此项服务或托运人不要求投保时此栏内必须打印"×××"符号。

17. 运输处理注意事项处填制相应的代码票航空公司注意事项（21）

（1）如果是危险货物，有两种情况，一种是需要附托运人危险品申报单的，则这栏内应打印"DANGEROUS GOODS AS PER ATTACHED SHIPPER'S DECLARATION"字样，对于要求装货机上的危险货物，还应再加上"CARGO AIRCRAFT ONLY"字样。另一种是属于不要求附危险品申报单的危险货物，则应打印"SHIPPER'S

DECLARATION NOT REQUIRED"字样。

（2）当一批货物中既有危险品也有非危险品时，应分别列明，危险货物必须列在第一项，此类货物不要求托运人附危险品申报单，只要危险货物不是放射性物质且数量有限。

（3）其他注意事项尽可能使用"货物交换电报程序"（CARGO-IMP）中的代号和简语，例如：

① 货物上的标志、号码以及包装方法；

② 货运单所附文件，如托运人的动物证明书（SHIPPER'S CERTIFICATION FOR LIVE ANIMAL），装箱单（PACKING LIST），发票（INVOICE）等；

③ 除收货人外，另请通知人的姓名、地址、国家，以及电话、电传或传真号码；

④ 货物所需要的特殊处理规定；

⑤ 海关规定等。

18. 货物运价细目（22A）至（22B）

货物运价细目（Consignment Rating Details）中，一票货物中如含有两种或两种以上不同运价类别计费的货物应分别填写，每填写一项另起一行，如果含有危险品，则该危险货物应列在第一项。

（1）件数/运价组合点（No. of Pieces Rcp）（22A）。

打印货物的件数；如果使用非公布直达运价计算运费时，在件数的下面还应打印运价组合点城市的 IATA 三字代号。

（2）毛重（Gross Weight）（22B）。适用于运价的货物实际毛重（以运价为单位时可保留至小数后一位）。

（3）重量单位（kg/Lb）（22C）。

以千克为单位用代号"K"；以磅为单位用代号"L"。

（4）运价等级（Rate Class）（22D）。

根据需要打印下列代号：

M——Minimum Charge（最低运费）；

N——Normal Rate[45千克以下（或100千克以下）运价]；

Q——Quantity Rate（45千克以上运价）；

C——Specific Commodity Rate（指定商品运价）；

R——Class Rate Reduction（等级货物附减运价）；

S——Class Rate Surcharge（等级货物附加运价）；

U——Unit load Device Basic Charge or Rate（集装化设备基本运费或运价）；

E——Unit load Device Additional Rate（集装化设备附加运价）；

X——Unit load Device Additional Information（集装化设备附加说明）；

Y——Unit load Device Discount（集装化设备折扣）。

（5）商品品名编号（Commodity Item No.）（22E）。

① 使用指定商品运价时，此栏打印指定商品品名代号（打印位置应与运价代号 C 保持水平）；

② 使用等级货物运价时，此栏打印附加或附减运价的比例（百分比）；

③ 如果是集装货物，打印集装货物运价等级。

(6) 计费重量（Chargeable Weight）（22F）。

打印与运价相应的货物计费重量；如果是集装货物则有如下要求：①与运价代号"U"对应打印适合集装货物基本运费的运价点重量；②与运价代号"E"对应打印超过使用基本运费的重量；③与运价代号"X"对应打印集装器空重。

(7) 运价/运费（Rate/Charge）（22G）。

① 当使用最低运费时，此栏与运价代号"M"对应打印最低运费；

② 打印与运价代号"N"、"Q"、"C"等相应的运价；

③ 当货物为等级货物时，此栏与运价代号"S"或"R"对应打印附加或附减后的运价；

④ 如果货物是集装货物则：与运价代号"U"对应打印集装货物的基本运费；与运价代号"E"对应打印超过基本运费的集装货物运价。

(8) 总计（22H）。

打印计费重量与适用运价相乘后的运费金额；如果是最低运费或集装货物基本运费时，本栏与（22G）内金额相同。

(9) 货物品名和数量（Nature and Quantity of Goods）（22I）。

本栏应按要求打印，尽可能地清楚、简明，以便涉及组织该批货物运输的所有工作人员能够一目了然。

① 打印货物的品名（用英文大写字母）；

② 当一票货物中含有危险货物时，应分列打印，危险货物应列在第一项；

③ 活动物运输，本栏内容应根据IATA活动物运输规定打印；

④ 对应集合货物，本栏应打印"Consolidation as Per Attached List"；

⑤ 打印货物的体积，用长×宽×高表示，如 DIMS：40×30×20cm；

⑥ 可打印货物的产地国。

(10) 总件数（22J）。

打印（22A）中各组货物的件数之和。

(11) 总毛重（22K）。

打印（22B）中各组货物毛重之和。

(12) 总计（22L）。

打印（22H）中各组货物运费之和。

(13) 一般不需打印，除非承运人需要，此栏内可打印服务代号：（22Z）

B——Service Shipment（公务货物）；

C——Company Material（公司货物）；

D——Door to Door Service（门到门服务）；

J——Priority Service（优先服务）；

P——Small Package（小件货服务）；

T——Charter（包机）。

19. 其他费用（23）

其他费用（Other Charges）栏包括如下内容。

(1) 打印始发站运输中发生的其他费用，按全部预付或全部到付。

(2) 作为到付的其他费用，应视为"代垫付款"托运人应按代垫付款规定支付手续费，否则，对其他运费应办理到付业务。

（3）打印"其他费用"金额时，应冠以下列代号：

AC——Animal Container（动物容器租费）；

AS——Assembly Service Fee（集中货物服务费）；

AT——Attendant（押运员服务费）；

AW——Air Waybill（货运单费）；

BR——Bank Release（银行放行）；

DB——Disbursement fee（代垫付款手续费）；

DF——Distribution Service（分发服务费）；

FC——Charges collect fee（运费到付手续费）；

GT——Government tax（政府捐税）；

HR——Human remains（尸体、骨灰附加费）；

IN——Insurance Premium（代办保险服务费）；

LA——Live Animals（动物处理费）；

MA——Miscellaneous—Due Agent（代理人收取的杂项费用）；

MZ——Miscellaneous—Due Carrier（填开货运单的承运人收取的杂项费用）；

PK——Packaging（包装服务费）；

PA——Dangerous goods Surcharge（危险品处理费）；

SD——Surface Charge Destination（目的站地面运输费）；

SI——Stop in transit（中途停运费）；

SO——Storage Origin（始发站保管费）；

SR——Storage Destination（目的站保管费）；

SU——Surface Charge（地面运输费）；

TR——Transit（过境费）；

TX——Taxes（捐税）；

UH——ULD Handling（集装设备操作费）。

（4）承运人收取的其他费用"C"表示，代理人收取的其他费用"A"表示。

如 AWC 为代理人收取的货运单费。

20. 预付

预付（Prepaid）栏包括如下内容。

（1）预付运费（Weight Charge）（24A）。

打印货物计费重量计得的货物运费，与（22H）或（22L）中金额一致。

（2）预付声明价值附加费［Valuation Charge (Prepaid)］（25A）。

如果托运人向货物运输声明价值的话，此栏打印根据公式：（声明价值－实际毛重×最高赔偿额）×0.5％。

计得的声明价值附加费金额。此项费用与（22H）或（22L）中货物运费一起必须全部预付或全部到付。

（3）预付的其他费用总额（Total Other Prepaid charges）。根据（23）内的其他费用打印。

① 预付由代理人收取的其他费用总额〔Total (Prepaid) Charges Due Agent〕(27A)。打印由代理人收取的其他费用总额。

② 预付由承运人收取的其他费用〔Total (Prepaid) Charges Due Carrier〕(28A)。打印由承运人收取的其他费用总额。

(4) 无名称阴影栏目(29A)。

本栏不需打印，除非承运人需要。

(5) 预付总计 Total Prepaid

打印(24A)(25A)(26A)(27A)(28A)等栏有关预付款项之和。

21. 到付

到付(Collect)栏包括如下内容。

(1) 到付运费 Weight Charge (24B)。

打印按货物计费重量计得的货物航空运费，与(22H)或(22L)中的金额一致。

(2) 到付声明价值附加费〔(Prepaid) Valuation Charge〕(25B)。

托运人向货物运输声明价值的话，此栏打印根据公式：(声明价值－实际毛重×最高赔偿额)×0.5%。

计得的声明价值附加费金额。此项费用与(22H)或(22L)中货物运费一起必须全部预付或全部到付。

(3) 到付税款〔(Prepaid) Tax〕(26B)。

打印适用的税款。此项费用与(22H)或(22L)中货物运费一起必须全部预付或全部到付。

(4) 预付的其他费用总额(Total Other Prepaid Charges)。有关栏内容根据(23)内的其他费用打印。

① 到付由代理人收取的其他费用总额〔Total (Prepaid) Charges Due Agent〕(27B)。打印由代理人收取的其他费用总额。

② 到付由承运人收取的其他费用〔Total (Prepaid) Charges Due Carrier〕(28B)。打印有承运人收取的其他费用总额。

(5) 无名称阴影栏目(29A)。

本栏不需打印，除非承运人需要。

(6) 预付总计(Total Prepaid)

打印(24B)、(25B)、(26B)、(27B)、(28B)等栏有关预付款项之和。

22. 托运人证明

托运人证明(Shipper's Certification Box)栏打印托运人名称(可参考托运人栏中内容)并令其在本栏内签字或盖章。

23. 承运人证明

承运人证明(Carrier's Execution Box)栏内容如下。

(1) 填开日期〔Executed on (Date)〕(32A)。

按日、月、年的顺序打印货运单的填开日期(月份可用缩写)，如 06SEP2000。

(2) 填开地点〔At (Place)〕(32B)。

打印机场或城市的全称或缩写。

(3) 填开货运单的承运人或其代理人签字（Signature of Issuing Carrier or Its Agent）(32C)。

填开货运单的承运人或其代理人在本栏内签字。

24. 仅供承运人在目的站使用（33）

仅供承运人在目的站使用（For Carrier's Use only at Destination）栏不需打印。

25. 用目的国家货币付费（仅供承运人使用）(30A)~(33D)

(1) 货币兑换比价（Currency Conversion Rate）(33A)。

打印目的站国家货币代号，后面是兑换比率。

(2) 用目的站国家货币付费（CC Charges in Destination Currency）(33B)。

将（29B）中所列到付总额，使用始发国的货币换算比率折算成目的站国家货币的金额，打印在本栏内。

(3) 在目的站的费用（Charges at Destination）(33C)。

最后承运人将目的站发生的费用金额包括利息等（自然增长的），打印在本栏。

(4) 到付费用总额（Total Collect Charges）。

打印（24B）与（29B）内的费用金额之和。

【相关单证】

单证4-2 国际货物托运书

中 国 民 用 航 空 局

THE CIVIL AVIATION ADMINISTRATION OF CHINA

国 际 货 物 托 运 书

SHIPPER'S LETTER OF INSTRUCTION

托运人姓名及地址 SHIPPER'S NAME AND AD-DRESS	托运人账号 SHIPPERS ACCOUNT NUMBER	供承运人用 FOR CARRIER USE ONLY	
		班期/日期 FLIGHT/DAY	航班/日期 FLIGHT/DAY
收货人姓名及地址 CONSIGNEE'S NAME AND ADDRESS	收货人账号 CONSIGNEE ACCOUNT NUMBER	已预留吨位 BOOKED	
		运费 CHARGES	
代理人的名称和城市 ISSUING CARRIERS AGENT NAME AND CITY		ALSO NOTIFY	
始发站 AIRPORT OF DEPARTUE			
到达站 AIRPORT OF DESTINATION			

托运人声明价值 SHIPPERS DECLARED VALUE		保险金额 AMOUNT OF INSURANCE	所附文件 DOCUMENT TO ACCOMANY AIR WAYBILL
运输费用 FOR CARRIAGE	供海关用 FOR CUSTOMS		

处理情况（包括包装方式、货物标志及号码）
HANDLING INFORMATION (INCL. METHOD OF PACKING IDENTIFING MARKS AND NUMBERS, ETC.)

件数 NO. OF PACKAGES	实际毛重/千克 ACTUAL GROSS WEIGHT/KG.	运价种类 RATE CLASS	收费重量/千克 CHARGEABLE WEIGHT/KG	费率 RATE/CHARGE	货物品名及数量（包括体积或尺寸）NATURE AND QUANTITY OF GOODS (INCL. DIMENSION OF VOLUME)

托运人证实以上所填全部属实并愿遵守承运人的一切载运章程
THE SHIPPER CERTIFIES THAT THE PARTICULARS ON THE PAGE HEREOF ARE CORRECT AND AGREES TO THE CONDITIONS OF CARRIAGE OF THE CARRIER

托运人签字 SIGNATURE OF SHIPPER	日期 DATE	经手人 AGENT	日期 DATE

单证 4-3 航空货运单

航空货运单

IATA-FIATA INTRODUCTORY COURE

(1A) | (1) | (1B)　　　　　　　　　　　　　　　　　　　　　　　　　(1A)　　　(1B)

Shipper's Name and Address (2)	(3) shipper's amount Number	Not Negotiable Air Waybill ISSUED BY　　　　　　　　　　　　　　　　(1C)
		Copies 1, 2 and 3 of this Air Waybill are originals and have the same validity. (1D)
Consignee's Name and Address (4)	(5) Consignee's Account Number	It is agreed that the goods described herein are accepted in apparent good order and condition (except as noted) for carriage SUBJECT TO THE CONDITIONS OF CONTRACCT ON THE REVERSE HEREOF. ALL GOODS MAY BE CARRIED BY ANY OTHER MEANS INCLUDING ROAD OR ANY OTHER CARRIER UNLESS SPECIFIC CONTRARY INSTRUCTIONS ARE GIVEN HEREON BY THE SHIPPER, AND SHIPPER AGREES THAT THE SHIPMENT MAY BE CARRIED VIA INTERMEDIATE STOPPING PLACES WHICH THE CARRIER DEEMS APPROPREATE. THE SHIPPER'S ATTENTION IS DRAWN TO THE NOTICE CONCERNING CARRIER'S LIMITATION OF LIABILITY. Shipper may increase such limitation of liability by declaring a higher value for carriage and paying a supplemental charge if require (1E)
Issuing Carrier's Agent Name and City　　　　　　(6)		Accounting Information (10)
Agent's IATA Code　(7)	Account No.　(8)	
Airport of Departure (Addr. Of First Carrier) and Requested Routing (9)		Reference Number　｜　Optional Shipping Information (34A)　｜　(34B)　｜　(34C)

续表

TO (11A)	By First Carrier (11B)	Routing and Destination					Currency (12)	CHGS Code (13)	WT/VAL OTHER				Declared Value for Carriage (16)	Declared Value for Customs (17)
		to (11C)	by (11D)	to (11E)	by (11F)				PPD (14A)	COL (14B)	PPD (15A)	COLL (15B)		

Airport of Destination (18)	Flight/date (19A)	for Carriage Use Only	Flight/date (19B)	Amount of insurance (20)	INSURANCE - If carrier offers insurance and such insurance is required in accordance with the conditions thereof, indicate amount to be insured in figures in box marked "amount of insurance" (20B)

Handling Information (21)				(20A)	(21A) SCI

No. of pieces RCP	Gross Weight	kg lb	Rate class		Chargeable weight	Rate / Charge	Total	Nature and Quantity of Goods (incl. Dimensions or Volume)
				Commodity Item No.				
(22A)	(22B)	(22C)	(22Z)	(22E)	(22F)	(22G)	(22H)	(22D)
			(22D)					
(22J)	(22K)						(22L)	

Prepaid	Weight charge	Contract	Other charges
	(24A)	(24B)	
Valuation Charge			(23)
	(25A)	(25B)	
Tax			
	(26A)	(26B)	
Total Other Charges Due Agent			
	(27A)	(27B)	
Total Other Charges Due Carrier			
	(28A)	(28B)	
	(29A)	(29B)	Shipper certify that the particulars on the face hereof are correct and that in so far as any part of the consignment contains dangerous goods, such part is properly described by name and is in proper condition for carriage by air according to the applicable dangerous goods Regulations. (31) Signature of shipper or his Agent
Total Prepaid	Total Collect		
(30A)	(30B)		
			(32A) (32B) (32C)
Currency Conversion Rates	CC Charges in Dest. Currency		
(33A)	(33B)		Executed on (date) at (place) Signature of Issuing carrier or its Agent
For Carrier's use only at Destination (33)	Charges at Destination (33C)	Total Collect Charges (33D)	

ORIGINAL 3 (FOR SHIPPER) A

【技能实训】

1. 根据以下销售确认书填写航空托运单

SALES CONFIRMATION

S/C NO.: JY-HSNSC05

DATE: APRIL 1ST 2003

The Seller: GUANGZHOU BAIYUN INDUSTRIAL TRADING COMPANY
ADDRESS: 906 PUBEI ROAD
        GUANGZHOU, CHINA
THE BUYER: HASSAN ALKAMAR FOR GENERAL TRADING
ADDRESS: P. O. BOX 20242 TAIZ STREET

	SANA'A - REPUBLIC OF YEMEN				
Item No.	Commodity & Specifications	Unit	Quantity	Unit Price/ US $	Amount/ US $
	Daily Brand Tumblers			CIF C 5% BARCELONA	
1	ART. SY001	PIECE	3 000	6.59	19 770.00
2	ART. BS007	PIECE	3 000	6.83	20 490.00
3	ART. WP101	PIECE	2 660	7.45	19 817.00
4	ART. AF022	PIECE	2 380	8.19	19 492.20
				TOTAL	65 401.50
TOTAL CONTRACT VALUE			SAY US DOLLARS SEVENTY NINE THOUSAND FIVE HUNDRED SIXTY NINE AND CENTS TWENTY ONLY		

PACKING: TO BE PACKED IN PLASTIC BAGS WITH ZIP OF ONE PC EACH, 20PCS TO A CARTON, TOTAL 552 CARTONS ONLY.

SHIPMENT: TO BE EFFECTED BY THE SELLER FROM GUANGZHOU TO HODEIDAH NOT LATER THAN MAY 31ST 2003 ON CONDITION THAT UPON RECEIPT OF THE RELEVANT L/C WITH PARTIAL SHIPMENT AND TRANSHIPMENT NOT ALLOWED

PAYMENT: THE BUYER SHALL OPEN THROUGH A BANK ACCEPTABLE TO THE SELLER AN IRREVOCABLE LETTER OF CREDIT AT 30 DAYS FROM AWB DATE TO REACH THE SELLER BEFORE APRIL 25TH 2003 AND VALID FOR NEGOTIATION IN CHINA UNTIL THE 15TH DAY AFTER THE DATE OF SHIPMENT.

INSURANCE: THE SELLER SHALL COVER THE INSURANCE FOR 110% OF TOTAL INVOICE VALUE AGAINST ALL RISKS AND WAR RISK AS PER AND SUBJECT TO THE RELEVANT OCEAN MARINE CARGO CLAUSES OF PEOPLE'S INSURANCE COMPANY OF CHINA DATED 1/1/1981.

THE SELLER
GUANZHOU BAIYU INDUSTRIAL
TRADING COMPANY

THE BUYER
HASSAN AL KAMAR FOR
GENERAL TRADING

2. 根据以下销售合同填写航空托运单

SALES CONTRACT

卖方	KKK TRADING CO., LTD.	编号 **NO.:**	NEO20060116
SELLER:	HUARONG MANSION RM2901 NO.	日期 **DATE:**	Nov. 8, 2006
	85 GUANJIAQIAO, NANJING 210005, CHINA	地点 **SIGNED IN:**	NANJING, CHINA
	TEL: 0086-25-4715004 FAX: 0086-25-4711363		
买方	NEO GENERAL TRADING CO.		
BUYER:	P.O. BOX 99552, RIYADH 22766, KSA		
	TEL: 00966-1-4659220 FAX: 00966-1-4659213		

买卖双方同意按以下条款达成交易:
This contract is made by and agreed between the BUYER and SELLER, in accordance with the terms and conditions stipulated below:

1. 品名及规格 Commodity & Specification	2. 数量 Quantity	3. 单价及价格条款 Unit Price & Trade Terms	4. 金额 Amount
CFR DAMMAM PORT, SAUDI ARABIA			
ABOUT 1 700 CARTONS CANNED MUSHROOMS PIECES & STEMS 24 TINS X 227 GRAMS NET WEIGHT (G.W. 425GRAMS) AT USD7.80 PER CARTON. ROSE BRAND.	1 700 CARTONS	USD 7.80	USD 13 260.00
Total	1 700 CARTONS		USD 13 260.00

允许　　　溢短装，由卖方决定
With　　　More or less of shipment allowed at the sellers' option

5. 总值　　　　　USD THIRTEEN THOUSAND TWO HUNDRED AND SIXTY ONLY.
   Total Value

6. 包装　　　　　EXPORTED BROWN CARTON
   Packing

7. 唛头　　　　　ROSE BRAND
   Shipping Marks　　178/2006
   　　　　　　　　RIYADH

8. 装运期及运输方式　　　　　　　　　　　Not Later Than JAN. 15, 2007 BY AIR
   Time of Shipment & means of Transportation

9. 装运港及目的地　　　　　　　From：SHANGHAI PORT, CHINA
   Port of Loading & Destination　　To：DAMMAM PORT, SAUDI ARABIA

10. 保险　　　　　TO BE COVERED BY THE BUYER.
    Insurance

11. 付款方式　　　The Buyers shall open through a bank acceptable to the Seller an Irrevocable Letter
    Terms of Payment　of Credit payable at sight of reach the seller 30 days before the month of shipment, valid for negotiation in China until the 15th day after the date of shipment.

12. 备注
    Remarks

　　　　　　　　The Buyer　　　　　　　　　　　　The Seller
　　　　　NEO GENERAL TRADING CO.　　　　　KKK TRADING CO., LTD.
　　　　　　　（signature）　　　　　　　　　　　（signature）

第5章

【本章导读】
进出口货物报检程序
进出口货物报检单据
商品检验证书

【学习目标和要点】
本章主要介绍进出口货物报检程序、商品检验证书的种类和内容。通过本章的学习，学生应熟练掌握商品报检的一般程序，能根据相关材料填制报检单，熟悉商品检验证书的内容。

商品检验是国际贸易发展的产物，且随之成为商品买卖的一个重要环节。作为必要的运作程序，商品检验的目的是保证进出口商品的质量，维护对外贸易各方的合法权益。商品检验的对象不仅针对货物，还包括与货物运输有关的一切运输工具。

货物出入境检验检疫

5.1 进出口货物报检程序

5.1.1 进出口商品的报检分类和范围

1. 法定检验报验

我国现行的法律、行政法规或国际条约、协议规定,有一部分进出口商品及其运输工具必须经过商检机构的检验。未经检验合格的,不能出口或不能在国内销售,使用这类商品及其运输工具的报检称为法定检验报验。

1) 进口商品法定检验的范围

(1) 列入《种类表》的进口商品。

(2) 有关国际条约、协议规定须经商检机构检验的进口商品。

(3) 其他法律、行政法规规定须经商检机构检验的进口商品。

2) 出口商品及其运载工具法定检验报验的范围

(1) 列入《种类表》的出口商品。

(2) 出口食品的卫生检验。

(3) 贸易性出口动物产品的检疫。

(4) 出口危险物品和《种类表》内商品包装容器的性能检验和使用鉴定。

(5) 装运易腐烂变质食品出口的船舱和集装箱。

(6) 有关国际条约、协议规定须经商检机构检验的出口商品。

(7) 其他法律、行政法规规定须经商检机构检验的出口商品。

2. 鉴定业务报检

根据《中华人民共和国进出口商品检验法》(以下简称《商检法》)及其实施条例的规定,对外经济贸易关系人或者外国商检机构可以根据有关合同的约定或自身的需要、申请或委托商检机构办理进出口商品鉴定业务,签发鉴定证书。

商检机构受理鉴定业务的范围主要有以下几个方面。

(1) 进出口商品的质量、数量、重量、包装鉴定和货载衡量。

(2) 进出口商品的监视装载和监视卸载。

(3) 进出口商品的积载鉴定、残损鉴定、载损鉴定和海损鉴定。

(4) 装载出口商品的船舶、车辆、飞机、集装箱等运载工具的适载鉴定。

(5) 装载进出口商品的船舶封舱、船舱检视、空距测量。

(6) 集装箱及集装箱货物鉴定。

(7) 与进出口商品有关的外商投资财产的价值、品种、质量、数量和损失鉴定。

(8) 抽取并签封各类样品。

(9) 签发价值证书及其他鉴定证书。

(10) 其他进出口商品鉴定业务。

3. 监督管理

据国家有关法律、行政法规的规定,出口食品的卫生检验和检疫工作由商检机构办理,做好卫生监督、检验。要从生产厂、库的卫生条件做起,商检机构对出口食品的加工厂、屠宰场、冷库、仓库，采用注册登记的形式对其卫生状况和卫生质量进行监督管理。

1）船舱和集装箱检验

对装运出口粮油食品、冷冻品等易腐食品的船舱和集装箱实施强制性检验。有关承运人和装箱部门应在装货前向商检机构申请检验，经商检符合装运技术条件并发给合格证书后方准装运。船舱检验包括干货舱检验、油舱检验、冷藏检验，以确认其对所装货物的适载性，对其他出口集装箱办理鉴定业务。

2）危险品的包装检验

对于生产危险货物包装容器的生产厂，在生产检验合格基础上，应申请包装容器的性能鉴定，检验合格后，签发包装容器性能检验结果单。对于生产危险品的单位，应申请包装容器的使用鉴定，合格后签发包装容器的使用鉴定结果单。

3）质量监督员制度

根据《商检法》及国家的有关规定，商检机构对管辖范围内加工生产大宗的或涉及卫生、安全等重要出口商品的生产企业派驻质量监督员，代表国家对派驻企业的出口商品质量和检验工作进行监督管理。

5.1.2 进出口商品的检验程序

凡属国家规定或协议规定必须经中国进出口商品检验机构检验出证的商品，在货物备齐后，必须向商检机构申请检验，取得商检机构颁发的合格的检验证书后，海关才准予放行。凡经检验不合格的货物，一律不得出口。有些合同中已明确规定呈交检验证明，即使没有规定，在海运出口托运环节中，未经海关检验合格是不能装船出运的。因而在托运的同时，应办理报检。进出口商品的检验程序如图5-1所示。

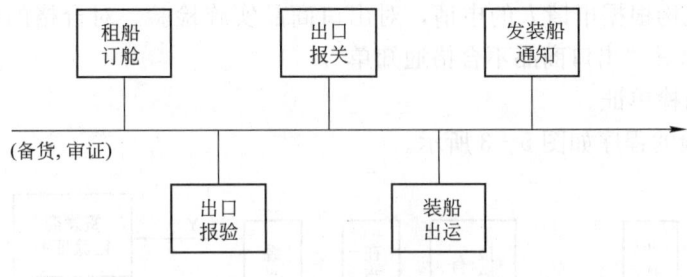

图5-1 出口报检程序

通过图5-1可以看出，通常在租船订舱的同时，卖方就需要安排出口报验。

1. 出口商品检验工作程序

总的来说，出口商品检验分为法定检验和非法定检验两大部分。其中，法定检验的范围包括《种类表》及其他法律、法规规定必须经过商检机构和国家商检部门、商检机构指定的检验机构检验的进出口商品。

1）法定检验出口的检验工作程序

（1）报检人填写"出口检验申请单"。

（2）提供合同、信用证及有关单证资料。

（3）商检机构对已报验的出口商品实施检验，并出具检验结果。直接出口的出口商品，经检验合格后出具放行单或商检证书。运往口岸或已出口的出口商品，经检验合格后出具"出口商品检验报验凭单"。经检验不合格的，出具"出口商品检验不合格通知单"。

（4）报检人领取商检单证。

法定检验的程序如图5-2所示。

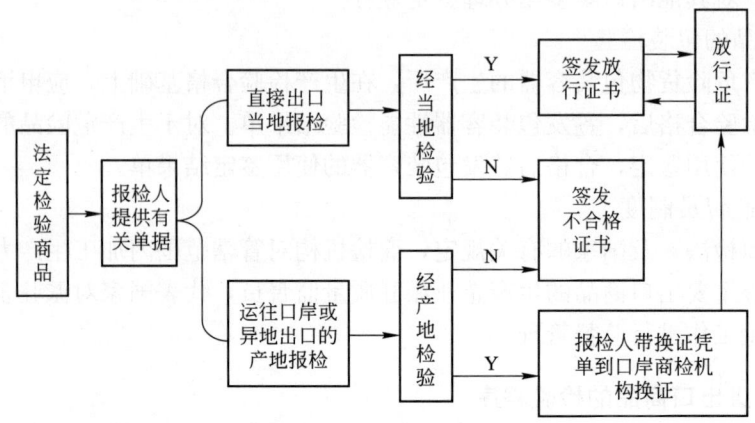

图5-2　法定检验程序

2）非法定检验出口的检验工作程序

（1）据合同、信用证的规定或申请人的要求，需商检机构检验出具商检证书的，可向商检机构报验。

（2）填写"出口检验申请单"，并提供有关单据及资料。

（3）商检机构根据申请人的申请，对出口商品实施检验。对合格的出具商检证书，对不合格的则出具"出口商品不合格通知单"。

（4）领取商检单证。

非法定检验的程序如图5-3所示。

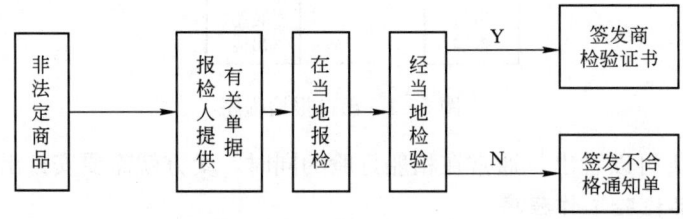

图5-3　非法定检验程序

2. 出口商品的报检程序

1）报检要求

（1）报检人在报验时应填写规定格式报检申请单，提供与出入境检验检疫有关的单证资料，按规定缴纳检验检疫费用。

（2）报检人申请撤销报验时，应书面说明原因，经批准后方可办理撤销手续。报检后 30 天内未联系检验检疫事宜的,作自动撤销报检处理。

(3) 应重新报检的情况有:①超过检验检疫有效期限的;②变更输入国家或地区,并又有不同检验检疫要求的;③改换包装或重新拼装的;④已撤销报检的。

(4) 报检人申请更改证单时,应填写更改申请单,交附有关函电等证明单据,并退还原证单,经审核同意后方可办理更改手续。品名、数(重)量、检验检疫结果、包装、发货人、收货人等重要项目更改后与合同、信用证不符的,或者更改后与输出、输入国家或地区法律法规不符的,均不能更改。

2) 填写《出(入)境货物报检单》

《出(入)境货物报检单》由各口岸出入境检验检疫局统一印刷,除编号由检验检疫机构指定外,其余各栏由报检单位填置并盖章确认,填制规范如下。

(1) 编号(NO.)。由检验检疫机构受代理人指定,前 6 位为检验检疫机关代码,第 7 位为报检类代码,第 8、9 位为年代码,第 10~15 位为流水号。

(2) 报检单位(Declaration Inspection Unit)。经国家质检总局审核,获得许可、登记,并取得国家质检总局颁发的《自理报检单位备案登记证明书》或《代理报检单位备案登记证明书》的企业。本栏填报报检单位的中文名称,并加盖与名称一致的公章。

(3) 报检单位登记号(Register No.)。其指报检单位在国家质检总局登记的登记证号码。本栏填 10 位数登记证号码。联系人:填报检人员姓名;电话号:填报检人员姓名联系电话。

(4) 报检日期(Declaration Inspect Date)。指检验检疫机构接受报检当天的日期。本栏填制的报检日期统一用数字来表示,而不用英文等来表示。

(5) 发货人(Consignor)。其指外贸合同中的出售商,或商业发票上的出票人。本栏分别用中、英文对照分行填报发货人名称。

(6) 收货人(Consignee)。其指外贸合同中的收购商,或商业发票上的受票人。本栏分别用中、英文对照分行填报收货人名称。

(7) 货物名称(中/外文)(Description of Goods)。其指被申请报检的出入境货物名称、规格、型号、成分并以中英文对照。本栏应按合同、信用证、商业发票中所列商品名称的中、英文填写。注意:废旧物资在此栏内需注明。

(8) H. S. 编码(H. S. Code)。其指海关《协调商品名称及编码制度》中所列编码。H. S. 编码为 8 位数字,并以当年海关公布的商品税则编码分类为准。本栏填报 8 位商品编码。注意:有些商品有最后两位补充编码时,应填报 10 位编码。

(9) 产地(Original Area)。在出境货物报检单中,其指货物生产地、加工制造地的省、市、县名。在进境货物报检单中,其指该进口货物的原产地国或地区。本栏填报出境货物生产地的省、市、县的中文名称。

(10) 数/重量(Quantity/Weight)。其指以商品编码分类中计量标准项下的实际检验检疫数量、重量。本栏按实际申请检验检疫的数/重量填写,重量还须列明毛/净/皮重。注意:本栏可以填报一个以上计量单位,如第一计量单位:"个";第二计量单位:"千克"等。

(11) 货物总值(Amount)。其指出境或入境货物的商品总值及币种。本栏应与合同、发票或报关单上所列货物总值一致。注意:本栏不需要填报价格术语,如"CIF"

或"FOB"等。

（12）包装种类及数量（Number and Type of Declaration）。本栏应按照实际运输外包装的种类及对应数量填报，如"136箱"等。注意：实际运输中，为了方便装卸，保护外包装，常用托盘运输包装，这时除了填报托盘种类及数量以外，还应填报托盘上装的包装数量及包装种类。

（13）运输工具名称号码（Means of Conveyance）。其指载运出境货物运输工具的名称和运输工具编号。本栏填制实际出境运输工具的名称及编号，如船舶名称及航次等。注意：实际报检申请时，若未定运输工具的名称及编号时，可以笼统填制运输方式总称。如填报"船舶"或"飞机"等。

（14）合同号（Contract No.）。其指对外贸易合同、订单、形式发票等的号码。本栏填报的合同号应与随附的合同号等号码一致。

（15）贸易方式（Means of Trading）。其指该批货物的贸易性质，即买卖双方将商品所有权通过何种方式转让。本栏填报与实际情况一致的贸易方式。常见的贸易方式有"一般贸易"、"来料加工贸易"、"易货贸易"、"补偿贸易"等九十多种贸易方式。

（16）货物存放地点（Place of Goods）。其指出口货物的生产企业所存放出口货物的地点。本栏按实际填报具体地点、仓库。

（17）发货日期（Shipment Date）。其指货物实际出境的日期。按实际开船日或起飞日等填报发货日期，以年、月、日的方式填报。

（18）输往国家（地区）(Destination Country/Area)。其指出口货物直接运抵的国家（地区），是货物的最终销售国。本栏填报输往国家（地区）的中文名称。

（19）许可证/审批号（Licence No./Approve No.）。凡申领进出口许可证或其他审批文件的货物，本栏应填报有关许可证号或审批号。无许可证或没有审批文件的出境货物报检单可以免报。

（20）生产单位注册号（Manufacture Register No.）。其指出入境检验检疫机构签发的卫生注册证书号或加工厂的注册号码等。本栏填报实际生产单位的注册号（10位数）。

（21）起运地（Place of Departure）。本栏填报出境货物最后离境的口岸或所在地的中文名称，如"上海口岸"等。

（22）到达口岸（Final Destination）。其指出境货物运往境外的最终目的港。本栏最终目的港可预知的，按实际到达口岸的中文名称填报；最终到达口岸不可预知的，可按尽可能预知的到达口岸填报。

（23）集装箱规格/数量及号码（Type of Container/Container Number）。集装箱规格是指国际标准的集装箱规格尺寸。常见的是4种箱型有A型、B型、C型、D型，它们的尺寸有十多种，主要有20'C型、40'A型等。集装箱的数量是指实际集装箱数量，而不是作为换算标准箱。集装箱号码是指国际集装箱号码的识别号码，其组成规则是：箱主代号（3位字母）+设备识别号（"U"为海运集装箱）+顺序号（6位数字）+检测号（1位），如TGHU8491952。本栏填报实际集装箱数量、规格、箱号，如"1×20'/TGHU8491952"。

（24）合同、信用证订立的检验检疫条款或特殊要求。在合同中订立的有关检验检疫的特殊条款及其他要求应填入此栏。

（25）标记号码（Marks and Number of Packages）。货物的标记号码又称为货物的唛头，主要用于识别货物。本栏应根据实际合同、发票等外贸单据上相同内容填报。注意：如没有唛头应填报"N/M"，不可以空缺。

（26）用途（Purpose）。从以下 9 个选项中选择符合实际出境货物的用途来填报：①种用或繁殖；②食用；③奶用；④观赏或演艺；⑤伴侣动物；⑥实验；⑦药用；⑧饲用；⑨其他。

（27）随附单据（画"√"或补填）（Attached Files in √ ）。按照实际随附的单据种类画"√"或补充填报随附单据。

（28）签名（Signature of Authorized Signatory）。由持有《报检员证》的报检员手签姓名。

（29）检验检疫费用。由检验检疫机构计费人员核定费用后填写，如熏蒸费和消毒费等。

（30）领取证单。报检人在领取证单时填写领证日期和领证人签名。

5.2　进出口货物报检单据

5.2.1　入境货物报检所需提供的单证

入境报检时，应填写入境货物报检单并提供合同、发票、提单等有关单证。

此外，还应按要求提供有关文件。

（1）凡实施安全质量许可、卫生注册或其他需审批审核的货物，应提供有关证明。

（2）品质检验的还应提供国外品质证书或质量保证书、产品使用说明书及有关标准和技术资料；凭样成交的，须加附成交样品；以品级或公量计价结算的，应同时申请重量鉴定。

（3）报检入境废物时，还应提供国家环保部门签发的《进口废物批准证书》和经认可的检验机构签发的装运前检验合格证书等。

（4）申请残损鉴定的还应提供理货残损单、铁路商务记录、空运事故记录或海事报告等证明货损情况的有关单证。

（5）申请重（数）量鉴定的还应提供重量明细单、理货清单等。

（6）货物经收、用货部门验收或其他单位检测的，应随附验收报告或检测结果以及重量明细单等。

（7）入境的国际旅行者，应填写入境检疫申明卡。

（8）入境的动植物及其产品，在提供贸易合同、发票、产地证书的同时，还必须提供输出国家或地区官方的检疫证书；需办理入境检疫审批手续的，还应提供入境动植物检疫许可证。

（9）过境动植物及其产品报检时，应持货运单和输出国家或地区官方出具的检疫证书；运输动物过境时，还应提交国家检验检疫机构签发的动植物过境许可证。

（10）报检入境运输工具、集装箱时，应提供检疫证明，并申报有关人员健康状况。

（11）入境旅客、交通员工携带伴侣动物的，应提供入境动物检疫证书及预防接种证明。

(12) 因科研等特殊需要，输入禁止入境物的，必须提供国家检验检疫机构签发的特许审批证明。

(13) 入境特殊物品的，应提供有关的批件或规定的文件。

5.2.2 出境货物报检所需提供的单证

出境报检时，应填写出境货物报检单并提供对外贸易合同（售货确认书或函电）、信用证、发票、装箱单等必要的单证。

此外，还应按要求提供有关文件。

(1) 生产经营部门出具的厂检结存件。

(2) 法定检验出口商品报检时，还应提供商检机构签发的"出口商品运输包装容器性能检验结果单"正本。

(3) 凭样成交的应提供成交样品。

(4) 经预验的商品，在向商检机构办理放行手续时，应加附该商检机构签发的"出口商品预验结果单"或"出境货物换证凭单"正本。

(5) 发货人委托其他单位代理报检时，应加附委托书（原件）。

(6) 经其他商检机构检验的商品，应加附发运地向商检机构签发的"出口商品查验报验凭单"正本。

(7) 按照国家法律、行政法规规定实行卫生注册及出口质量许可证的商品，必须提供商检机构批准的注册编号或许可证编号。

(8) 出口危险品货物时，必须提供危险品包装容器的性能检验和使用检定合格证（单）。

(9) 出口锅炉、压力容器，需提供锅炉监察机构（如市级劳动行政主管部门）审核盖章的安全性能检验报告（正本）。

5.3 商品检验证书

检验证书是商检机构对进出口商品执行法定检验或办理鉴定业务后，根据受验货物、鉴定对象的实际情况，对外签发的证件，又称商检证书。检验证书是具有法律效力的证明凭证，在国际贸易中起到公正性的证明作用，是交接货物、结算货款、银行议付、国外通关、核计关税、明确责任、计算费用、对外索赔以及仲裁、诉讼举证的重要证明文件。检验证书在对外贸易的各个环节中都发挥着重要作用，配合对外贸易的顺利进行，维护对外贸易有关方面的合法权益，促进对外贸易的发展。检验证书根据不同的检验项目和要求，分别签发品质、包装、重量、数量、兽医、卫生、残损鉴定以及其他各项检验、鉴定业务的证书。

5.3.1 商检证书的性质、作用和结构

商检机构根据申请人或合同、信用证的要求，以及有关国际条约的约定，对出口商品实施检验，检验合格后出具商检证书，它可作为报关验放、征收关税等的有效凭证。

1. 商检证书在国际贸易中的公证作用
（1）作为报关验放的凭证。
（2）作为履约、交接货物的有效凭证。
（3）作为结算货款的有效证件。
（4）作为银行议付货款和出口结汇的单据。
（5）作为征收关税和优惠减免关税的有效凭证。
（6）作为结算运费的有效证件。
（7）作为证明情况、明确责任的证件。
（8）作为办理索赔的有效证件。
（9）作为仲裁、诉讼举证的有效证件。

2. 商检证书的结构

商检证书由国家商检机构统一设计、印制。证书尺寸为 297 mm×210 mm，证书由 5 个部分组成，具体如下。

（1）签证机构的名称，包括地址、电报挂号和电话。

（2）证书名称和种类，包括正本或副本、证书印制顺序号、证书号（即报验号）和签证日期，此日期必须早于货运单据签发日期。

（3）商品识别部分，包括发货人、收货人、商品名称、报验数量/重量、标记及号码、运输工具、发货港、目的港等。

（4）证明内容，即检验或鉴定的结果和评定，这是证书的主要部分。

（5）签署部分，包括检验日期和地点，签证机构签证专用印章、签署人（主任检验员或主任兽医或主任鉴定人）的签字。并在证书右上角加盖钢印。检验证书的格式是由国家质量监督检验检疫部门统一制定的。出口商品检验证书的证明内容一般使用英文，也可根据报验人要求用中文表示；进口商品检验证书的证明内容，一般使用中文，证书最后加印"本证书译文如有任何异点，概以中文为主。"商检机构对外签发证书只发一份正本，并增发副本三份。检验证书发出后，不准任何人涂改证书或变造、伪造，违反者依法查处。证书发出后，报验人需要更改或补充内容时，应向原签发的商检机构申请按照规定办理。

此外，根据国家商检部门的规定，在证书的右上角（证书号码和日期部分）加盖 CCB 字样的钢印。只有经过签字和盖上商检机构签证章并加盖 CCB 钢印的证书方算有效。

5.3.2 商检证书的种类

目前，我国商检机构签发的检验检疫证书主要有以下几种。

（1）品质检验证书（Inspection Certificate of Quality），是证明进出口商品的质量、规格的证明文件，具体证明进出口商品的质量、规格是否符合买卖合同或有关规定。

（2）重量或数量检验证书（Inspection Certificate of Weight or Quantity），是证明进出口商品重量或数量的证件。其内容为货物经何种计重方法或计量单位得出的实际重量或数量，以证明有关商品的重量或数量是否符合买卖合同的规定。

（3）包装检验证书（Inspection Certificate of Packing），是用于证明进出口商品包

装情况的证书。进出口商品包装检验，一般列入品质检验证书或重量（数量）检验证书中证明，但也可根据需要单独出具包装检验证书。

（4）兽医检验证书（Veterinary Inspection Certificate），是证明出口动物产品经过检疫合格的证件，适用于冻畜肉、冻禽、禽畜肉、罐头、冻兔、皮张、毛类、绒类、猪鬃、肠衣等出口商品。凡加上卫生检验内容的，称为兽医卫生检验证书（Veterinary Sanitary Inspection Certificate）。

（5）卫生检验证书（Inspection Certificate of Sanitary），又称健康检验证书（Certificate of Health），是证明可供人类食用或使用的出口动物产品、食品等经过卫生检验或检疫合格的证件。其适用于肠衣、罐头、冻鱼、冻虾、食品、蛋品、乳制品、蜂蜜等。

（6）温度检验证书（Inspection Certificate of Temperature），是证明出口冷冻商品温度的证书。如国外仅需要证明货物温度，不一定要单独的温度证书，可将测温结果列入品质证书。

（7）消毒检验证书（Inspection Certificate of Disinfection），是证明出口动物产品经过消毒处理，保证卫生安全的证件。其适用于猪鬃、马尾、皮张、山羊毛、人发等商品。其证明内容也可在品质检验证书中附带。

（8）熏蒸证书（Inspection Certificate of Fumigation），是证明出口量谷、油籽、豆类、皮张等商品，以及包装用木材与植物性填充物等已经经过熏蒸灭虫的证件。其主要证明使用的药物、熏蒸的时间等情况。如国外不需要单独出证，可将其内容列入品质检验证书中。

在国际贸易实际业务中，买卖双方应根据成交货物的种类、性质、有关国家的法律和行政法规、政府的涉外经济贸易政策和贸易习惯等来确定卖方应提供何种检验证书，并在买卖合同中予以明确规定。

5.3.3 缮制商检证书应注意的事项

1. 发货人

发货人即申请人，在一般情况下，发货人应该是实际交货的出口公司，但是，当信用证的受益人不是实际交货人而是第三者时，这一栏的"发货人"应与信用证的受益人相同，即与提单的"托运人"一致，以便保持各种单据相互一致。

2. 收货人

一般不用填写，只有在转让检验证书时，可将该栏填成中性受让（To Whom It may Concern）或空白抬头（to order）。

3. 证明内容

若信用证规定检验证书由外国的公证行、公证人、鉴定人签发，由于外国机构的检验标准和出证时间各异，常会发生问题，受益人不宜接受。产地证的内容应严格遵循信用证的规定。有的来证规定品质证书和重量证书上必须标上出口商品的生产年份（INSPECTION CERTIFICATE IN 3 COPIES MANUFACTURE MONTH MUST BE MENTIONED），出口方应照办。

4. 掌握主动权

受益人不应接受检验货物权和签发证书权都被交易对方控制和掌握的信用证，如"Inspection Certificate must be issued and signed by the applicant whose authority and signature must be in conformity with the records held in ourt Band."对这样的信用证不宜接受。

【案例】

> 河北恒泰进出口贸易公司报检员张玲（电话：85126347）于2008年8月15日向检验机构报检，提交的单证包括合同、信用证、发票、装箱单、厂检单等，招检单如表5-1所示。生产单位注册号为3237000015，报检单位登记号为3256000023。纺织品临时出口许可证编号为5070809235。货物存放在天津新港保税仓库以备出口。要求出具品质证书和数量证书各1正1副。

表 5-1 恒泰公司填制的报检单

中华人民共和国出入境检验检疫
出境货物报检单

报检单位（加盖公章）：河北恒泰进出口贸易公司　　　　*编　号：
报检单位登记号：3256000023　联系人：张玲　电话：85126347　报检日期：2008年8月15日

发货人	（中文）河北恒泰进出口贸易公司
	（外文）HEBEI HENGTAI IMPORT & EXPORT CORPORATION
收货人	（中文）美国太平国际公司
	（外文）PACIFIC INTERNATION INC.

货物名称（中/外文）	H.S.编码	产地	数/重量	货物总值	包装种类及数量
全棉条纹毛巾 100% COTTON STIPE TOWEL	58021100	河北石家庄	4 500打 225包	22 050.00 美元	225包

运输工具名称号码	QINLUN V.1502	贸易方式	一般贸易	货物存放地点	天津新港保税仓库
合同号	02AG18185	信用证号	LC-710-076405	用途	其他
发货日期	2008.08.25	输往国家（地区）	美国	许可证/审批号	5070809235
起运地	天津	到达口岸	洛杉矶	生产单位注册号	3237000015
集装箱规格、数量及号码					

合同、信用证订立的检验检疫条款或特殊要求	标记及号码	随附单据（画"√"或补填）	
	PACIFIC 18185 LOS ANGELES 1-225	☑合同 ☑信用证 ☑发票 ☐换证凭单 ☑装箱单 ☑厂检单	☐包装性能结果单 ☑许可/审批文件 ☐ ☐ ☐ ☐

需要证单名称（画"√"或补填）		*检验检疫费	
☑ 品质证书　　1 正 1 副 ☐ 重量证书　　__正__副 ☑ 数量证书　　1 正 1 副 ☐ 兽医卫生证书　__正__副 ☐ 健康证书　　__正__副 ☐ 卫生证书　　__正__副 ☐ 动物卫生证书　__正__副	☐ 植物检疫证书　__正__副 ☐ 熏蒸/消毒证书　__正__副 ☑ 出境货物换证凭单 ☐ ☐ ☐	总金额 （人民币）	
		计费人	
		收费人	
报检人郑重证明： 1. 本人被授权报检。 2. 上列填写内容正确属实，货物无伪造或冒用他人的厂名、标志、认证标志。并承担货物质量责任。 　　　　　　签名：张玲		领取证单	
		日期	年　月　日
		签名	

注：有"*"的内容由报检单位填写或盖章　　　　　　　　◆国家出入境检验检疫局制

【相关单证】

单证 5-1　出境货物报检单

中华人民共和国出入境检验检疫
出境货物报检单

报检单位（加盖公章）：			*编　号_____	
报检单位登记号：	联系人：	电话：	报检日期：	年　月　日

发货人	（中文）
	（外文）

收货人	（中文）
	（外文）

货物名称（中/外文）	H.S. 编码	产地	数/重量	货物总值	包装种类及数量

运输工具名称号码		贸易方式		货物存放地点	
合同号		信用证号		用途	
发货日期		输往国家（地区）		许可证/审批号	
起运地		到达口岸		生产单位注册号	
集装箱规格、数量及号码					

合同、信用证订立的检验检疫条款或特殊要求	标记及号码	随附单据（画"√"或补填）	
		☐ 合同	☐ 包装性能结果单
		☐ 信用证	☐ 许可/审批文件
		☐ 发票	☐
		☐ 换证凭单	☐
		☐ 装箱单	
		☐ 厂检单	

续表

需要证单名称（画"√"或补填）		*检验检疫费	
□品质证书 __正__副 □重量证书 __正__副 □数量证书 __正__副 □兽医卫生证书 __正__副 □健康证书 __正__副 □卫生证书 __正__副 □动物卫生证书 __正__副	□植物检疫证书 __正__副 □熏蒸/消毒证书 __正__副 □出境货物换证凭单 □出境货物通关单	总金额（人民币）	
		计费人	
		收费人	
报检人郑重声明： 1. 本人被授权报检。 2. 上列填写内容正确属实，货物无伪造或冒用他人的厂名、标志、认证标志，并承担货物质量责任。 签名：_____		领取证单	
		日期	
		签名	

注：有"*"号栏由出入境检验检疫机关填写　　◆国家出入境检验检疫局制

[1-1 (2000.1.1)]

单证 5-2　入境货物报检单

中华人民共和国出入境检验检疫
入境货物报检单

报检单位（加盖公章）：　　　　　　　　　　　*编　号_____

报检单位登记号：　　联系人：　　电话：　　报检日期：　年　月　日

收货人	（中文）		企业性质（画"√"）	□合资 □合作 □外资
	（外文）			
发货人	（中文）			
	（外文）			

货物名称（中/外）	H.S.编码	原产国（地区）	数/重量	货物总值	包装种类及数量

运输工具名称号码		合同号	
贸易方式		贸易国别（地区）		提单/运单号	
到货日期		起运国家（地区）		许可证/审批号	
卸毕日期		启运口岸		入境口岸	
索赔有效期至		经停口岸		目的地	
集装箱规格、数量及号码			
合同订立特殊条款以及其他要求		货物存放地点	
		用　途	
随附单据（画"√"或补填）	标记及记号	*外商投资财产（画"√"）	□是　□否

续表

□合同 □发票 □提/运单 □兽医卫生证书 □植物检疫证书 □动物检疫证书 □卫生证书 □原产地证书 □许可/审批文件	□到货通知 □装箱单 □质保书 □理货清单 □磅码单 □验收报告 □ □ □		*检验检疫费	
			总金额 （人民币）	
			计费人	
			收费人	
报检人郑重声明： 1. 本人被授权报检。 2. 上列填写内容正确属实。 签名：_____			领取单证	
			日期	
			签名	

注：有"*"号栏由出入境检验检疫机关填写　　　　　　　　*国家出入境检验检疫局制

[1-1 (2000.1.1)]

单证 5-3　出境货物换证凭单

中华人民共和国出入境检验检疫
出境货物换证凭单

类别：	预检		编号	320800202016597
发货人	安徽省安庆市＊＊＊公司		标记及号码 暂　　无	
收货人	＊＊＊			
品名	经编晴纶毯			
H.S. 编码	63019000.10			
报检数/重量	---3 000---条			
包装种类及数量	纸箱---100---箱			
申报总值	美元：-9 300-元			
产地	江苏　无锡	生产单位（注册号）	无锡＊＊＊家用纺织品有限公司	
生产日期	2002 年 7 月	生产批号	02AQXH0405	
包装性能检 验结果单号	320800301003705	合同/信用证号	02AQXH0405/＊＊＊	
		运输工具名称及编号	＊＊＊　＊＊＊	
输往国家或地区	＊＊＊	集装箱规格及数量	＊＊＊＊＊＊	
发货日期	＊＊＊	检验依据	FZ61002-90 标准及合同	
检验检疫结果	本批产品共 100 箱/3 000 条，经按 FZ61002-91 标准，在仓库随机抽取代表性样品 150 条，根据检验依据要求进行检验，结果如下： 成　　　分：晴纶 规　　　格：100 cm×140 cm 重　　　量：0.7 kg/pc 外观检验评定：合格 评　　　定：上述货物符合检验依据要求。 ＊＊＊＊＊＊＊＊			
	签字：		日期：2002 年 7 月 8 日	

续表

分批出境核销栏	本单有效期	截止于 2003 年 7 月 7 日							
	备注	＊＊＊							
	日期	出境数/重量	结存数/重量	核销人	日期	出境数/重量	结存数/重量	核销人	

说明：1. 货物出境时，经口岸检验检疫机关查验货证相符，且符合检验检疫要求的予以签发通关单或换发检验检疫证书；2. 本单不作为国内贸易的品质或其他证明；3. 涂改无效。

A 5432818　　　　　　　　　　①办理换证　　　　　　　[5-3(2001.1.1)＊1]

单证 5-4　出入境货物代理报检委托书

出入境货物代理报检委托书

委托单位		十位编码	
地　　址		联系电话/经办人	

我单位将于＿＿＿＿年＿＿月进口 □ 出口 □ 以下货物

货物名称		H.S.编码		件数/重量	
货　　值		贸易性质		包装性质	
货物起运国		货物产地		合同号或发票号	
企业性质		运单号		信用证号	
经营范围					

随附单据名称、份数及编号：

1. 合同＿＿＿＿份；
2. 发票＿＿＿＿份；
3. 装箱清单＿＿＿＿份；
4. 登记手册＿＿＿＿本；编号：＿＿＿＿
5. 许可证＿＿＿＿份；编号：＿＿＿＿
6. 不办、免办证明＿＿＿＿份；编号：＿＿＿＿
7. 机电证明＿＿＿＿份；编号：＿＿＿＿
8. 海关免表＿＿＿＿份；编号：＿＿＿＿
9. 换证凭单或电子转单＿＿＿＿份；编号：＿＿＿＿
10.

我单位郑重声明，保证遵守中华人民共和国出入境检验检疫有关法律、法规的规定和检验检疫机构的各项规章制度。如有违反行为，自愿接受检验检疫机构的处罚并负法律责任。

我单位所委托受委托人向出入境检验检疫局提交的"报检单"和随附各种单据所列内容是真实无讹的。

（以上内容由委托单位填写）

被委托单位		报检单位注册号	
地　　址		联系电话	
经办人		报检证号	

（以上内容由被委托单位填写）

代理报检企业章		委托单位章及其法人代表章	

单证 5-5 出口商品品质检验证书

中华人民共和国上海进出口商品检验局
SHANGHAI IMPORT & EXPORT COMMODITY
INSPECTION BUREAU OF THE PEOPLE'S
REPUBLIC OF CHINA

地址：上海市中山东一路 13 号
Address：13, Zhongshan Road
(E.1), Shanghai

No.

品 质 检 验 证 书
QUALITY CERTIFICATE

日期
Date

电话：
Tel：8621-32155296

发货人：
Consignor：

受货人：
Consignee：

品名：
Description of Goods：

报验数量/重量：
Quantity/Weight Declared：

包装种类及数量：
Number and Type of Packages：

运输工具：
Means of Conveyance：

装运日期：
Date of Loading：

发票号：
Invoice No.：

合同号：
Contract No.：

结论：
Conclusion：

印章：
Official Stamp：

签证地点：
Place of Issue：

签证日期：
Date of Issue：

授权签字人：
Authorized Officer：

注意：本证书译文如有任何异点，概以中文为主。
(N. B. In case of divergence, the Chinese text shall be regarded as authentic)

单证 5-6　数量检验证书

中华人民共和国出入境商品检验检疫局
SHANGHAI IMPORT & EXPORT COMMODITY INSPECTION BUREAU OF THE PEOPLE'S REPUBLIC OF CHINA

地址：
Address：　　　　　　　　　　　　　　　No.×××

数　量　检　验　证　书
QUANTITY INSPECTION CERTIFICATE

　　　　　　　　　　　　　　　　　　　　日期：
　　　　　　　　　　　　　　　　　　　　Date：

电话：
Tel：

发货人：
Consignor：
受货人：
Consignee：
品名：
Commodity：
报验数量/重量：
Quantity/Weight：
包装种类及数量：
Number and Type of Packages：
运输工具：
Means of Conveyance：
检验结果：
Results of Inspection：

　　我们已尽所知和最大能力实施上述检验，不能因我们签发本证书而免除卖方或其他方面根据合同和法律所承担的产品数量责任和其他责任。
　　ALL INSPECTIONS ARE CARRIED OUT CONSCIENTIOUSLY TO THE BEST OF OUR KNOWLEDGE AND ABILITY. THIS CERTIFICATE DOES NOT IN ANY RESPECT ABSOLVE THE SELLER AND OTHER RELATED PARTIES FROM HIS CONTRACTUAL AND LEGAL OBLIGATIONS ESPECIALLY WHEN PRODUCT QUANTITY IS CONCERNED.

　　　　　　　　　　　　　　　　　　　　　　　　　　　×××
　　　　　　　　　　　　　　　　　　　　　　　　　　　OCT. 15，2005

单证 5-7 兽医检验证书

中华人民共和国出入境商品检验检疫局
SHANGHAI IMPORT & EXPORT COMMODITY INSPECTION BUREAU OF THE PEOPLE'S REPUBLIC OF CHINA

地址：
Address：

No.

检 验 证 书
INSPECTION CERTIFICATE

日期：
Date：

电话：
Tel：

发货人：
Consignor：

受货人：
Consignee：

品名：　　　　　　　　　　　　　　　标记及号码：
Commodity：　　　　　　　　　　　　Mark & No.：

报验数量/重量：
Quantity/Weight：
Declared：

官方兽医证明如下：
the undersigned Official Veterinarian, certify that：

主 任 兽 医
Chief Veterinarian

【技能实训】

请根据下面所给信用证以及相关资料缮制出境货物报检单和数量检验证书各一份

NATIONAL PARIS BANK
24 MARSHAL AVE DONCASTER MONTREAL, CANADA

WE ISSUE OUR IRREVOCABLE DOCUMENTARY CREDIT NUMBER: QQ2005 IN FAVOUR OF: SHANGHAI KNITWEAR AND MANUFACTURE GOODS IMPORT AND EXPORT TRADE CORPORATION.
321, CHONGSHAN ROAD SHANGHAI, CHINA
BY ORDER OF: YI YANG TRADING CORPORATION
88 MARSHALL AVE
DONCASTER VIC 3108
CANADA
FOR AN AMOUNT OF USD89 705.00
DATE AND PLACE OF ISSUE: SEPT. 18th, 2005 MONTREAL
DATE OF EXPIRY: NOV. 15th, 2005
PLACE: IN BENEFICARY'S COUNTRY
BY NEGOTIATION OF BENEFICIARY'S DRAFT DRAWN ON US AT SIGHT IN MONTREAL
THIS CREDIT IS TRANSFERABLE
AGAINST DELIVERY OF THE FOLLOWING DOCUMENTS
+ COMMERCIAL INVOICES IN 3 COPIES
+ CANADA CUSTOMS INVOICES IN 3 COPIES
+ ORIGINAL CERTIFICATE IN 3 COPIES
+ FULL SET OF NEGOTIABLE INSURANCE POLICY OR CERTIFICATE BLANK ENDORSED FOR 110 PERCENT OF INVOICE VALUE COVERING ALL RISKS.
+ FULL SET OF ORIGINAL MARINE BILLS OF LADING CLEAN ON BOARD PLUS 2 NON-NEGOTIABLE COPIES MADE OUT OR ENDORSED TO ORDER OF NATIONAL PARIS BANK 24 MARSHALL AVE DONCASTER MONTREAL, CANADA.
+ SPECIFICATION LIST OF WEIGHTS AND MEASURES IN 4 COPIES COVERING SHIPMENT OF COTTON TEA TOWELS.
AS PER S/C MN808
FOR 1-300 SIZE 10 INCHES * 10 INCHES 16 000 DOZ AT USD 1.31/DOZ.
301-600 SIZE 20 INCHES * 20 INCHES 6 000 DOZ AT USD 2.51/DOZ.
AND 601-900 SIZE 30 INCHES * 30 INCHES 11 350 DOZ AT USD 4.73/DOZ.
CIF MONTREAL
FROM SHANGHAI TO MONTREAL
NOT LATER THAN OCT. 31th, 2005
PARTIAL SHIPMENTS: ALLOWED
SPECIAL INSTRUCTIONS:
+ ALL CHARGES IF ANY RELATED TO SETTLEMENTS ARE FOR ACCOUNT OF BENEFICIARY.
+ IN CASE OF PRESENTATION OF DOCUMENTS WITH DISCREPANCY (IES) A CHARGE OF

USD 55.00 THIS CREDIT IS SUBJECT TO UCP DOCUMENTARY CREDITS（1993 REVISION）ICC PUBLICATION 500.

补充资料如下。

  （1）报检单位登记号：19866895；许可证号：2004122566。

  （2）货物存放地点：逸仙路1328号。

  （3）运输工具名称：PUDONG VOY.053。

  （4）贸易方式是一般贸易。

  （5）G.W.：19 911 kgs N.W.：19 339 kgs。

  （6）唛头：YI YANG MONTREAL C/NO.1－360。

  （7）报检日期是2005年10月10日；出证日期是2005年10月20日。

  （8）H.S.CODE：8204.6661。

第6章

【本章导读】
货物进出境报关程序
进出口货物报关单

【学习目标和要点】
我国《海关法》规定,货物进出境时,收发货人或其代理人必须向进出境口岸海关办理报关手续,交验规定的申报单证,接受海关依法进行审核、查验、缴纳海关税费,然后才能由海关批准提取或装运货物。通过本章的学习,学生应了解出口通关的业务程序,能够根据业务合同、发票、装箱单等单据填制出口货物报关单。

货物进出境报关

6.1 货物进出境报关程序

进出境报关制度是任何一个主权国家为维护本国政治、经济、文化利益,对进出口货物和物品在进出境口岸进行监督管理的基本制度。由于现代国际贸易方式的多元化,海关对不同贸易方式进出货物的通关,在办理手续管理办法上有不同的要求。

6.1.1 进出境报关的含义

报关是指进出口货物的收发货人及其代理人、进出境运输工具的负责人、进出境物品的所有人向海关办理有关货物、运输工具、物品进出境手续的全过程。

根据《中华人民共和国海关法》(以下简称《海关法》)的有关规定,国家在对外开放的口岸和海关监管业务集中的地点设立海关,进出境运输工具、货物、物品都必须通过设有海关的地点进境或者出境。在特殊情况下,经国务院或国务院授权的机关批准,可在未设海关的地点临时进境或出境,但必须依法办理海关手续。

6.1.2 货物进出境报关程序

为确保进出口货物合法进出境,我国海关根据国家有关法律法规的要求,对进出口货物的报关规定了一系列特定的手续和步骤,报关人必须遵守,否则要承担相应的法律责任。

根据进出境货物不同的性质及海关不同的监管要求,进出境货物的报关大体分为以下三个阶段。

1. 前期报关阶段

前期报关要在进出口货物实际进出境之前向海关办理,主要适用于保税进出口货物、特定减免税进出口货物和暂准进出口货物,其主要内容是进出口货物收发货人或其代理人向海关说明有关进出口货物的情况,申请适用特定的报关程序。这一环节根据通关制度的不同,主要有加工贸易备案申请、特定减免税进口货物的减免税申请、暂准(时)进口货物的备案、担保申请等海关手续。

2. 进出境报关阶段

进出境报关程序是指进出口货物在进出境环节需向现场海关履行的手续,这一环节主要包括申报、查验、征税、放行货物等海关手续,需要在货物实际进出境时向海关办理,进出境报关程序是任何通关制度下的进出口货物都必须履行经过的通关环节。

1) 申报

申报是指进出口货物的收发货人或其代理人,向海关交验规定的单证,申请办理查验、放行等后续事宜的行为。进出口货物的申报要由报关员代表报关单位向海关办理。我国海关对申报时间、申报单证、申报内容等都做了明确规定。

(1) 申报时间。《海关法》规定,进口货物的收货人及其代理人应当自运输工具申报进境之日起 14 日内向海关申报;出口货物的发货人除海关特准的外,应当在货物运抵海关监管区后,装货 24 小时以前,向海关申报。

(2) 申报单证。海关在接受申报时,将严格审核有关申报单证,申报单证主要包括三种类型：①基本单证，包括进出口货物报关单、发票、装箱单、提（装）货凭证；②特殊单证，包括配额许可证管理证件、出入境货物通关单、出口收汇核销单、海关签发的进出口货物征免税证明、进料（来料）加工登记手册等；③预备单证，包括贸易合同、货物原产地证明、委托单位的工商执照证书、委托单位的账册资料及其他有关单证等。

2）查验

查验是在海关接受报关员申报后，依法对申报人所申报的进出口货物进行实际的核对和检查，以确定单、证、货是否相符，有无违法情形，可否合法进出，并为下一通关程序准备条件。

3）征税

在审核单证、查验货物后，海关根据国家的有关政策、法规对进出口货物征收关税及进口环节的税费，对符合规定的货物依法实施减免税。

海关征税的一般程序包括：①海关按照《中华人民共和国海关进出口税则》（以下简称《海关进出口税则》）的归类规则将进出口货物进行税则归类，并确定其适用的税率；②海关按照《海关法》和《中华人民共和国进出口关税条例》（以下简称《进出口关税条例》）的有关规定审定进出口货物的完税价格，进口货物是以成交价格为基础的到岸价格为完税价格，出口货物以海关审定的货物售予境外的离岸价格，扣除出口税后作为完税价格；③海关根据进出口货物适用的税率和审定的完税价格计算应征关税、增值税、消费税税款，向纳税义务人填发税款缴款书。

（1）海关征税的范围。根据《海关法》和《进出口关税条例》的有关规定，进出口货物除国家另有规定外，均应征收关税。关税由海关依照《海关进出口税则》征收。对进出口货物除征收关税外，还要征收进口环节增值税，对少数商品征收消费税。

（2）纳税人的范围。进口货物的收货人、出口货物的发货人是进出境货物关税的纳税义务人。在我国境内销售货物或者提供加工、修理、修配、劳务以及进口货物的单位和个人是增值税的纳税义务人。在我国境内生产、委托加工和进口《中华人民共和国消费税暂行条例》规定的消费品的单位和个人，是消费税的纳税义务人。

（3）税款缴纳期限。经海关审定应征关税、增值税、消费税的货物，其纳税义务人应当在海关填发税款缴纳证之日起15日内向指定银行缴纳税款。

4）放行

放行是海关监管现场作业的最后一个环节。海关在接受进出口货物的申报后，经审核报关单据、查验实际货物，依法计征进出口税费后，在有关单据上签盖放行章。对一般进出口货物，海关的现场放行即为结关，进口货物可由收货人凭以提取、发运，出口货物可由发货人装船、起运。

3. **后续报关阶段**

后续报关程序主要是指进出口货物实际进出境以后，进出口货物收发货人或其代理人根据海关管理的要求向海关办理的旨在证明有关进出口货物合法进出口、在境内合规使用并已经完结有关海关监管义务的手续。这一环节主要有加工贸易核销、暂准（时）进出口货物的销案和特定减免税进口货物解除海关监管等海关手续。

应当指出的是，不同通关制度下的货物在报关程序的适用上会有所不同，一般进出口货物只需通过进出境报关程序即可完成全部报关活动，但对于保税、特定减免税、暂准（时）进出口等货物，除了进出境程序外，在货物实际进出境前，一般需要经过前期报关程序，办理相关的备案、申请手续；在货物实际进出境后，需经过后续报关程序，办理相应的核销、销案及解除海关监管手续后才能完成全部报关活动（见表6-1）。

表6-1 各类监管货物适用的报关程序

	前期报关	进出境报关	后续报关
一般进出口货物	无	申报—查验—征税—放行	无
保税进出口货物	登记备案		登记手册核销
减免税进出口货物	资格认定、备案		解除监管
暂准进出口货物	备案、担保		销案

6.2 进出口货物报关单

进出口货物报关单是向海关报告进出口货物情况，申请海关查验、放行货物的基本法律文件。作为报关员，一个主要工作任务就是填制报关单。报关单位必须对所填制报关单的真实性、合法性负责，承担相应的法律和经济责任。能否正确填写进出口货物报关单将直接影响通关速度，企业的经济效益和海关征、减、免、验、放等工作环节。因此，正确填写进出口货物报关单是报关企业和报关员必须履行的义务和责任。这就要求报关企业和报关人员在填报进出口货物报关单时必须做到真实、准确、齐全、清楚。

6.2.1 报关单种类

纸质进口货物报关单要求一式五联，分别是海关作业联、海关留存联、企业留存联、海关核销联和进口付汇证明联。

纸质出口货物报关单要求一式六联，分别是海关作业联、海关留存联、企业留存联、海关核销联、出口收汇证明联和出口退税证明联。

根据海关规定，按不同的用途，进（出）口货物报关单分别有以下几种情况。

（1）一般贸易进出口货物，填写白色报关单。

（2）进料加工进出口货物，填写粉红色报关单。

（3）来料加工装配和补偿贸易进出口货物，填写浅绿色报关单。

（4）外商投资企业进出口货物，填写浅蓝色报关单。

（5）出口后需国内退税的货物，填写浅黄色报关单。

各种报关单只是颜色有别，报关单所列项目及格式完全相同。

6.2.2 报关单填制的一般要求

进出境货物的收、发货人或其代理人向海关申报时，必须填写并向海关递交进出口货物报关单。申报人在填制报关单时,应当依法如实向海关申报,对申报内容的真实性、准确性、完整性和规范性承担相应的法律责任。

(1) 报关员必须按照《海关法》、《货物申报管理规定》和《报关单填制规范》的有关规定和要求,向海关如实申报。

(2) 报关单填报必须真实,做到"两个相符"。①单、证相符,即所填报关单各栏目的内容必须与合同、发票、装箱单、提单以及批文等随附单据相符。②单、货相符,即所填报关单各栏目的内容必须与实际进出口货物情况相符。

(3) 报关单的填报要准确、齐全、完整、清楚,报关单各栏目内容要逐项详细准确填报(打印),字迹清楚、整洁、端正,不得用铅笔或红色复写纸填写;若有更正,必须在更正项目上加盖校对章。

(4) 不同的批文或合同的货物、同一批货物中不同的贸易方式的货物、不同备案号的货物、不同提运单的货物、不同的运输方式或相同的运输方式但不同航次的货物,均应该分单填报。一份原产地证书只能对应一份报关单;同一份报关单上的商品不能够同时享受协定税率和减免税;在一批货物中,对于实行原产地证书联网管理的,如涉及多份原产地证书或含有非原产地证书商品,也应分单填报。

(5) 在反映进出口商品情况的项目中,需分项填报的主要有下列几种情况:①商品编号不同的;②商品名称不同的;③原产国(地区)/最终目的国(地区)不同的。

(6) 已向海关申报的进出口货物报关单,如原填报内容与实际进出口货物不一致而又有正当理由的,申报人应向海关递交书面更正申请,经海关核准后,对原填报的内容进行更改或撤销。

6.2.3 进出口货物报关单的填写

报关单共47栏,为保证报关单的填写质量,进出口货物报关单由海关统一印制,报关员需按照海关统一的填制规范要求填写。

1. 预录入编号

预录入编号是指预录入单位预录入报关单的编号,用于申报单位与海关之间引用其申报后尚未接受申报的报关单。

2. 海关编号

海关编号是指海关接受申报时给予报关单的编号。

3. 进口口岸/出口口岸

进口口岸/出口口岸是指货物进出境口岸海关的名称。

4. 备案号

本栏目填报进出口货物收发货人在海关办理加工贸易合同备案或征、减、免税备案审批等手续时,海关核发的《中华人民共和国海关加工贸易手册》、电子账册及其分册、《进出口货物征免税证明》或其他备案审批文件的编号。

一份报关单只允许填报一个备案号。

无备案审批文件的报关单,本栏目免予填报。

5. 合同协议号

本栏目应填报进出口货物合同(协议)的全部字头和号码。

6. 进口日期/出口日期

进口日期填运载进口货物的运输工具申报进境的日期。

出口日期填运载所申报货物的运输工具办结出境手续的日期。本栏目供海关打印报关单证明联用，在申报时免予填报。

7. 申报日期

申报日期是指海关接受进出口货物的收、发货人或受其委托的报关企业申请的日期。

8. 经营单位

经营单位是指对外签订并执行进出口贸易合同的中国境内企业、单位或个人的名称及海关注册编码。

9. 收货单位/发货单位

收货单位填报已知的进口货物在境内的最终消费、使用单位的名称，包括自行从境外进口货物的单位和委托进出口企业进口货物的单位。

发货单位填报出口货物在境内的生产或销售单位。

10. 申报单位

申报单位指对申报内容的真实性直接向海关负责的企业或单位。自理报关的，填报进出口企业的名称及海关注册编码；委托代理报关的，填报经海关批准的报关企业名称及海关注册编码。

11. 运输方式

运输方式是指载运货物进出关境所使用的运输工具的分类，如江海运输、汽车运输或航空运输。

12. 运输工具名称

运输工具名称是指载运货物进出境的运输工具的名称或运输工具编号，如船名、航次。

13. 航次号

航次号是指载运货物进出境的运输工具的航次编号。

14. 提运单号

提运单号是指进出口货物提单或运单的编号。

一份报关单只允许填报一个提单或运单号，一票货物对应多个提单或运单时，应分单填报。

15. 贸易方式（监管方式）

本栏目应根据实际情况按海关规定的《贸易方式代码表》选择填报相应的贸易方式简称或代码，如一般贸易、进料加工等。

一份报关单只允许填报一种贸易方式。

16. 征免性质

征免性质是指海关对进出口货物实施征、减、免税管理的性质类别。

本栏目应按照海关核发的《征免税证明》中批注的征免性质填报，或根据实际情况按海关规定的《征免性质代码表》选择填报相应的征免性质简称或代码，如一般征税、来料加工等。

一份报关单只允许填报一种征免性质。

17. 征税比例/结汇方式

进口报关单本栏目免予填报。

出口报关单填写出口货物的发货人或其代理人收结外汇的方式。本栏目应按海关规定的《结汇方式代码表》选择填报相应的结汇方式名称或代码，如 T/T、D/A、D/P、L/C。

18. 许可证号

应申领进（出）口许可证的货物，在此栏目填报商务部及其授权发证机关签发的进（出）口货物许可证的编号。

一份报关单只允许填报一个许可证号。

19. 起运国（地区）/运抵国（地区）

进口报关单的起运国（地区）填进口货物起始发出直接运抵我国或者在运输中转国（地）未发生任何商业性交易的情况下运抵我国的国家（地区）。

出口报关单的运抵国（地区）填出口货物离开我国关境直接运抵或者在运输中转国（地区）未发生任何商业性交易的情况下最后运抵的国家（地区）。

不经过第三国（地区）转运的直接运输进出口货物，以进口货物的装货港所在国（地区）为起运国（地区），以出口货物的指运港所在国（地区）为运抵国（地区）。

经过第三国（地区）转运的进出口货物，如在中转国（地区）发生商业性交易，则以中转国（地区）作为起运/运抵国（地区）。

20. 装货港/指运港

装货港填报进口货物在运抵我国关境前的最后一个境外装运港。

指运港填报出口货物运往境外的最终目的港；最终目的港不可预知的，按尽可能预知的目的港填报。

21. 境内目的地/境内货源地

境内目的地填报已知的进口货物在国内的消费、使用地或最终运抵地。

境内货源地填报出口货物在国内的产地或原始发货地。

22. 批准文号

填报《出口收汇核销单》编号。进口报关单中本栏目免予填报。

23. 成交方式

根据实际成交价格条款按海关规定的《成交方式代码表》选择填报相应的成交方式代码，如 CIF、FOB。

24. 运费

填报进口货物运抵我国境内输入地点起卸前的运输费用，出口货物运至我国境内输出地点装载出境后的运输费用。进口货物成交价格包含前述运输费用或者出口货物成交价格不包含前述运输费用的，本栏目免予填报。

运费可按运费单价、总价或运费率三种方式之一填报，注明运费标记（运费标记"1"表示运费率，"2"表示每吨货物的运费单价，"3"表示运费总价），并按海关规定的《货币代码表》选择填报相应的币种代码。

25. 保费

保费一栏填报进口货物运抵我国境内输入地点起卸前的保险费用,出口货物运至我国境内输出地点装载出境后的保险费用。进口货物成交价格包含前述保险费用或者出口货物成交价格不包含前述保险费用的,本栏目免予填报。

保费可按保险费总价或保险费率两种方式之一填报,注明保险费标记(保险费标记"1"表示保险费率,"3"表示保险费总价),并按海关规定的《货币代码表》选择填报相应的币种代码。

26. 杂费

杂费一栏填报成交价格以外的,按照《中华人民共和国进出口关税条例》相关规定应计入完税价格或应从完税价格中扣除的费用。可按杂费总价或杂费率两种方式之一填报,注明杂费标记(杂费标记"1"表示杂费率,"3"表示杂费总价),并按海关规定的《货币代码表》选择填报相应的币种代码。

应计入完税价格的杂费填报为正值或正率,应从完税价格中扣除的杂费填报为负值或负率。

27. 件数

件数一栏填报有外包装的出口货物的实际件数。本栏目不得填报为零,裸装货物填报为"1"。

28. 包装种类

本栏目填写进出口货物的实际外包装种类。

29. 毛重(千克)

本栏目填报货物实际毛重,计量单位为千克,不足一千克的填报为"1"。

30. 净重(千克)

本栏目填报货物的实际净重,计量单位为千克,不足一千克的填报为"1"。

31. 集装箱号

本栏目填报装载进出口货物(包括拼箱货物)集装箱的箱体信息。一个集装箱填一条记录,分别填报集装箱号(在集装箱箱体上标示的全球唯一编号)、集装箱的规格和集装箱的自重。非集装箱货物填报为"0"。

32. 随附单据

本栏目根据海关规定的《监管证件代码表》选择填报除18栏所列许可证件以外的其他进出口许可证件或监管证件代码及编号。

33. 用途/生产厂家

进口货物填报用途,应根据进口货物的实际用途按海关规定的《用途代码表》选择填报相应的用途代码。

出口货物填报其境内生产企业。

34. 标记唛码及备注

本栏目填写标记唛码中除图形以外的文字、数字以及其他申报时必须说明的事项。

35. 项号

本栏目分两行填报及打印。

第一行打印报关单中的商品排列序号。

第二行专用于加工贸易、减免税等已备案、审批的货物，填报和打印该项货物在《加工贸易手册》或《征免税证明》等备案、审批单证中的顺序编号。

36．商品编号

此为按商品分类编码规则确定的进出口货物的商品编号。

37．商品名称、规格型号

本栏目分两行填报及打印。

第一行打印进出口货物规范的中文商品名称；第二行打印规格型号，必要时可加注原文。

38．数量及单位

本栏目为进出口商品的实际数量及计量单位。

39．原产国（地区）/最终目的国（地区）

原产国（地区）应依据《中华人民共和国进出口货物原产地条例》、《中华人民共和国海关关于执行〈非优惠原产地规则中实质性改变标准〉的规定》以及海关总署关于各项优惠贸易协定原产地管理规章规定的原产地确定标准填报。

最终目的国（地区）填写已知的出口货物的最终实际消费、使用或进一步加工制造的国家（地区）。

40．单价

本栏目填报同一项号下进出口货物实际成交的商品单位价格。

41．总价

本栏目填报同一项号下进出口货物实际成交的商品总价。

42．币制

本栏目填写进出口货物实际成交价格的币种。

43．征免

本栏目指海关对进出口货物进行征税、减税、免税或特案处理的实际操作方式。按海关核发的《征免税证明》或有关政策规定，对报关单所列每项商品选择填报海关规定的《征减免税方式代码表》中相应的征减免税方式。

44．税费征收情况

本栏目供海关批注进（出）口货物税费征收及减免情况。

45．录入员

预录入操作人员的姓名。

46．录入单位

电子数据报关单的录入单位名称。

47．填制日期

本栏目指报关单的填制日期。

48．海关审单批注栏

本栏目是供海关内部作业时签注的栏目，由海关关员手工填写在预录入报关单上。

【相关单证】

单证 6-1　出口货物报关单

<h3 style="text-align:center">中华人民共和国海关出口货物报关单</h3>

预录入编号：　　　　　　　　　　　　　　　　　　　　　　　　　海关编号：

出口口岸		备案号		出口日期		申报日期	
经营单位		运输方式		运输工具名称		提运单号	
发货单位		贸易方式		征免性质		结汇方式	
许可证号		运抵国（地区）		指运港		境内货源地	
批准文号		成交方式		运费		保费	杂费
合同协议号		件数		包装种类		毛重（千克）	净重（千克）
集装箱号		随附单据				生产厂家	
标记唛码及备注							

项号	商品编号	商品名称、规格型号	数量及单位	最终目的国（地区）	单价	总价	币制	征免

税费征收情况

录入员　录入单位	兹声明以上申报无讹并承担法律责任	海关审单批注及放行日期（签章）	
报关员			
	申报单位（签章）	审单	审价
单位地址			
邮编	电话　　填制日期	征税	统计
		查验	放行

单证 6-2 进口货物报关单

中华人民共和国海关进口货物报关单

预录入编号：　　　　　　　　　　　　　　　　　　海关编号：

进口口岸		备案号		进口日期		申报日期	
经营单位		运输方式		运输工具名称		提运单号	
收货单位		贸易方式		征免性质		征税比例	
许可证号		起运国（地区）		装货港		境内目的地	
批准文号		成交方式		运费		保费	杂费
合同协议号		件数		包装种类	毛重（千克）		净重（千克）
集装箱号		随附单据			用途		
标记唛码及备注							

项号	商品编号	商品名称、规格型号	数量及单位	原产国（地区）	单价	总价	币制	征免

税费征收情况

录入员　　录入单位	兹声明以上申报无讹并承担法律责任	海关审单批注及放行日期（签章）	
报关员	申报单位（签章）	审单	审价
单位地址		征税	统计
邮编	电话　　　填制日期	查验	放行

【案例】

恒泰公司填制的报关单如表6-2所示。

表6-2 中华人民共和国海关出口货物报关单

预录入编号:				海关编号:
出口口岸 黄埔	备案号		出口日期 080826	申报日期 080823
经营单位 河北恒泰进出口贸易公司	运输方式 江海		运输工具名称 QINLUN V.1502	提运单号 COS07-25061
发货单位 河北恒泰进出口贸易公司	贸易方式 一般贸易		征免性质 一般征税	结汇方式 L/C
许可证号	运抵国(地区) 美国		指运港 洛杉矶	境内货源地 石家庄
批准文号 999123456	成交方式 CFR	运费 502/2200/3	保费	杂费
合同协议号 02AG18185	件数 150	包装种类 包	毛重(千克) 10 125	净重(千克) 9 450
集装箱号 COSX663209/20/2275	随附单据		生产厂家 高阳毛巾厂	
标记唛码及备注 N/M				

项号	商品编号	商品名称、规格型号	数量及单位	最终目的国(地区)	单价	总价	币制	征免
1	58021100	条纹毛巾 30″×60″ ART No. ABC69	4 500 打	美国	4.90	22 050	USD	

税费征收情况

录入员 录入单位 李欣 报关员 单位地址 中国河北石家庄和平路231号 邮编 050000	兹声明以上申报无讹并承担法律责任 申报单位(签章) 河北恒泰进出口贸易公司 电话: 0311-84576936 填制日期: 080823	海关审单批注及放行日期(签章)	
		审单	审价
		征税	统计
		查验	放行

【技能实训】

1. 根据所给的资料（见表6-3），填制报关单。

表6-3 上海翔宇国际贸易公司商业发票
上海翔宇国际贸易公司
SHANGHAI XIANGYU INTERNATIONAL TRADING CO.

Add：21/f, Finance Mansion 　　Contract No.：SYD0212
　　　235 ZhongShan Road 　　　Date：JUNE20，2006
　　　Shanghai 200437，China 　　L/C No.：56489
Tel：0086-21-65435189
Fax：0086-21-65435288

商 业 发 票
COMMERCIAL INVOICE

To：INCUERM INTERNATIONAL LTD.

Under mentioned goods from Shanghai to Penang via Singapore

Marks & Nos.	Quantities and Description	Unit Price	Amount
MDY PENANG VIA SINGAPORE	100%COTTON IMITATION WAX PRINTED FABRIC 全棉仿蜡染布 30×30　68×68　32"/33" 12YDS PIECE @600/120000YDS 200 CLOTH BALE GW：72 000KGS NW：67 000KGS 外汇核销 28/2345762 H.S No. 52085200 计量单位：米/千克 1码＝0.914 4米 B/LNO. OCE3426 上海闸北区景华印染厂生产并发货 附商检证 上海华安集装箱公司报关、录入 报关员：李卫　录入员：黄明 装"东方红 V209"于2006年8月15日出口 预录入编号：517001111 海关注册编码：3122200085	CIF PENANG USD0.6/YD	USD72 000.00 运费：5% 保费：0.25%

上海翔宇国际贸易公司
SHANGHAI XIANGYU INTERNATIONAL TRADING CO.

2. 根据提供的原始材料（见表 6-4～表 6-6），从下列出口货物报关单 20 个已填栏目中找出 7 个错误。

表 6-4 报关单样本
中华人民共和国出口货物报关单

预录入编号：   海关编号：

出口口岸		(A) 备案号 B09089400347	出口日期	(B) 申报日期 01.01.24
经营单位		运输方式	(C) 运输工具名称 MIN YUAN	(D) 提运单号 FC2000L077
发货单位		(E) 贸易方式 来料加工	(F) 征免性质 来料加工	(G) 结汇方式 电汇
许可证号	运抵国（地区）		指运港	(H) 境内货源地 大连（其他）
(I) 批准文号 FC2000L077	(J) 成交方式 FOB	运费	保费	杂费
(K) 合同协议号 BCHAI0818	(L) 件数 8 000 件	包装种类	(M) 毛重（kg） 294	净重（kg）
(N) 集装箱号	随附单据		生产厂家	
(O) 标记唛码及备注 N.D MBR-1101 CHINA				
(P) 项号 商品编码 商品名称、规格型号 (Q) 数量及单位 最终目的国（地区） (R) 单价 (S) 总价 币制 (T) 征免 01 8 000.00 件 0.23 4 000.00 全免 03 270.00 kg				
（以下略）				

表 6-5 发 票 样 本
中外合资大连东海服装有限公司发票
INVOICE

Consignee HAITASHI CO. LTD., JAPAN		Ref. No. FC2000L077
Notify THE SAME AS CONSIGNEE		Other references: CONTRACT No. MBR-1101
Departure date	Vessel/flight MIN YUAN/811W	来料加工手册 B09089400347 材料费 2160，列第 3 项 B/L No. DALUIP0202816
From DALIAN	To YOKOHAMA	Terms of delivery and payment M/T 核销单号 215134335
Shipping marks	No. & kind of pkgs	Goods description	Qty	Unit price	Amount
---	---	---	---	---	---
N.D MBR-1101 CHINA	12CTNS PACKING IN 12CTNS ONLY	MEN'S COAT H.S. CODE 62121010	8 000PCS	@USD0.23	USD1 840.00 FOBDALIAN CHINA (FOR PROCESSING PRICE)

表6-6 装箱单样本

中外合资大连东海服装有限公司装箱单
PACKING LIST

Consignee HAITASHI CO. LTD., JAPAN		Ref. No. FC2000L077			
Notify THE SAME AS CONSIGNEE		Other references: CONTRACT No. MBR-1101			
Departure date	Vessel/flight MIN YUAN/811W				
From: DALIAN	To YOKOHAMA	B/L No. DALUIP0202816			
Shipping marks	No. & kind of pkgs	Goods description	N.W.	G.W.	Measurement
N.D MBR-1101 CHINA	12CTNS	MEN'S COAT 8 000PCS TOTAL PACKAGE: TWELVE CTNS ONLY	270KGS	294KGS	1.60CBM

第 7 章

【本章导读】
出口货物投保概述
投保单的缮制
保险单的缮制

【学习目标和要点】
通过本章的学习，学生应了解国际货物运输保险的投保方式和投保程序，熟悉中国保险条款和伦敦保险协会条款的各种险别，掌握国际货物运输投保单以及保险单的内容和缮制要求，掌握保险单的作用和种类，能根据合同、发票和装箱单等单据的资料缮制货物运输投保单和保险单。

在进出口货物从卖方运到买方的长途运输和装卸过程中，常常会由于自然灾害、意外事故或其他外来原因遭受损失，为了在货物受损后获得经济补偿，货主在货物出运前就必须及时向保险公司办理投保。

进出口货物运输保险

7.1 进出口货物运输保险概述

货物的运输保险是指投保人(The Insured,在 FOB、CFR 术语下为买方,在 CIF 下为卖方)对一批或若干批货物向保险人(The Insurer,即保险公司),按一定的金额投保一定的险别,并缴纳保险费;保险人承保后签发保单作为承保的凭证,如果所保货物在运输过程中发生承保风险造成损失,则保险公司应按他出具的保单的规定给予被保险人补偿。

进出口货物在长途运送和装卸过程中,有可能会因自然灾害、意外事故或其他外来因素而导致受损。为了保障收货人在货物受损后获得经济补偿,一般在货物出运前,货主都向保险公司办理有关投保事宜,并按合同或信用证要求仔细、认真地填写货物运输险投保单交给保险公司,保险公司若接受了投保,就签发给投保人一份承保凭证即保险单(INSURANCE POLICY)。有时,出口方也可以出口货物明细单或出口发票副本来代替投保单,但必须加注如运输工具、开航日期、承保险别、投保金额或投保加成、赔款地、保单份数等内容。

7.1.1 保险条款及险别

1. 中国保险条款及险别

现行的中国保险条款(China Insurance Clause,CIC)是中国人民保险公司(PICC)制定的,其货物运输保险分为基本险和附加险两大类,基本险分为平安险、水渍险和一切险,可以单独投保其中一种,附加险不能单独投保。目前,在我国进出口业务中,一般多选用费用较高、但责任范围大的一切险。

1)基本险别

基本险又称主险,是可以独立承保的险别。我国海运货物保险的基本险分为平安险(Free from Particular Average,FPA)、水渍险(With Particular Average,WPA 或 WA)和一切险(All Risks)三种。

(1)平安险这一名称在我国保险行业中沿用甚久,其英文原意是指单独海损不负责赔偿。目前,平安险的责任范围包括:①在运输过程中,由于自然灾害和运输工具发生意外事故,造成被保险货物的实际全损或推定全损;②由于运输工具遭遇搁浅、触礁、沉没、互撞、与流冰或其他物体碰撞以及失火、爆炸等意外事故造成被保险货物的全部或部分损失;③只要运输工具曾经发生搁浅、触礁、沉没、焚毁等意外事故,不论这意外事故发生之前或者以后曾在海上遭遇恶劣气候、雷电、海啸等自然灾害造成的被保险货物的部分损失;④在装卸转船过程中,被保险货物一件或数件落海所造成的全部损失或部分损失;⑤被保险人对遭受承保责任内危险的货物采取抢救,防止或减少货损措施支付的合理费用,但以不超过该批被救货物的保险金额为限;⑥运输工具遭遇自然灾害或者意外事故,需要在中途的港口或者在避难港口停靠,因而引起的卸货、装货、存仓以及运送货物所产生的特别费用;⑦发生共同海损所引起的牺牲、分摊费和救助费用;⑧运输契约订有"船舶互撞条款",按该条款规定应由货方偿还船方的损失。

(2)水渍险英文原意是指单独海损负责赔偿。目前,水渍险的责任范围,除包括上列"平安险"的各项责任外,还负责被保险货物由于恶劣气候、雷电、海啸、地震、洪水等自然灾害所造成的部分损失。

(3) 一切险的责任范围除包括"平安险"和"水渍险"的所有责任外,还包括货物在运输过程中,因一般外来原因所造成的被保险货物的全损或部分损失。实际上,一切险是平安险、水渍险以及一般附加险的总和。

2) 附加险

附加险是不能单独承保的险别。它必须依附于基本险项下,即只有投保基本险其中的一种之后,才可加保附加险,并须另外支付一定的保险费。目前,我国海运货物保险的附加险有一般附加险和特殊附加险两种。

(1) 一般附加险归纳起来共有 11 种,包括:偷窃提货不着险(Theft, Pilferage and Non-delivery)、淡水雨淋险(Fresh Water Rain Damage)、短量险(Risk of Shortage)、混杂、沾污险(Risk of Intermixture & Contamination)、渗漏险(Risk of Leakage)、碰损、破碎险(Risk of Clash & Breakage)、串味险(Risk of Odour)、受热、受潮险(Damage Caused by heating & Sweating)、钩损险(Hook Damage)、包装破裂险(Loss or Damage Caused by Breakage Packing)、锈损险(Risks of Rust)。

(2) 特别附加险是指承保由于军事、政治、国家政策法令以及行政措施等特殊外来原因所引起的风险与损失的险别。中国人民保险公司承保的特别附加险,除包括下列战争险(War Risk)和罢工险(Strikes Risk)以外,还有交货不到险(Failure to Delivery Risks)、进口关税险(Import Duty Risk)、舱面险(On Deck Risk)、拒收险(Rejection Risk)、黄曲霉素险(Aflatoxin Risk)和出口货物到香港(包括九龙在内)或澳门存储仓火险责任扩展条款(Fire risk extension clause for storage of cargo at destination HongKong, including Kowloon or Macao)。

2. 伦敦保险协会条款

世界上保险业务中较多采用的是伦敦保险协会条款(Institute cargo clause, ICC),即现行的伦敦保险协会的海运货物保险条款,包括 ICC(A)险、ICC(B)险、ICC(C)险、协会战争险条款—货物(Institute War Clause-Cargo)、协会罢工险条款—货物(Institute Strikes Clause-Cargo)、恶意损坏险条款(Malicious Damage Clause)等。

1) ICC(A)承保风险和除外责任

(1) ICC(A)的承保风险。本条款对承保风险的规定有一切风险减除外责任和列明承保险两种方法,ICC(A)就是以一切风险减除外责任的形式出现,因为这一险别中承保的责任范围最大,采用除列明风险和损失之外,一切风险损失都予承保的规定,最为简单明了。

(2) ICC(A)的除外责任,包括:①一般除外责任,如归因于被保险人故意的不法行为造成的损失或费用,自然渗漏、自然损耗、自然磨损、包装不当或准备不足造成的损失或保险标的内在缺陷或特性造成的损失或费用,直接由于延迟所引起的损失或费用,船舶所有人、经营人、租船人的经营破产或不履行债务造成的损失或费用,由于使用任何原子或热核武器所造成的损失或费用;②不适航、不适货除外责任,所谓不适航、不适货除外责任,是指保险标的在装船时,如被保险人或其受雇人已经知道船舶不适航,以及船舶、装运工具、集装箱等不适货,保险人不负赔偿责任;③战争除外责任,如由于战争、内战、敌对行为所造成的损失或费用,由于捕获、拘留、扣留等所造成的损失或费用,由于漂流水雷、鱼雷等武器所造成的损失或费用;④罢工除外责任,由于罢工被迫停工所造成的损失或费用,由于任何恐怖主义者或任何出于政治目的所采取的行动。

2) ICC（B）承保风险和除外责任

（1）ICC（B）的承保风险。本险别采用列明风险的形式,凡属列出的就是承保的,没有列出的,不论何种情况均不负责,这种方法明确、肯定,便于选择投保,便于处理索赔,凡归因于下列情况者均予承保:①火灾、爆炸;②船舶或驳船触礁、搁浅、沉没;③陆上运输工具碰撞出轨;④船舶、驳船或运输工具同水以外的外界物体碰撞;⑤在避难港卸货;⑥地震、火山爆发、雷电;⑦共同海损牺牲;⑧抛货或浪击落海;⑨海水、湖水或河水进入运输工具或储存处所;⑩货物在装卸时落海或跌落造成的整件全损。

（2）ICC（B）的除外责任。ICC（B）的除外责任与ICC（A）的除外责任基本相同,只是对ICC（A）中的全部除外责任,因任何人故意损害或破坏、海盗等造成的损失或费用不负责。

3) ICC（C）的承保风险和除外责任

（1）ICC（C）的承保风险比ICC（A）、ICC（B）险要小得多,它只承保重大意外事故,而不承保自然灾害及非重大意外事故,其具体承保风险包括:①火灾、爆炸;②船舶或驳船触礁、搁浅、沉没;③陆上运输工具倾覆或出轨;④在避难港卸货;⑤共同海损牺牲;⑥抛货。

（2）ICC（C）的除外责任。其除外责任与ICC（B）完全相同。

ICC保险条款三种险别中保险人承保范围的比较如表7-1所示。

表7-1 三种险别中保险人承保范围的比较

承保风险	ICC（A）	ICC（B）	ICC（C）
（1）火灾、爆炸	√	√	√
（2）船舶、驳船的触礁、搁浅、沉没、倾覆	√	√	√
（3）陆上运输工具的倾覆或出轨	√	√	√
（4）船舶、驳船或运输工具同出水以外的任何外界物体碰撞	√	√	√
（5）在避难港卸货	√	√	√
（6）地震、火山爆发或雷电	√	√	
（7）共同海损牺牲	√	√	√
（8）共同海损分摊和救助费用	√	√	√
（9）运输合同订有"船舶互撞责任"条款,根据该条款的规定应由货方偿还船方的损失	√	√	√
（10）投弃	√	√	√
（11）浪击落海	√	√	×
（12）海水、湖水或河水进入船舶、驳船、运输工具、集装箱、大型海运箱或储存处所	√	√	×

续表

承保风险	ICC (A)	ICC (B)	ICC (C)
(13) 货物在船舶或驳船装卸时落海或跌落，造成任何整体的全损	√	√	×
(14) 由于被保险人以外的其他人（如船长、船员等）的故意违法行为所造成的损失或费用	√	×	×
(15) 海盗行为	√	×	×
(16) 由于一般外来原因造成的损失	√	×	×

注：① "√" 代表承保风险；"×" 代表免责风险或不承保风险；
② 第 13 项即 "吊索损害"，第 14 项即 "恶意损害"。

7.1.2 保险单据的种类

（1）保险单（Insurance Policy）。这是一种正规的保险合同，是完整独立的保险文件。保单背面印有货物运输保险条款（一般表明承保的基本险别条款之内容），还列有保险人的责任范围及保险人与被保险人各自的权利、义务等方面的条款，俗称 "大保单"。

（2）保险凭证（Insurance Certificate）。中国人民保险公司发出的保险凭证是表示保险公司已经接受保险的一种证明文件，这是一种比较简化的保险单据。它包括了保险单的基本内容，但不附有保险条款全文，这种保险凭证与保险单有同等的法律效力，俗称 "小保单"。

（3）联合凭证（Combined Certificate），又称承保证明（Risk Note）。这是我国保险公司特别使用的，比保险凭证更简化的保险单据。保险公司仅将承保险别、保险金额及保险编号加注在我国进出口公司开具的出口货物发票上，并正式签章即作为已经保险的证据。仅用于我国内地对港澳等地区的贸易，是最简单的保险单据，现已较少使用。

（4）预约保险单（Open Policy）。这是进口贸易中，被保险人（一般为进口人）与保险人之间订立的总合同。订立这种合同即可以简化保险手续，又可使货物一经装运即可取得保障。

（5）保险声明（Insurance Declaration）。预约保险单项下的货物一经确定装船，要求被保险人立即以保险声明书的形式，将该批货物的名称、数量、保险金额、船名、起讫港口、航次、开航日期等通知保险人，银行可将保险声明书当作一项单据予以接受。

（6）批单。保险单出立后，如需变更其内容，可由保险公司另出的凭证注明更改或补充的内容，称为批单。其必须粘在保险单上并加盖骑缝章，作为保险单不可分割的一部分。

（7）暂保单（Cover Note）。暂保单是保险人在出立正式保险单之前签发的证明保险人已同意给予投保人以保险保障的一种临时凭证。保险人在同投保人商订保险合同中接受投保的原则意合已定，但还有一些条件尚未完全谈妥，一般就使用这种凭证。如果洽商不能达成协议，暂保单可以取消。达成协议，可签发正式保险单代替暂保单。有效期一般为 1 个月，正式出立保单后即自动失效。如保险人事前通知，也可提前终止效力。除非信用证特别要求，银行不接受暂保单。

7.1.3 保险单的背书转让

保险单是可以经背书（Endorsement）转让的单据。根据国际保险行业的习惯，保险单据经被保险人背书后，即随着被保险货物的所有权转移自动转到受让人手中，背书前后均不需要通知保险公司。因此，出口方只需在保险单上背书就完成了转让手续。

保险单背书一般分为空白背书和记名背书。空白背书只注明被保险人（包括进出口公司的名称和经办人的名字）的名称。当来证没有明确使用何种背书时，可使用空白背书方式。记名背书在出口业务中较少使用。因为这一背书方式只允许被背书人（受让人）而限制其他任何人在被保险货物损失后享有向保险公司或其代理人索赔的权利，并得到合理的补偿。

7.2 投保单

如果是出口方投保，则根据合同或信用证的规定，在备齐货物确定装船出运后，向保险公司填制一份"运输险投保申请单"，这是保险公司接受投保、出具保险单的依据。投保单是投保人在投保时对保险标的及有关事实的告知和陈述，也是保险人签发保险单和确定保险费的依据，因此投保单的填写必须准确、真实。

投保单的具体内容一般主要有以下几项：被保险人、发票号码和合同号码、包装数量、保险货物项目、保险金额、装载运输工具、航次、航班、开航日期、运输路线、承保险别、赔款地、投保人签章及企业名称、电话、地址、投保日期等。

应该注意的是，投保单的内容必须同买卖合同及信用证上的有关规定一致。如果投保人不按合同的规定填写投保单，保险人据此出立的保险单就会与合同的规定不符，收货人就可以拒绝接受这种保险单。在信用证支付方式下，投保单的内容还应符合信用证的有关规定，否则保险单也会因"单证不符"遭到银行的拒收。

不同的保险公司投保单的格式和内容略有不同，但相差不大。投保单的缮制一般要求如下。

（1）被保险人：信用证下按信用证要求；除非信用证有特别规定，一般应为信用证的受益人或合同的卖方即发货人。

（2）保单号（Policy No.）（如果有）：暂空。

（3）发票号（Invoice No.）、合同号（Contract No.）、信用证号（L/C No.）：分别根据相关单证规定填写。

（4）唛头（Marks & Nos）：要求按信用证规定，或与发票等其他单据上的唛头一致。

（5）数量和保险货物项目（Quantity & Description of goods）：数量是出口货物的总数量，如总重量或总包装件数；保险货物项目是货物的品名或规格，一般按提单的填法，填大类名称或货物的统称，不必详细列明各种规格等细节。

（6）发票金额（Amount Invoice）：依商业发票。

（7）保险金额（Amount Insured）：填写计算投保加成后的总保险金额，或成交金额，但需标明成交价格条件。

（8）运输相关项目：即装于何种运输工具、开航日期（即为提单签发日期）、运输路线（即货物装运地和目的地）。

（9）提单、通知单或邮局收据号次：根据不同的运输方式，填写运单号，如提单号、航空运单号或其他运输单据号。

（10）保费给付地点及赔款地点（Claims Payable At）：一般在 CIF 条件下，卖方支付保险费，保费给付地点为卖方所在地，赔款偿付地点一般为买方所在地。

（11）保险险别：按合同规定或信用证条款。

（12）加成（Value Plus About）：按规定，保险公司一般能接受的最高加成是 30%，超过此，保险公司一般不予承保。

（13）包装情况：集装箱或散货运输等，据装箱单所示。

（14）费率和保险费（如果有）：由保险公司负责。

（15）投保日期：一般不能晚于提单日前。

（16）投保人签章：上述内容填完后投保人须签字盖章才能生效。

（17）其他项：如船龄等项不知道可以不必填写，或与保险公司联系后填写。

【相关单证】

单证 7-1 货物运输保险投保单

中国平安保险股份有限公司
PING AN INSURANCE COMPANY OF CHINA, LTD.
进出口货物运输险投保单
APPLICATION FOR IMP/EXP TRANSPORTATION INSURANCE

被保险人
Insured：

本投保单由投保人如实填写并签章后作为向本公司投保货物运输保险的依据，本投保单为该货物运输保险单的组成部分。
The Applicant is required to fill in the following items in good faith and as detailed as possible, and affix signature to this application, which shall be treated as proof of application to the Company for cargo transportation insurance and constitute an integral part of the insurance policy.

兹拟向中国平安财产保险股份有限公司投保下列货物运输保险： Herein apply to the Company for Transportation Insurance of following cargo：	请将投保的险别及条件注明如下： Please state risks insured against and conditions：
请将保险货物项目、标记、数量及包装注明此上。 Please state items, marks, quantity and packing of cargo insured here above.	( ) PICC (C.I.C.) Clause　　( ) S.R.C.C. ( ) ICC Clause　　　　　　( ) W/W ( ) All Risks　　　　　　　( ) TPND ( ) W.A.　　　　　　　　( ) FREC ( ) F.P.A.　　　　　　　 ( ) IOP ( ) ICC Clause A　　　　　( ) RFWD ( ) ICC Clause B　　　　　( ) Risk of Breakage ( ) ICC Clause C　　　　　( ) Risks during ( ) Air TPT All Risks　　　( ) transshipment ( ) Air TPT Risks ( ) O/L TPT All Risks ( ) O/L TPT Risks ( ) War Risks

续表

| 装载运输工具（船名/车号）： per conveyance | 船龄： Age of Vessel | 集装箱运输： Container Load | 是□ 否□ Yes No | 整船运输： Full Vessel Charter | 是□ 否□ Yes No |

| 发票或提单号 Invoice No. or B/L No. | 开航日期： Slg. On or abt. AS PER B/L. | 年 月 日 Year Month Day |

| 自： From： | 国 Country | 港/地 Port | 经： Via： | 港/地 Port | 至： To： | 国 Country | 港/地 Port |

| 发票金额 Invoice Value： | 保险金额 Amount Insured： |

| 费率 Rate： | 保险费 Premium： |

备注
Remarks：

投保人兹声明上述所填内容属实，同意以本投保单作为订立保险合同的依据；对贵公司就货物运输保险条款及附加险条款（包括责任免除和投保人及被保险人义务部分）的内容及说明已经了解。
I declare that above is true to the best of my knowledge and belief, and hereby agree that the application be incorporated into the policy. I have read and understand the Company's cargo transportation insurance and extensions (including the Exclusions and the applicant's or insured's Obligations).

| 投保人签章： Name/Seal of Proposer | 联系地址： Address of Proposer |

| 送单地址： Delivery Address： | 同上□ 或 Ditto or | 电话： Tel： | 日期： Date： | 年 月 日 year month day |

【案例】

根据合同和信用证要求，河北恒泰进出口贸易公司向中国平安保险公司投保一切险和战争险，缮制进出口货物运输险投保单如表7-2所示。

表7-2 进出口货物运输险投保单

中国平安保险股份有限公司
PING AN INSURANCE COMPANY OF CHINA，LTD.
进出口货物运输险投保单
APPLICATION FOR IMP/EXP TRANSPORTATION INSURANCE

被保险人
Insured：HEBEI HENGTAI IMPORT&EXPORT CORPORATION

本投保单由投保人如实填写并签章后作为向本公司投保货物运输保险的依据，本投保单为该货物运输保险单的组成部分。
The Applicant is required to fill in the following items in good faith and as detailed as possible, and affix signature to this application, which shall be treated as proof of application to the Company for cargo transportation insurance and constitute an integral part of the insurance policy.

续表

兹拟向中国平安财产保险股份有限公司投保下列货物运输保险：	请将投保的险别及条件注明如下：
Herein apply to the Company for Transportation Insurance of following cargo:	Please state risks insured against and conditions:

100% COTTON STRIPE TOWEL
4500DOZS
20DOZS IN A BALE
MARKS:
  PACIFIC
  18185
  LOS ANGELES
  1-225

请将保险货物项目、标记、数量及包装注明此上。
Please state items, marks, quantity and packing of cargo insured here above.

(×) PICC (C. I. C.) Clause   ( ) S. R. C. C.
( ) ICC Clause   ( ) W/W
(×) All Risks   ( ) TPND
( ) W. A.   ( ) FREC
( ) F. P. A.   ( ) IOP
( ) ICC Clause A   ( ) RFWD
( ) ICC Clause B   ( ) Risk of Breakage
( ) ICC Clause C   ( ) Risks during
( ) Air TPT All Risks   ( ) transshipment
( ) Air TPT Risks
( ) O/L TPT All Risks
( ) O/L TPT Risks
(×) War Risks

装载运输工具（船名/车号）： 船龄： 集装箱运输：是□ 否☒ 整船运输：是□ 否☒
per conveyance S.S. QINLUN V. 1502   Age of Vessel   Container Load Yes No   Full Vessel Charter Yes No

发票或提单号 开航日期：   年 月 日
Invoice No. or B/L No.   Slg. On or abt. AS PER B/L   Year 2008 Month Aug Day 23

自： 国 港/地 经： 港/地 至： 国 港/地
From: CHINA Country   TIANJIN Port   Via: Port   To: USA Country   LOS ANGELES Port

发票金额   保险金额
Invoice Value: USD22 050.00   Amount Insured: USD24 255.00

费率   保险费
Rate: RATE AS ARRANGED   Premium: PREMIUM AS ARRANGED

备注
Remarks:

投保人兹声明上述所填内容属实，同意以本投保单作为订立保险合同的依据；对贵公司就货物运输保险条款及附加险条款（包括责任免除和投保人及被保险人义务部分）的内容及说明已经了解。
I declare that above is true to the best of my knowledge and belief, and hereby agree that the application be incorporated into the policy. I have read and understand the Company's cargo transportation insurance and extensions (including the Exclusions and the applicant's or insured's Obligations).

投保人签章：河北恒泰进出口贸易公司 联系地址：No. 231 HEPING ROAD, SHIJIAZHUANG,
                     HEBEI, CHINA
Name/Seal of Proposer   Address of Proposer

送单地址： 同上☒ 或 电话： 日期： 年 月 日
Delivery Address: Ditto   or   Tel: Date: year   month   day

【技能实训】

1. 根据下面一些来自信用证和托运单的资料制作投保单。

SOME MSG FROM L/C:

L/C NO. DATED: 6104-309-2 NOV. 27, 2006

FROM: ... BEIRUT

IN FAVOUR OF: CHINA NATIONAL METALS AND MINERALS I/E CORP. NINGBO BRANCH 774, DONG FENG RD 9E NINGBO

AMOUNT: USD 3 375.45

EVIDENCING SHIPMENT OF:

15 M/T BLAKE (SILVER) OAMORPHOUS GRAPHITE POWDER 85 PCT CARTON 90 PCT PASSING 200 MESH FROM CHINESE NINGBO PORT TO BEIRUT. PARTIAL SHIPMENTS AND TRANSHIPMENT ALLOWED...

DOCUMENTS:

...

INSURANCE POLICY OR CERTIFICATE IN DUPLICATE ISSUED IN AN IRREVOCABLE FORM BLANK ENDORSED COVERING THE GOODS FOR INVOICE AMOUNT PLUS 10 PENCENT AGAINST THE FOLLOWING RISKS: ALL RISKS AND WAR RISKS AS PER OCEAN MARINE CARGO CLAUSES OF THE PICC DATED 01, 01, 1981.

...

SOME MSG FROM S/O:

THE GOODS ARE PACKED IN BAGS OF 0.025MT EACH. AND THE GOODS SHIPPED FROM NINGBO BY YUETKONG-542 (S.S) ON FEB. 08, 2006 WITH TRANSHIPMENT AT HONGKONG.

SHIPPING MARKS: KSSAR
       BEIRUT
  INVOICE NO: AG (29) 88012

2. 根据下面资料制作投保单。

SHIPPING ADVICE

Messrs: MASON METAL INDUSTRY CO., LTD., NO. 13, Wu-chun 2nd, Wu-ku Ind, Park

Dear Sirs:

Re: Invoice No. EX0362T/2   L/C No. LC0440-8657

We hereby inform you that the goods under the above mentioned credit have been shipped. The details of the shipment are as follows:

 Commodity: Hot Rolled Steel Sheet In Coil

 Quantity: 20 PALLETS

 Amount: USD20 669.65

 Bill of Lading No.: YMLUI206070704

 Ocean Vessel: WING CHEONG V. WN095

 Port of Loading: TAIWAN

 Port of Destination: SHANGHAI, CHINA

 Date of Shipment: MAR. 30, 2005

COVERING ALL RISKS AND WAR RISK AS PER OCEAN MARINE CARGO CLAUSES OF THE PICC DATED 01,01,1981.

We hereby certify that the above content is true and correct.

SUZHOU LIYAN MACHINERY CO., LTD., South block, Digangang, Tanshu, Changxi Rd., SUZHOU, JIANGSU, P.R.C.

7.3 保险单

保险单（Insurance Policy/Certificate）是保险人（承保人）与被保险人（投保人或要保人）之间订立的保险合同的凭证，它既反映保险人与被保险人之间的权利和义务关系，又是承保证明。不同保险公司出具保险单据内容大同小异，多以英国劳合社船货保险单（S.G. Policy）为蓝本。

7.3.1 保险单填制的一般规范

1. 保险合同的当事人

保险合同的当事人包括保险人、被保险人、保险经纪人、保险代理人、勘验人、赔付代理人等。

被保险人（Insured）即保险单的抬头，正常情况下应是信用证的受益人，但如信用证规定保单为 To order of ×××bank 或 In favor of ×××bank，应填写"受益人名称+held to order of ×××bank 或 in favor of ×××bank"；如信用证要求所有单据以××为抬头人，保单中应照录；如信用证要求中性抬头（third party 或 in neutral form），填写"To whom it may concern"；如要求保单"made out to order and endorsed in blank,填写"受益人名称+to order"；信用证对保单无特殊规定或只要求"endorsed in blank"或"in assignable/negotiable form"，填受益人名称。

中外保险公司都可以以自己名义签发保单并成为保险人，其代理人是保险经纪人；保险代理人代表货主；勘验人一般是进口地对货物损失进行查勘之人；赔付代理人指单据上载明的在目的地可以受理索赔的指定机构，应详细注明其地址和联系办法。

2. 保险货物项目

唛头、包装及数量等保险货物项目（Description Of Goods）应与提单保持一致。标记（MARKS&NO.S）：按信用证规定，应与发票、提单相一致，可单独填写，也可填"AS PER INV. NO. ***"。包装及数量：如以单位包装件数计价者，可只填总件数，若为散装货，则应注明"IN BULK"，再填重量。保险物资项目：根据投保单填写，要与提单一致。

3. 保险金额

保险金额（Amount Insured）是所保险的货物发生损失时保险公司给予的最高赔偿限额，一般按 CIF/CIP 发票金额的 110%投保，加成如超出 10%，超过部分的保险费由买方承担可以办理，信用证项下的保单必须符合信用证规定，如发票价包含佣金和折扣，应先扣除折扣再加成投保，被保险人不可能获得超过实际损失的赔付，保险金额的大小写应一致，保额尾数通常要"进位取整"或"进一取整"，即不管小数部分数字是多少，一律舍去并在整数部分加"1"。信用证支付方式下，严格按信用证规定。大小写要一致，币种要用英文全称。币制应与信用证规定相符。

4. 保费和费率

通常事先印就"As Arranged"（按约定）字样，除非信用证另有规定，保费（Premium）和费率（Rate）在保单上可以不具体显示。如"INSURANCE POLICY ENDORSED IN BLANK FULL INVOICE VALUE PLUS 10% MARKED PREMIUM PAID"时，此栏就填入"PAID"或把已印好的"AS ARRANGED"删去加盖校对章后打上"PAID"字样。

保险费通常占货价的比例为1%～3%，险别不同，费率不一（水渍险的费率约相当于一切险的1/2，平安险约相当于一切险1/3；保一切险，欧美等发达国家费率可能是0.5%，亚洲国家是1.5%，非洲国家则会高达3%以上）。

5. 运输方面的要求

开航日期（Date Of Commencement）通常填提单上的装运日，也可填写提单签发日前5天内的任一日期，也可填"As Per B/L"或"As per Transportation Documents"；起运地、目的地、装载工具（Per Conveyance）的填写与提单上的操作相同。转运时，填"一程船/二程船"，可填 AS PER B/L；陆运填 BY RAILWAY 或 BY TRAIN：WAGON NO. ***；空运填 BY AIR；邮包运输填 BY PARCEL POST。

当信用证中未明确列明具体的起运港口和目的地港口时，如 ANY CHINESE PORT 或 ANY JAPANESE PORT，填制时一般应根据货物实际装运选定一个具体的港口，如 SHANGHAI 或 OSAKA 等。

6. 承保险别

承保险别（Conditions）是保险单的核心内容，填写时应与信用证规定的条款、险别等要求严格一致，如 AS PER ICC（A），1982.1.1，COVERING ALL RISKS AS PER OCEAN MARINE CARGO CLAUSES（1981.1.1）OF THE PICC。在信用证无规定或只规定"Marine/Fire/Loss Risk"、"Usual Risk"或"Transport Risk"等，可根据所买卖货物、交易双方、运输路线等情况投保 All Risks、WA 或 WPA、FPA 三种基本险中的任何一种；如信用证中规定使用中国保险条款（CIC）、伦敦保险协会货物条款（ICC）或美国协会货物条款（AICC），应按信用证规定投保、填制，所投保的险别除明确险别名称外，还应注明险别适用的文本及日期；某些货物的保单上可能出现 IOP（不考虑损失程度/无免赔率）的规定；目前许多合同或信用证都要求在基本险的基础上加保 War Risks 和 SRCC（罢工、暴动、民变险）等附加险；集装箱或甲板货的保单上可能会显示 JWOB（抛弃、浪击落海）险；货物运往偷盗现象严重的地区/港口的保单上频现 TPND（偷窃、提货不着险）。

在实际操作中，一般是由出口公司在制单时，先在副本上填写这一栏的内容，当全部保险单填好交给保险公司审核确认时，才由保险公司把承保险别的详细内容加注在正本保单上。例如，来证要求"INSURANCE POLICY COVERING THE FOLLOWING RISKS：ALL RISKS AND WAR RISK AS PER CHINA INSURANCE CLAUSE

(C.I.C)",则制单时应打上"ALL RISKS AND WAR RISK AS PER CHINA INSURANCE CLAUSE (C.I.C)"。

7. 赔付地点

赔付地点（Claim Payable At/In）栏应严格按照信用证或合同规定填制地点和币种两项内容，地点按信用证或投保单，币种应与保险金额一致。

如来证未具体规定，一般将目的地作为赔付地点，将目的地名称填入这一栏目，赔款货币为投保险金额相同的货币。如信用证规定不止一个目的港或赔付地，则应全部照打。如来证要求"INSURANCE CLAIMS PAYABLE AT A THIRD COUNTRY CHINA"。此时，应把第三国"CHINA"填入此栏。

8. 日期

日期（Date）指保单的签发日期。由于保险公司提供仓至仓（W/W）服务，所以出口方应在货物离开本国仓库前办结手续，保单的出单时间应是货物离开出口方仓库前的日期或船舶开航前或运输工具开行前。除另有规定，保单的签发日期必须在运输单据的签发日期之前。

9. 签章

签章（Authorized Signature）是指由保险公司签字或盖章以示保险单正式生效。单据的签发人必须是保险公司/承保人或他们的代理人，在保险经纪人的信笺上出具的保险单据，只要该保险单据是由保险公司或其代理人，或由承保人或其代理人签署的可以接受；UCP规定除非信用证有特别授权，否则银行不接受由保险经纪人签发的暂保单。实际操作中其签章一般已经印刷在保险单上。

10. 保单的背书

一般保险单据的背书有两种，即空白背书和记名背书。

空白背书的具体做法是在保险单据背面打上被保险人公司的名称或盖上公司图章，再加上背书人签字，此外不再作任何批注。如信用证规定"ENDORSED IN BLANK"或"BLANK ENDORSED"就需这样做。如果信用证对保险单据的背书无明确规定，也应做成空白背书。保险单据做成空白背书意味着被保险人或任何保单持有人在被保货物出险后享有向保险公司或其代理人索赔的权利并得到合理的补偿。

记名背书的具体做法除了在保险单据背面做成上述"空白背书"外，还应在被保险人的名称上面打印上"DELIVERY TO (THE ORDER OF)××BANK (Co.,)"，即[交由××银行（或公司）的（指示）]。记名背书必须以银行或公司为背书人，记名背书大都给开证行。记名背书在日常业务中较少使用。保险单据做成记名背书意味着保险单据的受让人在被保货物出险后享有向保险公司或其代理人索赔的权利。保险单据的被保险人，如果不是我国出口公司，而是其他国家或地区的"××Co.，LTD"，我国出口公司不用背书。如被保险人需转让海运提单，保险单据上则由其他国家或地区的"××Co.，LTD."背书。必须注意，如果保险单据的被保险人是托运人即我国外贸进出口公司或企业，根据信用证的不同规定，有时可做成空白背书，有时也可做成记名背书。

11. 保单的份数

当信用证没有特别说明保单份数时，出口公司一般提交一套完整的保险单，如有具体份数要求，应按规定提交，注意提交单据的正本（Original）、副本（Copy）不同要求。

12. 保单的其他规定

号码（Policy Number）由保险公司编制，投保及索赔币种以信用证规定为准，投保地点一般为装运港/地的名称，如信用证或合同对保单有特殊要求也应在单据的适当位置加以明确。

7.3.2 缮制保险单注意事项

在实践操作中，缮制保险单时应注意以下几点。

（1）出口公司在取得保险公司出具的保单后，凡以出口方为投保人的保险单均需背书，以利转让。

（2）保单内容必须与信用证要求及商业发票、提单等相互核对一致，严格做到单、单一致，单、证一致。

（3）超过合同所规定的附加险或超额险加成时，须事先与保险公司联系是否能办到，否则必须改证或由开证人本人负担。

（4）信用证应规定所需投保险别的种类，以及必要的附加险别。诸如"通常险别"、"惯常险别"一类意义不明确的条文不应使用。如使用此类条文，银行当按照所提示的保险单据予以接受，并对未经投保的任何险种不予负责。除非信用证另有规定，银行将接受证明受免赔率或免赔额约束的保险单据。

（5）关于投保一切险。当信用证规定投保一切险时，银行将接受含有任何一切险批注或条文的保险单据，不论其有无一切险标题，甚至表明不包括某种险别。银行对未经投保的任何险别不予负责。

【相关单证】

单证 7-2　保险单

中国人民保险公司
THE PEOPLE'S INSURANCE COMPANY OF CHINA
总公司设于北京　　一九四九年创立
Head office：BEIJING　Established in 1949
第一正本　　　　保　险　单　　　　保险单号次：
THE FIRST ORIGINAL　　INSURANCE POLICY　　POLICY NO.
中国人民保险公司（以下简称本公司）
THIS POLICY OF INSURANCE WITNESSES THAT THE PEOPLE'S INSURANCE COMPANY OF CHINA（HEREINAFTER CALLED "THE COMPANY"）
根据
AT THE REQUEST OF ＿＿＿＿＿＿＿＿＿＿＿＿＿＿＿1）＿＿＿＿＿＿＿＿＿＿＿＿＿＿＿
（以下简称被保险人）的要求，由被保险人向本公司缴付约
(HEREINAFTER CALLED "THE INSURED") AND IN CONSIDERATION OF THE AGREED PREMIUM PAID TO THE COMPANY BY THE COMPANDY BY
定的保险，按照本保险单承保险别和背面所载条款与下列

THE INSURED UNDERTAKES TO INSURE THE UNDERMENTIONED GOODS IN TRANSPORTATION SUBJECT TO THE CONDITIONS OF THIS
特款承保下述货物运输保险，特立本保险单
POLICY AS PER THE CLAUSES PRINTER OVERLEAF AND OTHER SPECIAL CLAUSES ATTACHED HEREON

标记 MARKS NOS	包装及数量 QUANTITY	保险货物项目 DESCRIPTION OF GOODS	保险金额 AMOUNT INSURED
2)	3)	4)	5)

总保险金额
TOTAL AMOUNT INSURED：_____ 6) _____
保费　7)　　　　　　　费率　　　　　　8) 装载运输工具
PREMIUM AS ARRANGED　RATE AS ARRANGED　PER CONVEYANCE SS. _____
_____ 9) _____
开航日期　10)　　　　　　　　　自　　　　　至
SLG. ON OR ABT.　FROM ____ 11) ___ TO ____ 12) ____
承保险别：
CONDITION

13)

所保货物，如遇出险，本公司凭本保险单及其他有关证件给付赔款。
CLAIMS, IF ANY, PAYABLE ON SURRENDER OF THE POLICY TOGETHER WITH OTHER RELEVANT DOCUMENTS
所保货物，如发生本保险单项下负责赔偿的损失或事故，
IN THE EVENT OF ACCIDENT WHEREBY LOSS OR DAMAGE MAY RESULT IN A CLAIM UNDER THIS POLICY IMMEDIATE NOTICE
应立即通知本公司下述代理人查勘。
APPLYING FOR SURVEY MUST BE GIVEN TO THE COMPANY'S AGENT AS MENTIONED HEREUNDER：

14)

　　　　　　　　　　　　　　　　中国人民保险公司上海分公司
　　　　　　　　　　　　　　THE PEOPLE'S INSURANCE COMPANY OF CHINA
赔款偿付地点　　　　　　　　　　SHANGHAI BRANCH
CLAIM PAYABLE AT/IN ____ 15) ____
　日期　　　　　　上海　　　_____
DATE　16)　SHANGHAI　　　　　　General Manager
地址：中国上海中山东一路 23 号　TEL：3234305 3217466-44　Telex：33128 PICCS CN.
Address：23 Zhongshan Dong Yi Lu Shanghai，China. Cable：42001 Shanghai

单证 7-3　货物运输保险单

PICC 中国人民保险公司 河北省分公司
THE PEOPLE'S INSURANCE COMPANY OF CHINA, HEBEI BRANCH

总公司设于北京　　一九四九年创立
Head office：BEIJING　Established in 1949

货物运输保险单
CARGO TRANSPORTATION INSURANCE

发票号（Invoice No.）　　　　　　　　　保单号次
合同号（Contract No.）　　　　　　　　Policy No.
信用证号（L/C No.）
被保险人：
Insured：_____

中国人民保险公司（以下简称本公司）根据被保险人的要求，由被保险人向本公司缴付约定的保险费，按照本保险单承保险别和背面所载条款与下列条款承保下述货物运输保险，特立本保险单
THIS POLICY OF INSURANCE WITNESSES THAT THE PEOPLE'S INSURANCE COMPANY OF CHINA (HEREINAFTER CALLED "THE COMPANY") AT THE REQUEST OF THE INSURED AND IN CONSIDER-ATION OF THE AGREED PREMIUM PAID TO THE COMPANY BY THE COMPANDY BY THE INSURED UNDERTAKES TO INSURE THE UNDERMENTIONED GOODS IN TRANSPORTATION SUBJECT TO THE CONDITIONS OF THIS POLICY AS PER THE CLAUSES PRINTER OVERLEAF AND OTHER SPECIAL CLAUSES ATTACHED HEREON

标记 MARKS NOS	包装及数量 QUANTITY	保险货物项目 DESCRIPTION OF GOODS	保险金额 AMOUNT INSURED

总保险金额
TOTAL AMOUNT INSURED：_____

保费　　　　　　　　　　起运日期　　　　　　　　　　　　　　　　装载运输工具
PREMIUM　AS ARRANGED　　DATE OF COMMENCEMENT _____　PER CONVEY-ANCE _____

自　　　　　　　　　经　　　　　　　　　至
FROM _____ VIA _____ TO _____

承保险别：
CONDITION

所保货物，如发生保险单项下可能引起索赔的损失或损坏，应立即通知本公司下述代理人查勘，如有索赔，应向本公司提交保单正本（本保险单共有__份正本）及有关文件，如一份正本已用于索赔，其余正本自动失效。
IN THE EVENT OF LOSS OR DAMAGE WHICH MAY RESULT IN A CLAM UNDER THIS POLICY. IMMEDIATE NOTICE MUST BE GIVEN TO THE COMPANY'S AGENT AS MENTIONED HEREUNDER. CLAIMS IF ANY. ONE OF THE ORIGINAL POLICY WHICH HAS BEEN ISSUED IN __ ORIGINAL(S) TOGETHER WITH THE RELEVENT DOCUMENTS SHALL BE SURRENDERED TO THE COMPANY IF ONE OF THE ORGINAL POLICY HAS BEEN ACCOMPLISHED. THE OTHERS TO BE VOID.

赔款偿付地点
CLAIM PAYABLE AT
签单日期（Issuing Date）
核保人：_____　制单人：_____　经办人：_____　　　_____
　　　　　　　　　　　　　　　　　　　　　　　　　　　　　Authorized Signature

注：此保险单中若干项目未显示，在实务中一般加盖批注章或相应批语用来补充完善相关内容。

【技能实训】

1. 根据以下资料填制保险单。

COMMERCIAL BANK OF CEYLON LIMITED

L/C NO.:	CBCL34,1520
DATE OF ISSUE:	NOV.18,2008
DATE AND PLACE OF EXPIRY:	JAN.18,2008,CHINA
APPLICANT:	RAIN DREANS I/E CORP
	NO.80,MOSQUE ROAD, GORAKANA, MORATUWA SRI LANKA
BENEFICIARY:	GUANGDONG FOREIGH TRADE I/E CORP
	123 TINAGE ROAD. GUANGZHOU/P.R. CHINA
AMOUNT:	USD 30 000.00 (SAY US KOLLARS THIRTY THOUSAND ONLY)
PARTIAL SHIPMENTS:	ALLOWED
TRANSHIPMENT:	ALLOWED
LOADING IN CHAR:	GUANGZHOU PORTS
TRANSPORTATION TO:	COLOMBO PORTS
LATEST DATE OF SHIPMENT:	JAN.3,2008
DESCRIPTION OF GOODS:	ENERGY SAVING LAMP
	1 000PCS. FCL-22 ELECTRIC ADAPTORS 22W/B22 USD 8.00 PER/PCS
	2 000PCS. FCL-32 ELECTRIC ADAPTORS 32W/B22 USD 11.00 PER/PCS
	ACCORDING TO SALES CONTRACT NO. A97-2360
	CIF COLOMBO
SHIPPING MARKS:	RAIN DREANS/A97-2360/COLOMBO
DOCUMENTS REPUIRED:	

1. SIGNED COMMERCIAL INVOICE IN 3-FOLD.

2. FULL SET OF CLEAN ON BOARD OCEAN BILLS OF LADING MADE OUT TO ORDER OUR ORDER MARKED: "FREIGHT PRIPAID". NOTIFY: APPLICANT (AS INDICATED ABOVE) AND SHOUN L/C NO.

3. INSURANCE POLICY/CERTIFICATE, COVERING RISKS AS PER "INSTITUTE CARGO CLAUSES (A)", AND "INSTITUTE WAR CLAUSES (CARGO)" INCLUDING W/W CLAUSE 110PCT OF CIF-VALUE, MARKED: "PREMIUM PAID".

ADDITIONAL CONDITIONS:	IF AN AMENDMENT TO THAT CREDIT IS NOT ACCEPTED BY THE BENEFICIARY THE BENEFICIARY'S SIGNED STATEMENT TO THAT EFFECT IS REQUIRED

相关资料如表7-2所示。

表 7-2 填制保险单的相关资料

发票号码	CD-88987	发票日期	DEC. 10th, 2008
保单号码	FC97-3491	产地证号码	GZ3/2234/298876
提单号码	GFT23556	提单日期	DEC. 28th, 2008
装箱情况	10PCS/CTN	集装箱号码	XULU1029975（20'）
单位尺码	(20*20*30) CM/CTN	船名	DIANG FENG V032

2. 根据以下资料填制保险单。

SALES CONFIRMATION

卖方 Jiangsu Easter Import and Export Corporation　　　　NO.：04DGU208
Seller：40 Mochou Road　　　　　　　　　　　　　　　　**DATE**：April 1, 2004
　　　　Nanjing China

买方 J. L. Colebrook (Division of G-X Apparel Group Limited)
Buyer：345 West 37th Street, New York
　　　　N. Y. 10018 U. S. A.

经买卖双方同意成交下列商品，订立条款如下：
This contract is made by and agreed between the BUYER and SELLER, in accordance with the terms and conditions stipulated below：

唛头 Marks and Numbers	名称及规格 Description of goods	数量 Quantity	单价 Unit Price	金额 Amount
	MENS NELON DOWN JACKETS HS NO. 6201.9310	11 900PCS	CIF NEW YORK	USD247 677.00
	JHK-001 J7612NY SHIPPED DURING APR 2004	1 800PCS	USD21.68	USD39 024.00
	JHK-003 J7514NY SHIPPED DURING MAY 2004	5 600PCS	USD19.38	USD108 528.00
	JHK-004 J7612NY SHIPPED DURING JUN 2004	4 500PCS	USD22.25	USD100 125.00

总值 TOTAL：USD247 677.00

Insurance（保险）：
COVERING ALL RISKS AND WAR RISK FOR 110% INVOICE VALUE SUBJECT TO THE RELEVANT OCEAN MARINE CARGO CLAUSES OF P. I. C. C. (DATED1/1/1981).

Payment（付款方式）：

By 100% irrevocable L/C available by 60 days sight draft, reaching the sellers 10 days before the month of shipment, remaining valid for negotiation in china for further 10 days after the prescribed time of shipment, transshipment not allowed & partial shipments allowed.

SHIPMENT：Before 20040630
PORT OF LOADING：CHINA
DESTINATION：New York

Force Majeure(人力不可抗拒):
如因人力不可抗拒的原因造成本合同全部或部分不能履约,卖方概不负责,但卖方应将上述发生的情况及时通知买方。

The sellers shall not hold any responsibility for partial or total non-performance of this contract due to Force Majeure. But the sellers advise the buyers on time of such occurrence.

Disputes settlement(争议之解决方式):
凡因执行本合约或有关本合约所发生的一切争执,双方应协商解决。如果协商不能得到解决,应提交仲裁。仲裁地点在被告方所在国内,或者在双方同意的第三国。仲裁裁决是终局的,对双方都有约束力,仲裁费用由败诉方承担。

All disputes in connection with this contract of the execution thereof shall be amicably settled through negotiation. In case no amicable settlement can be reached between the two parties, the case under dispute shall be submitted to arbitration, which shall be held in the country where the defendant resides, or in third country agreed by both parties. The decision of the arbitration shall be accepted as final and binding upon both parties. The Arbitration Fees shall be borne by the losing party.

Law application(法律适用):
本合同之签订地,或发生争议时货物所在地在中华人民共和国境内或被诉人为中国法人的,适用中华人民共和国法律,除此规定外,适用《联合国国际货物销售公约》。

It will be governed by the law of the People's Republic of China under the circumstances that the contract is signed or the goods while the disputes arising are in the People's Republic of China or the defendant is Chinese legal person, otherwise it is governed by Untied Nations Convention on Contract for the International Sale of Goods.

The Buyer   **The Seller**

第 8 章

【本章导读】
原产地证书
一般原产地证书
普惠制原产地证书

【学习目标和要点】
本章主要介绍一般原产地证书和普惠制原产地证书的主要内容。通过本章的学习，学生应了解原产地证书的分类以及签证程序，掌握一般原产地证书和普惠制原产地证书的缮制。

原产地证书

8.1 原产地证书

原产地证书（Certificate of Origin）是一种证明货物的原产地或制造地的文件，是商品进入国际贸易领域的"经济国籍"。原产地证书的主要作用在于证明货物的原产国，从而根据国别的不同实行差别关税、实行数量限制（如配额、许可证等）或者其他进口管制政策。该文件具有法律效力，也是通关、结汇、进行贸易统计的重要证明文件。

8.1.1 原产地证书的种类

按照签发原产地证书的机构不同、使用范围不同、证书格式不同，原产地证书主要有以下几种。

1. 一般原产地证书

一般原产地证书（Certificate of Origin）又称普通原产地证书，是证明货物原产于某一特定国家或地区的文件，是国际贸易中使用最多的一种。在我国，系指中华人民共和国原产地证书（Certificate of Origin of the People's Republic of China），简称"产地证（C.O.）"，由中国国际贸易促进委员会（民间签证机构，以下简称"中国贸促会"）和国家质量监督检验检疫总局（官方签证机构，以下简称"国家质检总局"）出具。两种证书的格式、内容、项目完全一样，只是签发单位名称和签章不同。签发的依据是：经国务院常务会议通过的《中华人民共和国出口货物原产地规则》及原对外经济贸易部制定的《中华人民共和国出口货物原产地规则实施办法》。提供哪一种证书，应该依据合同和信用证的规定，如果合同或信用证规定产地证由商业公会等民间机构提供，则一般由中国贸促会出具产地证；如果要求由商检机构提供，一般由国家质检总局出具产地证。如果信用证不明确证书由谁出具，银行应该接受任何一种证书。习惯上如果信用证未明确出具单位，一般由商检机构出具原产地证书。

2. 普惠制原产地证书格式 A

普惠制原产地证书格式 A（Generalized System of Perferences/Certificate of Origin Form A, GSP FORM A），全称是《普遍优惠制原产地证明书（申报与证明联合）格式A》，以下简称"格式A证书"，是受惠国的原产品出口到给惠国时，产品享受普惠制关税减免待遇时官方凭证。格式A证书相当于一种有价证券，因而联合国贸易和发展会议优惠特别委员会规定，仅证书的正本有效，证书只能使用英文或法文填制。

格式A证书由受惠国的出口商填制并申报，受惠国签证机构审核、证明及签发。签证机构还负责对已签证书的事后查询工作，答复给惠国对已签证书的查询。签证机构必须是受惠国政府指定的，其名称、地址、印模都要在给惠国注册登记，向联合国贸易和发展会议秘书处备案。在我国，国家质检总局及所属机构是签发普惠制产地证的唯一机构。

3. 区域优惠原产地证书

区域优惠原产地证书是订有区域性贸易协定的经济集团内的国家享受互惠的、减免关税的官方凭证，如曼谷协定产地证、英联邦特惠税产地证等。

在我国，目前主要有《〈中国—东盟自由贸易区〉优惠原产地证明书》（FORM E）、

《〈亚太贸易协定〉原产地证明书》(FORM B)、《〈中国与巴基斯坦自由贸易区〉优惠原产地证明书》(FORM P)、《〈中国—智利自由贸易区〉原产地证书》(FORM F)等。

4. 专用原产地证书

专用原产地证书是国际组织和国家根据政策与贸易措施的特殊需要，针对某一特殊行业的特定产品规定的原产地证书，主要有输往欧盟蘑菇罐头原产地证明书、烟草真实性证书等。

8.1.2 原产地证书的签证程序

1. 一般原产地证书签证程序

1) 注册登记与审核

申请单位必须向签证机构办理注册登记手续，经签证机构审核合格后，享有申办原产地证书的资格。申请单位向签证机构办理注册登记手续时，应当提交下列文件。

(1)《中华人民共和国非优惠原产地证书注册登记申请表》。

(2) 由工商行政管理部门颁发的当年有效的或经年审的营业执照副本复印件一份。

(3)《对外贸易经营者备案登记表》或《中华人民共和国进出口企业资格证书》；外商投资企业应当同时提供《中华人民共和国外商投资企业批准证书》。

(4)《组织机构代码证》有效复印件。

(5)《原产地证书申领员及手签人员授权书》。

(6)《原产地证书申领员证》。

(7) 签证机构要求的其他相关资料。

申请单位注册手签人员、申领员的授权人应为企业法人代表，若授权人不是企业法人代表，须提供企业法人代表的授权书。手签人员和申领员可以是同一人，也可以是不同人。每一个申请企业允许授权三名手签人员和三名申领员。

经注册登记的企业，须按签证机构的要求建立出口货物进料、生产、出货记录。对注册登记的企业及产品，签证机构将派专人到企业进行实地核查。签证机构有权对出口货物实行随机抽查。

2) 原产地证书的申领与签发

企业经注册登记后，其授权及委派的手签人员和申领员应接受签证机构的业务培训。申请原产地证书应当由指定的原产地证书申领员办理。申领员应当取得《原产地证书申领员证》，凭证申报。持证人因故不能办证时，企业可指定其他人员凭单位证明申办原产地证。申领员证不得转借、涂改，也不得用此证代替他人领取证书。若有遗失，应立即向发证机关申明，并凭单位证明申请补办。

企业最迟于货物报关出运前三天向签证机构申请办理原产地证书，并按签证机构要求，提交以下材料。

(1)《中华人民共和国出口货物原产地证明书/加工装配证明书申请书》一份。

(2)《中华人民共和国出口货物原产地证明书》一式四份。

(3) 出口货物商业发票。

(4) 其他证明文件。

签证机构对上述材料审核无误后，签发原产地证书。签证机构通常不接受货物出运后才递交的原产地证书申请，但特殊情况除外。

2. 普惠制原产地证书签证程序

普惠制原产地证书签证手续按《中华人民共和国普遍优惠制原产地证明书签证管理办法》办理。

1) 注册登记

凡申请办理普惠制原产地证书的单位，必须预先在当地商检机构办理注册登记手续。办理注册登记时，必须提供以下资料。

（1）政府主管部门授予申请单位进出口经营权的文件或证书，根据企业性质不同分为《中华人民共和国进出口企业资格证书》、《对外贸易经营者备案登记表》、《中华人民共和国外商投资企业批准证书》或《中华人民共和国台港澳侨投资企业批准证书》。

（2）企业工商营业执照。

（3）《申请签发普惠制原产地证明书（FORM A）注册登记表》。

（4）其他证明文件。

从事来料加工、来件装配及补偿贸易的单位还得提交承办对外加工装配业务或补偿贸易的协议，合同副本及本批产品成本明细单等有关文件。

商检机构对申请单位提交的表格和资料进行严格审查，并派员深入调查。经审查合格的，准予注册，发给《普惠制原产地证明书注册登记证》。

已经注册的企业、工厂必须建立完整的进料记录、生产记录和出货记录。其中，出货记录必须记载出口产品的品名、规格、数量、重量、包装、标记唛头、出厂价格、出运日期和进口国别等内容。上述记录和资料应保存两年以上，供商检机构及给惠国海关复查。

申请单位的印章和证书手签人员必须在注册的同时进行登记。手签人员应是申请单位法人代表（或法人代表授权的人员）并应保持相对稳定，如有变动，应及时向原登记机构申报。

2) 申请出证

申请单位在本批货物出运前 5 日到商检机构办理申请事宜。申请时一般提交以下资料。

（1）普惠制原产地证书申请书一份。

（2）缮制正确、清楚，并经申请单位手签和加盖公章的普惠制原产地证书格式 A 一式三份。

（3）出口商品商业发票副本一份。

（4）含有进口成分的产品，还得提交《含进口成分商品成本明细单》一式三份。

（5）复出口去日本的来料加工产品以及以进养出商品，还应提交缮制清楚的、经申请单位手签并加盖公章的《从日本进口原材料的证明》（CERTIFICATE OF MATERIALS IMPORTED FROM JAPAN）一式两份，及来料（或进料）发票副本和装箱单。

（6）其他被认为有必要提供的相关单证（如信用证、合同、报关单等）。

3）签发证书

出入境检验检疫机构接受申请后，认真审核证书各栏内容，必要时派人去生产厂核查，经查无误的，即予签发。

4）申请更改、后发

普惠制原产地证书经签发后，申请人如需要更改证书内容的，必须征得原签证机构的同意，全数退回原证书，填写更改单，提交更改凭证和重新缮制的普惠制原产地证书一式三份，经审核后予以重新签发。

特殊情况下，货物出运时未申请签发普惠制原产地证书，出运后外商又要求格式A证书时，申请单位可办理申请后发手续，但必须向出入境检验检疫机构提交货物确已出运的证明文件，经审核同意后，方能予以签发，并加盖"后发"印章。

8.2 一般原产地证书

在我国出口业务中采用一般原产地证书（Certificate of Origin of the People's Republic of China），证明出口货物的原产地是中华人民共和国，而且符合《中华人民共和国货物原产地规则》，该文件是进口国海关对该进口货物按何种税率征收进口税的依据。一般原产地证书的填写方法如下。

1. Certificate No. （证书编号）

证书编号位于证书右上方，由签证机构指定的号码编制。此栏不得留空，否则，证书无效。

2. Exporter (full name and address) （出口商名称、地址、国家）

本栏填写出口公司的详细地址和名称，一般包括企业全称、详细地址和国家名称。信用证业务一般为受益人，托收业务为托收人。此栏出口商公司名称应与注册时相同。若经其他国家或地区需填写转口商名称时，可在出口商后面加填英文 VIA 或 ON BEHALF OF，然后再填写转口商名称、地址、国家。举例如下。

ZHEJIANG NATIVE PRODUCE & ANIMAL BY - PRODUCTS I/E CORP.
NO. 368 NORTH ZHONGSHAN ROAD, HANGZHOU, CHINA.
VIA HONGKONG DAMING CO. LTD NO. 656, GUANGDONG ROAD, HONGKONG.

3. Consignee (full name and address) （收货人名称、地址、国家）

本栏应填写最终收货方的名称、详细地址及国家（地区）；通常是外贸合同中的买方或信用证上规定的提单通知人。但往往由于贸易的需要，信用证规定所有单证收货人一栏留空，在这种情况下，此栏加注"To Whom It May Concern"或"To Order"，但不得留空。如果需要转运，可在收货人后面加填英文 VIA，然后再填写转口商名称、地址、国家。

4. Means of Transport and Route （运输方式和路线）

本栏填报装运港、目的港、中转港的名称，并说明运输方式和运输路线，应注明起运地、目的地以及运输方式等内容。如经转运，应注明转运地。例如：FROM SHANGHAI TO HONGKONG ON APR. 6, 2005, THENCE TRANSHIPPED TO

ROTTERDAM BY VESSEL 或 FROM SHANGHAI TO ROTTERDAM BY VESSEL VIA HONGKONG.

5. Country/Region of Destination（目的地或最终目的国）

本栏填写货物最终到达的国家或地区。一般应与最终收货人或最终目的港国别一致，也可以将目的地和国名同时列出，但不得填写中间商客商国别。例如，New York USA。

6. For certify authority use only（供签证机构使用）

此栏为签证机构在签发后发证书、重发证书或加注其他声明时使用。正常情况时，此栏空白。如果是"后发"，加盖"ISSUED RETROSPECTIVELY"的红色印章。应当注意日本一般不接受"后发证书"。

7. Marks and Numbers（唛头和包装号）

本栏填写唛头和包装号。应按照出口发票上所列唛头填写完整图案、文字标记及包装号码，不可简单地填写"AS PER INVOICE NO...."（按照发票）或者"AS PER B/L NO...."（按照提单）。包装无唛头，应填写"N/M"或者"NO MARK"。此栏不得留空。如唛头多本栏填写不开，可填写在第7～9栏的空白处。如还不够，可用附页填写（附页的纸张要与原证书一样大小），在右上角打上证书号，并由申请单位和签证当局授权签字人分别在附页末页的左下角和右下角手签、盖印。附页手签的笔迹、地点、日期均与证书第11、12栏相一致。

注意：有附页时，请在申请书备注栏注明"唛头见附页 SEE ATTACHED SHEETS"，否则计算机退回。

8. Number and kind of packages description of goods（商品名称、包装数量及种类）

商品名称要填写具体名称，如睡袋（SLEEPING BAGS）、杯子（CUPS），不得用概括性表述。包装数量及种类要按具体单位填写，例如，100 箱彩电，填写为"100 CARTONS (ONE HUNDRED CARTONS ONLY) OF COLOR TV SET"。在阿拉伯数字后加注英文表述，如货物系散装，在商品名称后加注"散装"（IN BULK），例如，1 000 公吨生铁，填写为"1 000 M/T (ONE THOUSAND M/T ONLY) PIGIRON IN BULK"。有时信用证要求在所有单证上加注合同号、信用证号码等，可加在此栏。本栏的末行要打上表示结束的符号"*******"，以防添加内容。

9. H. S. Code（商品编码）

该栏应按照商品在《商品名称和编码协调制度》（Harmonized Commodity Description & Coding System）中的编码填写，应该与报关单中的商品编码一致。若同一份证书包含有几种商品，则应将相应的 H. S. 品目号全部填写。此栏不得留空。有时候此栏填报10位商品编号，其中最后两位为补充号；填报的商品编号，必须与实际货名一致，并与报关单中显示的 H. S. CODE 一致。

10. Quantity or Weight（数量或重量）

应按提单或其他运输单据中的有关毛重、数量等正常计量单位填写。一般填写出口货物的数量并与商品计量单位联用。如果计量单位为重量，应该以千克为单位，同时标明毛重和净重。例如，"G. W. 400 kg"或"N. W. 390 kg"。

11. Number and Date of Invoice（发票号码和日期）

应按照申请出口货物的商业发票填写。此栏日期应早于或同于实际出口日期，为避免对月份、日期的误解，月份一律用英文表述，此栏不得留空。

12. Declaration by the Exporter（出口商声明）

本栏必须由申领单位已在签证机构注册的人员签字并加盖有中英文的印章，并填写申领地点和日期。该日期不能早于发票的签发日期，一般与发票的日期相同；同时不能迟于装运日期和第13栏签证机关的签发日期。

13. Certification（签证机关证明）

由签证机构签字、盖章，签字和盖章不得重合，并填写签证地点、日期。签发日期不得早于发票日期（第11栏）和申请日期（第12栏）。

凡进口方要求由我官方机构签发一般原产地证的，申请单位应向国家质检总局出入境检验检疫局申请办理；凡进口方要求由我民间机构签发一般原产地证的，申请单位应向中国贸促会申请；未明确要求的，可向国家质检总局出入境检验检疫局或中国贸促会申请。

8.3 普惠制原产地证书

普惠制原产地证书主要书面格式为 GSP FORM A。在我国普惠制原产地证书由出口人填写后连同普惠制原产地证申请书和商业发票等单据资料一起送交国家质检总局出入境检验检疫局签发。GSP FORM A 的填写方法如下。

1. Reference No.（编号）

证书编号位于证书右上方，填写出入境检验检疫局指定的编号。此栏不得留空，否则，证书无效。

2. Issued in...（签发国别）

本栏位于证书名称栏下方，填上"THE PEOPLE'S REPUBLIC OF CHINA"，一般来说，出入境检验检疫局在印刷证书时已印妥。

3. Goods consigned from (Exporter's business name, address, country)（出口商名称、地址、国家）

本栏出口商公司名称应与注册时相同。必须打上国名、地址。

例如，ZHEJIANG NATIVE PRODUCE & ANIMAL BY-PRODUCTS I/E CORP. NO. 368 NORTH ZHONGSHAN ROAD, HANGZHOU, CHINA.

4. Goods consigned to (Consignee's name, address, country)（收货人名称、地址、国家）

本栏填写给惠国最终收货人名称和地址。一般可以为信用证的开证申请人，如果不明确最终的收货人，则可以填写提单通知人或发票抬头人。当然，也可以采用"To Whom It May Concern"表达方法。

除欧盟25国、挪威外，此栏须填上给惠国最终收货人名称，不可填中间转口商的名称，此栏须打上国名，欧盟25国、挪威对此栏是非强制性要求，若第2栏进口商国家和第12栏最终目的国都是欧盟国家，则可以与第12栏国家不同，也可以不填详细地址，只填上 To Order 或留空。

5. Means of Transport and Route（as far as known）（运输方式和路线，就所知而言）

本栏填报装运港、目的港、中转港的名称，并说明运输方式和运输路线，应注明起运地、目的地以及运输方式等内容。转运商品应加上转运港，如 FROM SHANGHAI TO HAMBURG BY SEA VIA HONGKONG。对输往内陆给惠国的商品，如瑞士、奥地利，由于这些国家没有海岸，因此如系海运，都须经第三国，再转运至该国，填证时应注明，例如，BY VESSEL FROM SHANGHAI TO HAMBURG, IN TRANSIT TO SWITZERLAND。

6. For Official use（供签证方使用）

本栏供签证当局（出入境检验检疫局）填写。正常情况时，此栏空白。如果是"后发"，加盖"ISSUED RETROSPECTIVELY"的红色印章。应当注意日本一般不接受"后发证书"。如是证书遗失、被盗或者损毁，签发"复本"证书时盖上"DUPLICATE"红色印章，并在此栏注明原证书的编号和签证日期，并声明原发证书作废，其文字是"THIS CERTIFICATE IS IN REPLACEMENT OF CERTIFICATE OF ORIGIN NO. . . . DATED. . . WHICH IS CANCELLED"。

7. Item Number（项目号）

如果同一批出口货物有不同种类商品品种，则按不同品种分列"1"、"2"、"3"…以此类推。单项商品，此栏填"1"。

8. Marks and Numbers（唛头和包装号）

本栏填写与一般原产地证书基本一致。

9. Number and kind of packages description of goods（商品名称、包装数量及种类）

本栏填写与一般原产地证书基本一致，但是需要注意以下几点。

（1）如果包件数量上了千以上，则千与百单位之间不能有"AND"连词，否则计算机退回。应填：TWO THOUSAND ONE HUNDRED AND FIFTY（2 150）CARTONS OF WORDING GLOVES。

（2）数量、品名要求在一页内打完，如果内容过长，请先在证书第七栏打上"总箱数和总品名"并打上"DETAILS SEE ATTACHED SHEETS"，附页做法可参照"唛头附页"。例如，ONE HUNDRED AND FIFTY（150）CARTONS OF SMALL COMMODITY（DETAILS SEE ATTACHED SHEETS）。

（3）包装必须打具体的包装种类，如 POLYWOVEN BAG, DRUM, PALLET, WOODEN CASE 等，不能只填写"PACKAGE"。如果没有包装，应填写"NUDE CARGO"（裸装货），"IN BULK"（散装货），"HANGING GARMENTS"（挂装）。

（4）商品名称必须具体填明（具体到能找到相对应的 4 位 H. S. 编码），不能笼统填"MACHINE"（机器）、"GARMENT"（服装）等。对一些商品，如玩具电扇应注明为"TOYS: ELECTRIC FANS"，不能只列"ELECTRIC FANS"（电扇）。

（5）商品的商标、牌名（BRAND）及货号（ARTICLE NUMBER）一般可以不填。商品名称等项列完后，应在下一行加上表示结束的符号，以防止加填伪造内容。国外信用证有时要求填写合同、信用证号码等，可加填在此栏空白处。

当一份 FORM A 的货物不止一种时，第 7~9 栏要做到一一对应。

10. Origin Criterion (See Notes Overleaf)（原产地标准）

该栏应按照普惠制原产地证申请书对货物原料的成分比例的不同填写"P"、"W"、"F"等字母。具体来说填法如下：

（1）不含任何进口成分，出口到所有给惠国，填写"P"。

（2）含有进口成分的产品，出口到欧盟25国、瑞士、挪威和日本，符合有关给惠国的加工标准的，应填写"W"，经过出口国充分加工的产品输往欧盟等国时，在"W"后加注出口产品在海关合作理事会税则目录（Customs Cooperation Council Nomenclature，CCCN）的税目号。例如："W" 62.03。条件如下：①产品列入了上述给惠国的"加工清单"符合其加工条件；②产品未列入"加工清单"，但产品生产过程中使用的非原产原材料和零部件经过充分的加工，产品的 H.S. 品目号不同于所用的原材料和零部件的 H.S. 品目号。

（3）含有进口成分的商品，出口到加拿大，如含有进口成分占产品出厂价的40%以下，使用"F"。

（4）出口到俄罗斯、白俄罗斯、哈萨克斯坦、乌克兰、捷克和斯洛伐克的，进口成分的价值不超过商品离岸价50%的，填"Y"，并在"Y"下方加注该商品进口成分的价值占商品离岸价的百分比，例如"Y" 38%。

（5）出口到澳大利亚、新西兰的产品，此栏可以空白。

11. Gross Weight or other Quantity（毛重或其他数量）

本栏填写与一般原产地证书基本一致。以商品的正常计量单位填，例如"只"、"件"、"双"、"台"、"打"等。例如，3 200 DOZ. 或 6 270 KGS。只有净重的，标净重亦可，但要标上 N.W.（NET WEIGHT）。

12. Number and Date of Invoice（发票号码和日期）

此栏不得留空，填写与一般原产地证书基本一致，发票日期不得迟于出货日期。

13. Certification（签证机关证明）

此栏由签证当局填写机构的名称并由其授权人手签。其一般由以下内容组成：①出入境检验检疫局盖公章，只签一份正本，副本不予签章，如"中华人民共和国上海市出入境检验检疫局"；②出入境检验检疫局授权人或手签人手签；③签证日期不得早于第12栏的发票日期和第14栏的申请日期，也不能晚于提单的装运日期；④签发地点应包括城市名称和国家名称。

14. Declaration by the Exporter（出口商申明）

本栏包括产品原产国、进口国（给惠国）国名、出口公司、出口公司指派的专人签字和申报地点、时间。进口国横线上填最终进口国，进口国必须与第3栏目的港的国别一致。另外，申请单位应授权专人在此栏手签，标上申报地点、日期，如 JINHUA CHINA APR. 6，2005 并加盖申请单位中英文印章。手签人员笔迹必须在检验检疫局注册登记，并保持相对稳定。此栏日期不得早于发票日期（最早是同日）。盖章时应避免覆盖进口国名称和手签人员姓名。本证书一律不得涂改，证书不得加盖校对章。该日期不能早于发票的签发日期，一般与发票的日期相同；同时不能迟于装运日期和第13栏签证机关的签发日期。

【相关单证】

单证 8-1 一般原产地证书

ORIGINAL

2. Exporter (full name and address)	1. CERTIFICATE No.： **CERTIFICATE OF ORIGIN** **OF** **THE PEOPLE'S REPUBLIC OF CHINA**
3. Consignee (full name, address, country)	
4. Means of transport and route	6. For certifying authority use only
5. Country/region of destination	

7. Marks and numbers	8. Number and kind of packages description of goods	9. H. S. Code	10. Quantity or Weight	11. Number and date of invoices

12. Declaration by the exporter The undersigned hereby declares that the above details and statement are correct; that all the goods were produced in China and that they comply with the Rules of Origin of the People's Republic of China.	13. Certification It is hereby certified that the declaration by the exporter is correct.
Place and date, signature and stamp of authorized signatory	Place and date, signature and stamp of certifying authority

单证 8-2　普惠制原产地证书

ORIGINAL

3. Goods consigned from (Exporter's business name, address, country)	1. Reference No.: **GENERALIZED SYSTEM OF PREFERENCES** **CERTIFICATE OF ORIGIN** (Combined declaration and certificate) **FORM A** 2. Issued in <u>THE PEOPLE'S REPUBLIC OF CHINA</u> 　　　　　　　　(country) 　　　　　　　　　　See Notes, overleaf
4. Goods consigned to (Consignee's name, address, country)	
5. Means of transport and route (as far as known)	6. For official use

7. Item number	8. Marks and numbers of packages	9. Number and kind of packages; description of goods	10. Orign criterion (See Notes overleaf)	11. Gross weight or other quantity	12. Number and date of invoices

13. Certification 　　It is hereby certified, on the basis of control carried out, that the declaration by the exporter is correct. ------------------------------- Place and date, signature and stamp of certifying authority	14. Declaration by the exporter 　　The undersigned hereby declares that the above details and statements are correct; that all the goods were produced in ＿＿＿**CHINA**＿＿＿ 　　　　　　　　　　(country) and that they comply with the origin requirements specified for those goods in the Generalized System of Preferences for goods exported to ------------------------------- 　　　　　　(importing country) ------------------------------- Place and date, signature of authorized signatory

【技能实训】

1. 根据以下材料填制一般原产地证书一份。

山西食品进出口有限公司报检登记号为3806000019。公司备好货（H.S 编码为0713.3190）后，将货物运至大连新港保税仓库，并于2008年3月7日原产地证书申领员刘丽在大同申领原产地证书，原产地证书编号为 DTCSF001/050001。发票如表8-1所示。出口装运日期为2008年3月22日。

表8-1 商业发票

山西食品进出口有限公司
SHANXI FOODSTUFFS IMP/EXP CO., LTD
NO. 345 ZHONGSHAN ROAD, TAIYUAN, CHINA
商业发票
COMMERCIAL INVOICE

Messrs:
VICTOR CO., LTD
LONG BEACH, USA

INVOICE NO.: ZW780321
DATE: MAR. 05, 2008
L/C NO: LC7584076584

Exporter:
SHANXI FOODSTUFFS IMP/EXP CO., LTD
NO. 345 ZHONGSHAN ROAD, TAIYUAN, CHINA

PORT OF LOADING: DALIAN CHINA	CONTRACT NO.: GHRU2908
PORT OF DISCHARGE: LONG BEACH USA	VESSEL: STAR RIVER V.092

MARK&NO.	DESCRIPTION OF GOODS	QUANTITY/UNIT	UNIT PRICE	AMOUNT
GHRU2908 SHANXI CHINA	SHANXI GREEN BEANS PACKING: IN BAG ORIGIN: SHANXI CHINA CONTRACT NO: GHRU2908	300BAGS/50KGS EACH PACKAGE	USD400.00/TON	
	USD6 000.00			

SHANXI FOODSTUFFS IMP/EXP CO., LTD
SIGNED BY..............

2. 根据信用证有关内容，缮制普惠制产地证一份。

DOC. CREDIT NUMBER: LRT9802457
DATE OF ISSUE: 20040428
EXPIRY: DATE 20040615 PLACE IN THE COUNTRY OF BENEFICIARY
APPLICANT: ABC. CORPORATION
　　　　　　AKEKSANTERINK AUTOP.O. BOX 9, FINLAND
BENEFICIARY: SHANGHAI IMP AND EXP CORPORATION
　　　　　　27 ZHONGSHAN ROAD, SHANGHAI, CHINA
AMOUNT: USD 30 000.00 (SAY US DOLLARS THIRTY THOUSAND ONLY)
AVAILABLE WITH/BY: ANY BANK IN ADVISING COUNTRY BY NEGOTIATION

DRAFTS AT…:	DRAFTS AT SIGHT FOR FULL INVOICE VALUE		
DRAWEE:	METIT BANK LTD, FINLAND		
PARTIAL SHIPMENTS:	ALLOWED		
TRANSSHIPMENT:	ALLOWED		
LOADING IN CHARGE:	SHANGHAI PORT		
FOR TRANSPORT TO:	TORONTO, CANADA		
LATEST DATE OF SHIP:	20040531		
DESCRIPT. OF GOODS:	ENERGY SAVING LAMP AS PER S/C NO. C972360,		
	1 000 PCS. F-22 USD 8.00 PER PCS.		
	2 000 PCS. F-32 USD 11.00 PER PCS.		
	PACKING: 5 PCS/CTN		
PRICE TERM:	CIF TORONTO (INCOTERMS 2000)		
DOCUMENTS REQUIRED:	1) 3/3 SET OF ORIGINAL CLEAN ON BOARD OCEAN BILLS OF LADING MADE OUT TO ORDER OF US ANDMARKED "FRIGHT PRE-PAID" NOTIFY APPLICANT (WITH FULL NAME AND ADDRESS)		
	2) ORIGINAL SIGNED COMMERCIAL INVOICE IN 5 FOLD		

相关资料如表 8-2 所示。

表 8-2 实训 2 相关资料

发票号码	IV-88987	发票日期	May2, 2004
单位毛重	18KGS/CTN	单位净重	15KGS/CTN
船名	DIANG FENG V032	原材料情况	完全自产品
提单号码	BFL23556	提单日期	May15, 2004

第 9 章

【本章导读】

汇票

发票

包装单据

运输单据

其他单据

【学习目标和要点】

制单结汇是出口业务的一项重要环节,及时、准确地缮制和转交各种单据不仅是卖方的义务,也是其安全收汇的重要保证。通过本章的学习,学生应熟悉在不同结汇方式下,各种结汇单证的制作方法,能准确缮制各种结汇单据并树立风险防范意识,对不能安全结汇的业务能及时采取措施加以补救。

主要结汇单据

在国际贸易中，一般情况下，买卖双方从贸易磋商、签订合同，到一方交货装货、另一方提货缴款，每个环节都有相应的单证需要缮制、交接和传递，以满足有关各方的要求，顺利完成进出口交易。同时，买卖双方也主要是以单证为媒介进行交货付款。在信用证付款的条件下，开证行审核单证与信用证要求完全相符后，才承担付款的责任，如发现任何不符之处，均有拒绝付款的可能，因此，准确、完整地制作各种单据，并及时送交银行，才能确保安全、迅速收汇。

9.1 结汇单据概述

在货物装箱托运以后，出口公司应立即按合同或信用证要求准备好各种单据，在信用证有效期或特定交单期内向出口地银行交单。制单前的主要准备工作是找全"合同"和"信用证"。在信用证付款的条件下，要分析判断信用证对单证的具体要求，并将有关内容一一列表，以便办理单证时查核，防止发生差错和遗漏。

9.1.1 结汇单据制作要领

总体来说，信用证方式下经常要求出口商提交的单据包括汇票、商业发票、包装单据、运输单据、保险单据、产地证明书、检验证书、受益人证明、装船通知副本、船公司证明等。

1. 单据制作要求

（1）正确。其指缮制的单据应单单一致、单证一致、单同一致、单货一致。

（2）完整。其指内容完整、份数上完整、种类的完整。凭单据买卖的合同或信用证都会明确要求出口方需提交哪些单据、提交几份、几份正本、几份副本、单据是否需要背书、由谁背书以及单据应标明的内容。所有这些都必须得到满足，否则就不能构成有效文件，银行将拒绝接受。

（3）及时。其指单据制作不迟延，即及时制单、及时审单、及时交单、及时收汇。

（4）简明。其指单据内容要简明扼要，防止复杂烦琐。

（5）整洁。其指单据的格式设计要标准化和规范化、内容排列主次分明、重点项目醒目突出。不应出现涂抹现象，应尽量避免或减少加签修改。

2. 单据制作的依据

（1）单据应符合相关法律、惯例和规则。国际贸易中所要求的单据都有相应的法律、惯例和规则与之对应，在我国较常见的有《中华人民共和国合同法》、《中华人民共和国票据法》（以下简称《票据法》）、《中华人民共和国对外贸易法》、《中华人民共和国海商法》（以下简称《海商法》）、《中华人民共和国保险法》、《联合国国际货物销售合同公约》以及《UCP600》、《〈跟单信用证统一惯例〉电子交单补充规则》（eUCP）、《关于审核跟单信用证项下单据的国际银行实务》（ISBP）、《托收统一规则》（URC522）、《跟单信用证项下银行间偿付统一规则》（URR525）、《2000年国际贸易术语解释通则》（INCOTERMS2000）等。

（2）单据应以合同、信用证和货物实际情况为准缮制。实践中主要指单单、单证、单同、单货的一致。

(3) 单据制作应满足各行业、部门的特殊要求。

3. 单据制作的时间顺序

各单据日期关系如下：①发票日期应在各单据日期之首；②提单日不能超过信用证规定的装运期，也不得早于信用证的最早装运期；③保险单的签发日应早于或等于提单日期（一般早于提单2天），不能早于发票；④箱单应等于或迟于发票日期，但必须在提单日之前；⑤产地证不早于发票日期，不迟于提单日；⑥商检证书日期不晚于提单日期，但也不能过早于提单日，尤其是鲜货，容易变质的商品；⑦受益人证明等于或晚于提单日；⑧装船通知等于或晚于提单日后三天内；⑨船公司证明等于或早于提单日。

9.1.2　交单注意事项

我国出口结汇主要有汇付（M/T、T/T、D/D）、托收（D/P、D/A）、信用证（L/C）三种方式。在实际业务中可能规定以信用证付款为主，结合汇付或托收方式的综合运用；可能是信用证与汇付的结合或信用证与托收的结合；也可能是信用证、汇付、托收的三结合。

(1) 采用信用证收汇的，出口方应在规定的交单时间内，备齐全部单证，并严格审核，确保没有错误后再交银行议付。

(2) 采用汇付收汇的，出口方在取得提单后应立即传真提单给进口方要求付款，确认收到余款后再将提单正本及其他文件寄给进口方。

(3) 如果汇付收汇的，要求收全款才能做柜的，要等收款后再安排拖柜，拿到提单后可立即寄正本提单给进口方。

9.2　汇票

汇票（DRAFT/BILL OF EXCHANGE）是出票人（DRAWER）签发的，要求受票人（DRAWEE）在见票时或在指定的日期无条件支付一定金额给其指定的受款人（PAYEE）的书面命令。

汇票的当事人一般有三个即出票人、受票人和受款人。出票人即签发汇票的人，在进出口业务中，通常是出口商；受票人即汇票的付款人，在进出口业务中，通常是进口商或其指定的银行。在信用证结算方式下，若信用证没有指定付款人，根据《UCP600》规定，开证行即是付款人；受款人即汇票规定的可受领金额的人，在进出口业务中，若信用证没有特别指定，受款人通常是出口商本人或其指定银行。除此之外，汇票在使用中还可能出现一些非基本当事人，如背书人（ENDORSER）、保证人（GUARANTOR）等。

9.2.1　汇票的使用

汇票是出口商凭以向进口商要求付款的收款工具，也是进口商付款的重要凭证。以票汇（D/D）方式结算货款时，使用的汇票属银行汇票，一般为光票。以托收和信用证方式结算货款时，使用的汇票，通常由出口商向进口商或银行签发，属商业汇票，一般都附有货运单据,为跟单汇票。

汇票属于资金单据,它可以代替货币进行转让或流通。为防止丢失,商业汇票通常一式两份,两份具有同等的法律效力,分别标明 FIRST OF EXCHANGE (1)、SECOND OF EXCHANGE (2),意为"付一不付二"或"付二不付一",即付款人仅凭其中一份付一次款,先到先付,后到无效。

在进出口贸易中,托收方式下必须使用汇票。信用证方式下,除延期付款信用证不需要汇票外,其他情况下都可能使用汇票,凡信用证中有"BY PAYMENT"字样的,则需附带汇票。

9.2.2 汇票的缮制

汇票是一种要式的有价证券,其填制内容应正确无误,且不得涂改,否则无效。汇票没有统一的标准格式,实践中,卖方可向银行购买,也可自行设计,但其项目和内容基本上都应包括汇票名称、出票依据、书面的无条件支付命令、出票地点和日期、汇票编号、汇票的大小写金额、付款期限、受款人、付款人、出票人签字等。不同付款方式下某些汇票内容的填写会略有区别。托收方式下的汇票应依据合同条款编制,信用证支付方式下应根据信用证的要求缮制汇票,方法如下。

1. 出票依据/出票条款(DRAWN UNDER)

信用证项下,出票依据(DRAWN UNDER)填写开证行名称及地址、信用证号码(L/C NO.)、开证日期(DATED)。托收项下,留空不填或者填写"FOR COLLECTION"。

2. 年息(PAYABLE WITH INTEREST@...% PER ANNUAL)

具体由银行填写,留空不填。

3. 出票地点及出票日期(DATE AND PLACE OF ISSUE)

在信用证项下地点为议付地,托收项下为办理托收的地点。一般都已事先印好,若未印好则由银行填写。日期由银行收到出口商提交单证时填写,是向银行议付的日期或委托银行收款的日期。该日期不得早于所有单据出单日期,且必须在信用证的有效期及议付期之前。

4. 汇票编号(NO.)

一般填写商业发票的号码。

5. 汇票金额(THE AMOUNT OF EXCHANGE)

汇票必须载明它的金额,汇票金额应写出明确的数目和货币,要用数字小写和文字大写分别表明。"Exchange for"后面是汇票的小写金额,填货币名称缩写和阿拉伯数字,保留至小数点后两位。"THE SUM OF"后面是汇票的大写金额,填写货币全称和金额数目文字。习惯上,货币前写"SAY"(合计),金额后写"ONLY"(整),要求顶格,不留空隙。

填制注意事项如下。

(1) 大小写金额应一致,不得涂改。若不一致,按中国《票据法》的规定,该汇票无效。金额零头的写法,如数字 0.35 的表达方法有以下几种:①CENTS THIRDTY-FIVE;②POINT THIRDTY-FIVE;③35% OR 35/100。

(2) 信用证项下，除非另规定，汇票金额所使用的货币应与信用证和发票所使用的货币一致。在通常的情况下，汇票金额为发票金额的 100%，但不得超过信用证规定的最高金额为限。如果信用证金额有"大约"等字样，则有 10% 的增减幅度。

(3) 如信用证中：DRAFT... FOR 100% OF INVOICE VALUE 或 DRAFT AT SIGHT... FOR FULL INVOICE VALUE，或者当实际装运的数量少于规定的数量，在信用证允许分批时，每一批出货的发票金额是实际应收金额。此时，汇票金额等于发票金额。

(4) 当发票金额含佣金或折扣时，信用证表示发票含佣金或折扣，议付时佣金或折扣必须在汇票上予以扣除，即汇票上应填制实际所能收回的除去佣金或折扣的金额，如 INVOICE SHOWING CFR VALUE INCLUDING 5% COMMISSION，AT THE TIME OF NEGOTIATION 5% COMMISSION MUST BE DEDUCTED FROM DRAWINGS UNDER THIS CREDIT。此时，汇票额等于发票额减去佣金。

(5) 当来证要求两张汇票分别支付一笔交易额，如 US $ 25 600.00 PAYABLE AGAINST SIGHT DRAFT ACCOMPANYING ABOVE DOCUMENTS，US $ 3 850.00 PAYABLE AGAINST SIGHT DRAFT AND PRESENTATIOM OF INDEPENDENT SURVEYORS REPORT... 这两张汇票上的各自的金额数也小于发票金额。

6. 付款期限（TENOR）

付款期限在汇票中用"AT... SIGHT"表示，主要有即期和远期两种，信用证项下，按规定填写，托收项下应注明 D/P 还是 D/A。

即期汇票（SIGHT DRAFT）是指在汇票的出票人按要求向银行提交单据和汇票时，银行应立即付款，一般在 AT 和 SIGHT 之间的横线上打上"…"、"－－－"或"＊＊＊"等。

远期汇票（TIME DRAFT）表示在将来的某个时间付款。具体付款时间应按照规定的"远期"起算日算起的几天内，不同的起算日，付款的日期也不同。

(1) DRAFT AT 30DAYS SIGHT。这是以见票日为"远期"起算日，即为见票日后 30 天付款，填写时，在付款期限一栏内填上 30DAYS 即可。

(2) DRAFT AT 30DAYS FROM THE DATE OF B/L。这是以提单日期作为"远期"起算日，即提单签发日后的 30 天付款。填写时，只要打上"30DAYS AFTER B/L DATE"。

(3) THIS L/C IS AVAILABLE WITH US BY PAYMENT AT 30DAYS AFTER RECEIPT OF FULL SET OF DOCUMENTS AT OUR COUNTERS。这是一张以付款银行收到全套单据为"远期"起算日的远期算付款信用证。在填制时，应打上"30DAYS AFTER RECEIPT OF FULL SET OF DOCUMENTS AT YOUR COUNTERS"。注意：信用证内容填写 OUR COUNTERS（我方柜台），在汇票上应作相应调整为"YOUR COUNTERS"，作为受益人对付款银行的称呼。

(4) DRAFT AT 30DAYS FROM THE DATE OF INVOICE。这是以发票日期为"远期"起算日，即发票日期后 30 天付款。填写汇票时应打上"30DAYS FROM THE DATE OF INVOICE"。对于此类要求，发票制作时应尽量提前日期以便卖方尽早收汇。

7. 受款人（PAY TO THE ORDER OF/PAYEE）

通常汇票的受款人处已印就"Pay to the order of"。一般在空处填银行的名称（一般为出口地银行），信用证方式下，受款人通常为议付行；托收方式下，受款人可以是托收行，也可将出口方写成受款人（已收汇票），然后由受款人作委托收款背书给托收行。实际上，在"pay to order of"栏中填写，国际上有三种写法：限制性抬头（PAY TO ××× ONLY）、指示式抬头（PAY TO THE ORDER OF ×××）、持票人抬头（PAY TO THE BEARER）。在我国出口业务中，一般银行为受款人，汇票上通常已事先印好，无须填写。

8. 付款人（DRAWEE/PAYER）

该栏即在汇票左下角"To"栏，必须按规定填写付款人名称、地址。在信用证业务中，汇票付款人是按信用证"draw on ×××"、"draft on ×××"或"drawee"确定。通常为开证行或指定的付款行（一般为通知行），不能填开证申请人，否则该汇票就成为附加单据。托收业务一般填写进口商。

9. 出票人（DRAWER）

一般在汇票的右下角，即签发汇票的人，写明全称和详细地址，并由负责人签署或盖章，否则无效。信用证项下，填信用证受益人；托收项下，填托收委托人。

【相关单证】

单证 9-1　跟单信用证项下汇票样本

```
凭
Drawn under _____
信用证号
L/C No. _____
日期          年      月      日
Date _____                                    1
按          息          付款
Payable with interest @ _____%per annum
号码          汇票金额                    中国  河北  石家庄  年  月  日
No. _____ Exchange for _____, Shijiazhuang Hebei, China. _____
见票                                       日后（本汇票之副本未付）付
At _____ sight of this  FIRST of Exchange (Section of exchange being unpaid)
受款人
pay to the order of _____
金    额
the sum of _____
_____
此致
To: _____
                              _____
```

单证9-2 托收项下汇票样本

凭
Drawn under _____

_____

按　　　息　　　　　　　　付款
Payable with interest @_____%per annum

号码　　　汇票金额　　　　　　　中国　河北　石家庄　年　月　日
No. _____ Exchange for _____, Shijiazhuang Hebei, China. _____

见票　　　　　　　　　　　　　　日后（本汇票之副本未付）付
At _____ sight of this　SECOND of Exchange（Section of exchange being unpaid）

受款人
pay to the order of _____

金　额
the sum of _____

此致
To: _____

【案例】

河北恒泰进出口贸易公司业务员杨光在货物装运后，随即根据信用证的要求和具体装运情况缮制汇票。

凭
Drawn under　CATHAY BANK, LOS ANGELES, USA

信用证号
L/C　　No.　LC-710-086405

日期　　　年　　月　　日
Date　JUL.6, 2008

按　　　息　　　　　　　　付款
Payable with interest @_____%per annum

号码　　　汇票金额　　　　　　　中国　河北　石家庄　年　月　日
No.　HT07110　Exchange for　USD 22 050.00　, Shijiazhuang Hebei, China.

见票　　　　　　　　　　　　　　日后（本汇票之副本未付）付
At　＊＊＊　sight of this　FIRST　of Exchange（Section of exchange being unpaid）

受款人
pay to the order of　BANK OF CHINA, HEBEI BRANCH

金　额
the sum of　SAY U.S DOLLARS TWENTY TWO THOUSAND AND FIFTY ONLY

此致
To:　CATHAY BANK, LOS ANGELES, USA

HEBEI HENGTAI IMPORT & EXPORT CORPORATION
NO.231 HEPING ROAD, SHIJIAZHUANG, CHINA
（签章）

【技能实训】

1. 根据下列信用证内容填制汇票一份。

ISSUING BANK: DEUTSCHE BANK (ASIA) HONGKONG
L/C NO. AND DATE: DBH35278, SEP. 20, 2007
AMOUNT: USD26 780.00
APPLICANT: BUBBLEM (H.K) LTD., ROOM1756, HANG LUNG CENTRE, PATERSON STREET, CAUSEWAY BAY, HONGKONG
BENEFICIARY: CHINA NATIONAL ARTS AND CRAFTS I/E CORP. HEBEI BRANCH.
ADVISING BANK: BANK OF CHINA, HEBEI BRANCH
WE OPENED IRREVOCABLE DOCUMENTS CREDIT AVAILABLE BY NEGOTIATION AGAINST PRESENTATION OF THE DOCUMENTS DETAILED HEREIN AND OF BENEFICIARY'S DRAFTS IN DUPLICATE AT SIGHT DRAWN ON OUR BANK.
INV. NO.: HBI00651
DATE OF NEGOTIATION: OCT. 20, 2007

2. 根据下列资料缮制汇票。

L/C NO.: 123456 DATED: NOV. 11, 2006
ISSUING BANK: ISREAL DISCOUNT BANK OF NEW YORK, NEW YORK BRANCH
APPICANT: BLACK CO., LTD.
BENEFICIARY: HEBEI TEXITILES IMPORT & EXPORT CORPORATION
ADVISING BANK: BANK OF CHINA, HEBEI BRANCH
AMOUNT: USD 25 000.00
COVERING: 1 000PCS of 100% COTTON BEDSPREADS
WE HEREBY ESTABLISH OUR IRREVOCABLE DOCUMENTARY CREDIT IN YOUR FAVOUR AVAILABLE AGAINST YOUR DRAFT AT SIGHT DRAWN ON OUR BANK BY NEGOTIATION.
OTHER TERMS AND CONDITIONS: INVOICE NOT TO SHOW ANY COMMISSION COMMISSION OF 2% TO SHOW ONLY ON BILL OF EXCHANGE.
INVOICE NO.: 37256

3. 根据下述的信用证缮制一份对应的汇票。

From: OVERSEAS UNION BANK LTD., SINGAPORE
To: BANK OF CHINA, HEBEI BRANCH
Form of Doc. Credit * 40 A: IRREVOCABLE
Doc. Credit Number * 20: 07-4-1520
Date of Issue   31C: 2007/11/18
Expiry   * 31 D: DATE 2008/01/24 PLACE AT OUR COUNTER
Applicant   * 50: UNIWORLD INTERNATIONAL CO.
                    34 JALAP STREET,
                    SINGAPORE
Beneficiary   * 59: HEBEI MACHINERY IMP. AND EXP. CORP (GROUP)
                    50 HUAIAN ROAD, SHIJIAZHUANG
                    HEBEI PROV., P. R., CHINA

Amount	*32B:	USD 70 600.00
Available with/by	*41D:	AVAILABLE WITH US BY DEFERRED PAYMENTAT 30 DAYS SIGHT FOR 100% INVOICE VALUE AGAINST THE BENEFICIARY'S DOCUMENTS
Partial Shipments	43P:	ALLOWED
Transshipment	43T:	ALLOWED
Loading in Charge	44A:	XINGANG
For Transport to	44B:	SINGAPORE
Latest Date of Ship.	44C:	2008/01/03
Descript. of Goods	45A:	STAINLESS STEEL SPADE HEAD, ART. NO. S701 3 500PCS, USD12.60 PER PC., ART. NO. F715 2 500PCS, USD10.60 PER PC., AS PER S/C NO. 07—00235 DATED NOV. 15, 2007 CIF SINGAPORE
Documents required	46A:	+SIGNED COMMERCIAL INVOICE IN TRIPLICATE. ....
Additional Cond.	47A:	1. A HANDING FEE OF USD 80.00 WILL BE DEDUCTED IF DISCREPANCY DOCUMENTS PRESENTED. 2. ALL DOCUMENTS INDICATING THIS L/C NUMBER.
Presentation Period	48:	DOCUMENTS TO BE PRESENTED WITHIN 21 DAYS AFTER THE DATE OF SHIPMENT, BUT WITHIN THE VALIDITY OF THE CREDIT.
Details of Charges	71B:	ALL BANKING CHARGES AND EXPENSES OUTSIDE THE ISSUING BANK ARE FOR BENEFICIARY'S ACCOUNT.

9.3 商业发票

发票由于不同的需要可分为不同的种类，如商业发票（Commercial invoice）、形式发票（Proforma Invoice）、领事发票（Consular invoice）、样品发票（Sample invoice）、厂商发票（Manufactures' invoice）、收讫发票（Receipt invoice）、详细发票（Detailed invoice）、海关发票（Customs invoice）等。实务中最为常见的是商业发票，通常简称为发票。

9.3.1 商业发票的含义及作用

商业发票（COMMERCIAL INVOICE）是卖方向买方开立的，对所装运货物的全面、详细说明，并凭以向买方收取货款的货款价目总清单，是进出口贸易结算中使用的最主要的单据之一。

商业发票是卖方向买方发送货物的凭证，使进口商对货物的品名、规格、单价、数量、总价等能够有一个全面的了解，并凭以对货物进行验收与核对。同时，商业发票也是进出口商记账、收付汇、进出口报关及海关统计的依据。在即期付款条件下，不需卖方出具汇票时，发票可替代汇票作为付款的依据。除此之外，发票还作为海关数据统计，保险索赔时可为价值的证明等。

商业发票是全套进出口单据的核心，其他单据均以它为中心来缮制，在外贸制单工作程序中，一般也先缮制好商业发票，然后才制作其他单据。

9.3.2 商业发票的内容和缮制

商业发票根据信用证或合同条款要求由各出口公司自行制定，一般无统一格式，但基本栏目大致相同。发票在结构上分首文、本文、结尾三部分，具体内容如下。

1. 首文部分

（1）单据名称。商业发票上应在明显位置上标明"INVOICE"（发票）或"COMMERCIAL INVOICE"（商业发票）字样，一般大多已事先印制。在信用证项下，为防止单证不符，发票名称应与信用证一致。

（2）出票人（ISSUER）。填写出口商的名称和地址。信用证项下即为受益人，一般表示为"BENEFICIARY：×××"；托收项下为合同的卖方，有时也包括电传、电话号码等。注意：该项目必须与销售合同及信用证的相关描述一致。

（3）受票人（TO:...）。本栏为发票抬头，如果是信用证项下的发票，除信用证有其他要求之外，一般填写开证申请人（APPLICANT）。信用证中一般表示为"FOR ACCOUNT OF×××"，或"TO THE ORDER OF×××"中"×××"部分。当采用托收或其他方式支付货款时，填写合同中买方的名称和地址。在实际操作中，公司名称和地址要分两行打，名称一般一行打完，不能换行，地址则可合理分行。

（4）发票号码（INVOICE NO.）。商业发票是出口单证的核心单据，因此它的编号可以代表整套单据的号码，一般由出口方自行编制，但编制规则并不统一。

（5）发票日期（INVOICE DATE）。一般而言，发票是全套单据中出具最早的。其日期应早于提单的出具日期而且不可迟于信用证规定的议付期。有时卖方在签订合同后即开立发票，其日期也就早于信用证开立日期，根据《UCP600》的规定，这是允许的，但必须在信用证及《UCP600》惯例规定的期限内提交。

（6）合同号码及信用证号码（S/C NO.，L/C NO.）。根据实际填写，一笔交易若有多个合同号应分别列出。实践中，买卖合同并不都以"CONTRACT"为名称，有时出现"S/C"，"ORDER"，"P.O."等，应根据信用证中所规定的作出相应的改变，以求单证一致。若来证中未规定合同号，此栏也可不填。托收方式下的发票必须填写合同号。

（7）支付方式（TERMS OF PAYMENT）。应填写该笔业务的付款方式，是T/T、托收或者信用证结算方式等。

（8）运输说明（TRANSPORT DETAILS）。货物的运输信息，包括运输的起讫口岸和转运地点以及运输方式（必要时加列运输工具名称）。一般只简单地表明运输路线及运输方式，如 FROM×××TO×××BY SEA/AIR。如果货物需经转运，应把转运港的名称打上。如 FROM SHANGHAI TO HAMBURG WITH TRANSSHIPMENT AT HONGKONG BY VESSEL（装运自上海到汉堡，在香港转运）。缮制此栏时应注意：起运地和目的地应明确具体，不能笼统；应与其他运输单据保持一致。

(9) 开证行（ISSUING BANK）。若信用证有要求则需注明。

2. 本文部分

(1) 货物描述（DESCRIPTION）。包括货物的品名、规格、等级、尺寸、颜色等，信用证方式下，品名规格应严格按照信用证的规定或描述填写，货物数量既应与实际装运相符，又应符合信用证的要求。此栏内容应严格与信用证的规定一致，不得随意减少内容，以防国外银行故意挑剔而拖延或拒付货款。若来证对货物的描述较合同简略，此时按信用证打印完毕后，再按合同要求列明货物具体内容，但应注意避免把过多的细节列入，以免发生差错。托收方式下可按买卖合同有关内容结合实际装运情况填制。

(2) 唛头（SHIPPING MARKS）。一般由卖方自行设计，但若合同或信用证规定了唛头，则须按规定。若无唛头，应注明 N/M。

(3) 数量（QUANTITY）。与计价单位连用。注意该数量和计量单位既要与实际装运货物情况一致，又要受信用证和提单约束，不能有出入。一般按合同标明装运货物数量，还必须标明数量单位，如 PIECE、SET、KG 或 METER 等。若货物品种规格较多，则每种货物应写明小计数量，最后再进行合计。

(4) 单价（UNIT PRICE）、总价（AMOUNT）。这是商业发票中一项极为重要的内容，包括币值、单位数额、计价单位和价格术语。一般要与信用证或合同一致。对应不同货物标明相应单价，注意货币单位及数量单位要与信用证或合同一致。总价即实际发货金额，应与信用证或合同规定一致，同时还应注明贸易术语。

(5) 合计。应有小写和大写两部分，若只有一种货物，也必须进行合计。

3. 结文部分

(1) 签字盖章。可有可无，若信用证要求 SIGNED INVOICE，就要求出口商签字或加盖图章。否则，按《UCP600》的规定，发票可不需签章。若加盖了公章则要与首文部分印好的出口公司名称一致。

(2) 其他。由于各国法令、习惯不一，有些国家要求在发票上注明一些特殊内容，应一一照办。如必须在商业发票上注明船名、重量、成本、保费、运费、进口许可证号码、无木制包装等字样，需根据具体业务及信用证要求具体对待。

在信用证实务中，发票缮制方式可能引起开证行的争议。各国或各地区制作发票的模式不尽相同，在国际结算实务中，因制作发票格式有异，而造成收汇拖延的事例时有发生。因此，对于各国制单的方式，出口商应尽量适应，以避免不必要的争议。

国际贸易单证实务

 【相关单证】

单证9-3 发票的样本

ISSUER		COMMERCIAL INVOICE	
TO			
		NO.	DATE
TRANSPORT DETAILS		S/C NO.	L/C NO.
		TERMS OF PAYMENT	
Marks and Numbers	Number and kind of package Description of goods	Quantity	Unit Price	Amount
	Total:			
SAY TOTAL:				

【案例】

河北恒泰进出口贸易公司业务员杨光根据信用证的要求与货物实际装运情况缮制商业发票（见表9-1）。

表 9-1 恒泰公司商业发票

ISSUER HEBEI HENGTAI IMPORT & EXPORT CORPORATION NO. 231 HEPING ROAD, SHIJIAZHUANG, HEBEI, CHINA	HEBEI HENGTAI IMPORT & EXPORT CORPORATION NO. 231 HEPING ROAD, SHIJIAZHUANG, HEBEI, CHINA
TO PACIFIC INTERNATIONAL INC. 129 HAYWARD WAY STREET MONTE, CA 91513	**COMMERCIAL INVOICE**
	NO. HT07110 DATE AUG.12, 2008
TRANSPORT DETAILS FROM XINGANG TO LOS ANGELES PORT BY S.S QINLUN V. 1502	S/C NO. 02AG18185 L/C NO. LC-710-076405
	TERMS OF PAYMENT BY L/C

Marks and Numbers	Description of goods	Quantity	Unit Price	Amount
PACIFIC 18185 LOS ANGELES 1-225	100% COTTON STRIPE TOWEL ART NO. ABC69 SIZE: 30″×60″	4 500 DOZENS	CIF LOS ANGELES USD4.90/DOZ	USD 22 050.00
	Total:	4 500 DOZENS		USD 22 050.00

SAY TOTAL: SAY U.S DOLLARS TWENTY TWO THOUSAND AND FIFTY ONLY

PACKING: ONE DOZEN IN A POLYBAG, 20DOZENS IN A BALE

THIS IS TO CERTIFY THAT THE GOODS NAMED HEREIN ARE OF CHINESE ORIGIN.
WE HEREBY CERTIFY THAT THE ABOVEMENTIONED PARTICULARS
AND FIGURES ARE TRUE AND CORRECT.

HEBEI HENGTAI IMPORT & EXPORT CORPORATION
NO. 231 HEPING ROAD, SHIJIAZHUANG,
HEBEI, CHINA
（手签名）

【技能实训】

1. 根据所给销售合同制作商业发票，设发票开票日期为 2007 年 8 月 15 日，号码为 YT070569。

SALES CONFIRMATION NO.: 07-2568
DATE: JUL. 8, 2007

THE SELLER: HEBEI YONGJIA IMP. & EXP. CORP. LTD.
  80 ZHONGSHAN ROAD, SHIJIAZHUANG, CHINA
THE BUYER: SHEMSY NEGOCE ID CORP.
  VIA ARZAGA 28, MILANO ITALY
THIS SALES CONFIRMATION IS HEREBY MUTUALLY CONFIRMED, TERMS AND CONDITIONS ARE AS FOLLOWS:

MARKS	DESCRIPTION OF GOODS	QUANTITY	UNIT PRICE	AMMOUNT
SN CO VIA TRADVERSA DI	5 PANEL CAP IN COTTON TWILL	CFR MILANO		
	N. BLUE	2 800 DOZ.	USD 4.80/DOZ.	USD13 440.00
	RED	1 100 DOZ.		USD5 280.00
	WHITE	1 200 DOZ.		USD5 760.00
	R. BLUR	500 DOZ.		USD2 400.00
	YELLOW	500 DOZ.		USD2 400.00
	GREEN	1 500 DOZ.		USD7 200.00
TOTAL		7 600 DOZ.		USD 36 480.00

PACKING: TO BE PACKED IN CARTON, 12DOZ IN A POLYBAGE, 25DOZ IN A CARTON
  GW: 18.00KGS/CTN, NW: 15.00KGS/CTN, MEAS: 50×20×10CM/CTN
SHIPMENT: FROM XINGNAG CHINA TO MILANO ITALY, NOT LATER THAN NOT LATER AUG. 31, 2007, PARTIAL SHIPMENTS AND TRANSHIPMENT TO BE ALLOWED.
PAYMENT: 30% T/T IN DEPOSIT, 70% D/P AT SIGHT
INSURANCE: TO BE EFFECTED BY THE BUYER
SELLER: HEBEI INTERNATIONAL IMP. & EXP. CORP. LTD.
BUYER: SHEMSY NEGOCE ID CORP.
2. 根据下列所给资料缮制发票一份，发票时间、号码、唛头由受益人决定。
FROM: BRITISH BANK OF THE MIDDLE EAST, JEBEL HUSSEIN, AMMAN, JORDAN.
TO: THE HONG KONG AND SHANGHAI BANKING CORPORATION LIMITED.
BENEFICIARY: ABC ARTS AND CRAFTS IMP. & EXP. CO.
  185 ZHONGHUA STREET, SHIJIAZHUANG, HEBEI, CHINA
APPLICANT: WHITE TRADING CO.
  P. O. BOX 11181. AMMAN JORDAN.
DC NO.: MEH87652
FORM OF DC: IRREVOCABLE
DATE OF ISSUE: 20 NOV., 2007
EXPIRY DATE AND PLACE: 30 DEC., 2007, CHINA
AMOUNT: USD19 200.00, CIF AQABA, JORDA
MAX CR AMT: NOT EXCEEDING...
AVAILABLE WITH/BY: ANY BANK BY NEGOTIATION

DRAFTS AT: AT SIGHT FOR FULL INVOICE VALUE, MENTIONING THIS DC NO.
DRAWEE: ISSUING BANK
LATEST DATE OF SHIPMENT: 15 NOV., 2007
COVERING: COTTON SLIPPER
    MODEL CA05 SIZE 35 - 40 6 000 PAIRS, USD1.60 PER PAIR.,
    MODEL YA10 SIZE 35 - 40 6 000 PAIRS, USD1.60 PER PAIR,
ALL IN 4 ASSORTED COLORS, BLUE, RED, PINK AND VIOLET
AS PER S/C ABC37412 DATED SEP. 8, 2007
DOUMENTS REQUIRED:
SIGNED INVOICES IN THREE COPIES SHOWING THAT THE GOODS EXPORTED ARE OF CHINESE ORIGIN, THE ORIGINAL INVOICE IS TO BE DULY CERTIFIED BY THE CHINA COUNCIL FOR THE PROMOTION OF INTERNATIONAL TRADE.
...
ADDITIONAL CONDITIONS:
    ① "MADE IN CHINA" MUST BE STICKED ON EACH PAIR AND THE RELATIVE INVOICES MUST CERTIFY TO THIS EFFECT.
    ② ALL DOCUMENTS REQUIRED UNDER THIS DOCUMENTARY CREDIT SHOULD BE ISSUED IN ENGLISH.
    ③ ALL DOCUMENTS REQUIRED UNDER THIS DOCUMENTARY CREDIT MUST MENTION THIS L/C NUMBER AND THE ISSUING BANK NAME.

3. 根据下列信息制作商业发票，要求格式清楚、内容完整。

L/C NO.: CN060/1181 DATED: SEP. 2, 2006
DATE AND PLACE OF EXPIRY: OCT. 15, 2006 IN COUNTRY OF BENEFICIARY
APPLICANT: GOODTIME CO. LTD.
           266 CASTLE PEAK ROAD, KOWLOON., HONGKONG.
BENEFICIARY: HEBEI YONGAN TOYS CO. LTD.
            76 ZHANGDE ROAD, HANDAN, CHINA
L/C AMOUNT: USD17 976.00
LOADING IN CHARGE: XINGANG, CHINA
FOR TRANSPORTATION TO: HONGKONG
LATEST DATE OF SHIP: AUG. 30, 2007
DESCRIPTION OF GOODS: 1 600DOZENS OF PLUSH STUFFED TOY AS PER SALES CONTRACT YG05789 DATED MAY 8, 2007.

STYLE NO.	QUANTITY	UNIT PRICE
BD075	600SETS	USD8.60/SET
BL065	720SETS	USD7.70/SET
DA090	720SETS	USD10.10/SET

                        FOB XINGANG
DOCUMENTS REQUIRED: + COMMERCIAL INVOICE IN 1 ORIGINAL AND 3 COPIES
                      LESS 5% COMMISSION AND HANDSIGNED BY BENEFICIARY.

```
ADDITIONAL COND.：+PACKING IN CARTONS OF 10 DOZS EACH.
               +CARTONS TO BE MARKED WITH:
                         GOODTIME
                         HONGKONG
                        C/NO. 1 - 170
                    +----------------
```

9.4 包装单据

出口商品在运输过程中，除散装货（PACKED IN BULK），如谷物、煤炭、矿砂等不需包装外，大多数商品为了避免在搬运、装卸和运输途中发生碰撞、振动或受外界其他影响而遭受损伤，改变货物的质量，都需要经过适当的包装才能装运出口，以便买方对货物进行分拨转售或对进口商品的包装、数量及重量等进行了解和掌握，也便于货物到达目的港时，供国外海关检查和核对。所以买方往往要求提供包装单据。

9.4.1 包装单据的定义与作用

包装单据（PACKING DOCUMENTS）是指一切记载或描述商品包装情况的单据，是商业发票的补充单据，也是货运单据中的一项重要单据。进口地海关验货、公证行检验、进口商核对货物时都必须以包装单据为依据。在向银行交单时，要求付款、承兑或议付，除散装货外，一般均要求提供包装单据。

包装单据是出口商缮制商业发票及其他单据时计量、计价的基础资料，是进口商清点数量或重量以及销售货物的依据，是海关查验货物的凭证，是公证行或商检机构查验货物的参考资料。

9.4.2 常见的包装单据

1. 装箱单/包装单

装箱单/包装单（PACKING LIST）是商业发票的补充，表明出口货物的包装情况，内容包括从最小包装到最大包装所有使用的包装材料、包装方式及包装规格等。对于重量和尺码内容，在装箱单中一般只体现它们的累计总额。

装箱单无统一的格式和内容，出口商可根据货物的种类和进口商的要求仿照商业发票的格式来制作。一般情况下，装箱单除注明合同编号、发票号码外，还应包括商品名称、唛头、装箱编号、包装类型、颜色与尺寸搭配、货物数量、包装数量、重量、体积等。

缮制装箱单/包装单时，对包装方面的说明、有关货物的描述及唛头等内容要与发票及其他单据相符，或者不相互矛盾。定量包装只需说明总件数、单件的重量和总重量。对不定量的包装，应逐件列出每种商品的包装方式、大小、重量等。

2. 规格单

规格单（SPECIFICATION LIST）在内容上与装箱单/包装单基本一致，但要重点说明包装的规格，如每箱装 20 打，每两打装一盒。

3. 重量单/磅码单

重量单/磅码单（WEIGHT LIST/NOTE/MEMO）是在装箱单的基础上，着重说明重量情况。一般列明每件包装商品的毛重和净重、整批货物的总毛重和总净重；有的还须增列皮重；按公量计量、计价的商品，则须列明公量及计算公量的有关数据。当商品以重量计价时，或当商品的重量对其质量能有一定的反映时，收货人一般会要求重量单。凡是提供重量单的商品，一般不需提供其他包装单据。

4. 尺码单

尺码单（MEASUREMENT LIST）偏重于说明所装运货物的体积，即每件商品的包装尺码以及总尺码。一般要用"M^3"表示货物的体积，其他内容基本与重量单相同。

5. 中性包装单

中性包装单（NEUTRAL PACKING LIST）上不表明出具单位和收货人名称，且不签字、不盖章。只注意与信用证上规定的有关包装条件、包装规格、包装重量等的一致性，一般情况下，可直接将包装要求按原句抄在单据上。

6. 包装声明

美国、加拿大规定，木质包装货物均需进行杀虫处理，按《国际植物保护公约》，对木质包装进行热处理时，一般要求温度达到56℃，并持续30分钟以上，有些木质包装还建议采取烘干或化学处理，熏蒸时要采用甲基溴化处理。新西兰、澳大利亚等国规定，凡进口货物使用木材为包装材料，木材必须无虫、无菌、经过熏蒸处理才准许入境。凡是向以上这些国家出口时，就需要采用包装声明（PACKING DECLARATION），如下。

DECLARATION FOR WOODEN PACKING

TO WHOM IT MAY CONCERN：

I, ×× CORPORATION, HEREBY DECLARE THAT ALL TIMBER USED FOR PACKING THE GOODS LISTED BELOW HAS BEEN INSPECTED BY CIQA AND WAS TO THE BEST OF MY KNOWLEDGE FREE FROM BARK AND FROM VISIBLE SIGNS OF INSECT AND FUNGI ATTACK WHEN THE GOODS WERE SHIPPED TO ×××.

×× CORPORATION (SIGNATURE)

若货物的包装并非木材，而是用纸箱、铁桶、麻袋等，则出具以下声明。

DECLARATION

TO WHOM IT MAY CONCERN：

WE HEREBY DECLARE THAT NO TIMBER HAS BEEN USED IN THE PACKING OF THE GOODS UNDER L/C NO. ××.

×× CORPORATION (SIGNATURE)

除此之外，常用的包装单据还有包装明细单/说明（PACKING SPECIFICATION）、包装提要（PACKING SUMMARY）、重量证书（WEIGHT CERTIFICATE）、详细装箱单（DETAILED PACKING LIST）、花色搭配单（ASSORTMENT LIST）等。

9.4.3 包装单据的内容

包装单据并无统一固定的格式，制单时可以根据信用证或合同的要求和货物的特点自行设计，一般仿照商业发票的大体格式来制作，出口商制作的装箱单格不尽相同，但基本栏目内容相似。其主要包括单据名称、编号、出单日期、货物名称、唛头、规格、件数、毛重与净重、签章等内容。

1. 单据名称

在实务中，应与信用证规定的名称相符，如信用证规定为"Weight Memo"，则单据名称（Name of Document）不能用"Weight List"。在实际应用中，Packing List，Packing Note，Packing Specification List，Detail Packing List，Neutral Packing List，Weight List，Weight Memo，Measurement List，Assortment List 等，这些都是类似包装单据的内容。由于这些单据名称不同，其具体内容也有差异。如要求 Detailed Packing List，则须在单据中详细显示单件货物的毛、净重和体积，如要求 Neutral Packing List，所提供的单据就不能打印受益人名称，不能签章。

2. 编号

包装单据编号（No.）一般都填发票号码，所以在有的包装单据上会直接出现商业发票编号栏。

3. 出单日期

一般来说，出单日期（Date）填发票日期。出单日不得早于发票日期，但不得晚于提单日期。

4. 买方名称和地址

买方名称和地址（Buyer's Name and Address）即抬头，合同的买方或信用证的开证申请人。

5. 品名和规格

品名和规格（Name of Commodity and Specifications）的填写必须与发票、合同和信用证相一致。除非信用证另有规定，如果货物有不同规格，或者规格价格不同，则各种规格的数量、重量应分别列出，货物以包装单位计价时，要表示货物包装单位的数量或件数。

6. 唛头

唛头（Shipping Marks）应与发票、提单、托运单等单据上的唛头保持严格一致。如果信用证规定了唛头，必须依照规定制唛。如果信用证未规定唛头，一般由出口商自行设计；如果无唛头，填写"N/M"。

7. 数量

数量（Quantity）填写实际件数，如品质规格不同，应将不同规格的数量分别列出，并累计出合计数。

8. 毛重（单件/合计）[Gross Weight (per package/total)]

毛重填入外包装每件重量。如果有几种规格，每种规格的毛重不同，则应分别列出毛重，并累计其总量。

9. 净重（单件/合计）[Net Weight (per package/total)]

填写每件货物的净重并合计总净重。

10. 尺码（单件/合计）[Measurement (per package/total)]

填写每件货物的体积及合计体积。

11. 签章（Signature）

由出具本单据的单位和负责人签字盖章，应与发票的签章一致。如果信用证要求中性包装或规定中性包装单，本栏应空白不签章。

9.4.4 制作包装单据的注意事项

（1）单据名称必须完全符合信用证的规定，无论信用证要求的包装单据是什么名称，都必须按其规定名称照打。

（2）如果信用证要求列明内包装情况，必须在单据中充分体现出来。如信用证规定每件装一袋、每 5 打装一盒、每 10 打装一箱，则必须注明。

（3）如果信用证条款只要求提供装箱单（PACKING LIST），而无任何特殊规定，则只需提供一般装箱单，将货物的包装情况作一般简要说明就可以了。如果信用证条款要求提供"详细装箱单"（DETAILED PACKING LIST），那么就必须提供详细的装箱内容，如描述每件包装的具体细节，包括商品的货号、色号、尺寸搭配、毛重、净重及尺码等。

（4）如果要求在装箱单、重量单或尺码单等出现特殊条款，应根据信用证或合同的要求填写。如来证只要求装箱单中标明信用证号码、合同号码或特殊包装文字说明，那么按照信用证或合同要求填写。

（5）一般不应在包装单据中显示货物的单价、总价，因为进口商在转移这些单据给实际买方时大多不愿泄露其购买的实际成本。

（6）包装单据都由出口商出具，其号码、出单日期完全同发票，毛重、净重方面，应列明单件的毛重和净重、总毛重和总净重，必须与发票和运输单据、产地证、出口许可证的数字相符。对于计价的重量，其数字更需注意。

（7）信用证若规定"不接受联合单据"，可以利用装箱单分别冠以重量单和尺码单的单据名称，一次缮制，按照信用证规定的份数提供给银行即可。

（8）签署。如果信用证无特别规定，装箱单、重量单和尺码单无签署。

【相关单证】

单证 9-4　装箱单样本

ISSUER			PACKING LIST			
TO						
			INVOICE NO.		DATE	
MARKS AND NUMBERS	NUMBER AND KIND OF PACKAGE DESCRIPTION OF GOODS	QUANTITY	PACKAGE	G. W	N. W	MEAS.

【案例】

河北恒泰进出口贸易公司业务员杨光于2008年8月12日根据信用证的要求缮制装箱单（见表9-2），货物尺码80×60×50CM/BALE，毛重45 KGS/BALE，净重42KGS/BALE。

表9-2 恒泰公司装箱单

ISSUER HEBEI HENGTAI IMPORT & EXPORT CORPORATION NO. 231 HEPING ROAD, SHIJIAZHUANG, HEBEI, CHINA	HEBEI HENGTAI IMPORT & EXPORT CORPORATION NO. 231 HEPING ROAD, SHIJIAZHUANG, HEBEI, CHINA ||
	PACKING LIST ||
TO PACIFIC INTERNATIONAL INC. 129 HAYWARD WAY STREET MONTE, CA 91513	INVOICE NO.	DATE
	HT07110	AUG. 12, 2008

MARKS AND NUMBERS	DESCRIPTION OF GOODS	QUANTITY	PACKAGE	G.W.	N.W.	MEAS.
PACIFIC 18185 LOS ANGELES 1-225	100% COTTON STRIPE TOWEL ART NO. ABC69 SIZE: 30″×60″	4 500 DOZENS	225BALES	10 125 KGS	9 450 KGS	54M³

TOTAL QUANTITY: 225BALES
TOTAL: SAY TWO HUNDERED AND FIFTY BALES ONLY
PACKING: ONE DOZEN IN A POLYBAG, 20DOZENS IN A BALE

HEBEI HENGTAI IMPORT & EXPORT CORPORATION
NO. 231 HEPING ROAD, SHIJIAZHUANG,
HEBEI, CHINA
（签名）

【技能实训】

1. 根据本章商业发票之练习 2 提供的信用证有关内容,缮制装箱单一份。

装箱单上需表明总箱数(数字、文字两种表示方法)、总毛重、总净重、总数量及总体积,并且要有唛头(由卖方决定),还须表明每箱毛重、净重、体积,设每箱毛重、净重、体积的资料如下。

ART NO.	SIZE	QTY. (PAIR)	CTNS.	G.W. (KG)	N.W. (KG)	MEAS. (CM)
MODEL CA05	35-40	6 000	200	14/2 800	12/2 400	60×50×45
MODEL YA10	35-40	6 000	200	14/2 800	12/2 400	60×50×45

2. 根据本章商业发票之练习 3 提供的信用证有关内容,缮制装箱单一份。

装箱单上需表明总箱数(数字、文字两种表示方法)、总毛重、总净重、总数量及总体积,并且要有唛头,还须表明每箱毛重、净重、体积,设每箱毛重、净重、体积的资料如下。

STYLE NO.	QTY. (SET)	CTNS.	G.W. (KG)	N.W. (KG)	MEAS. (CM)
BD075	600	50	26/1 300	24/1 200	80×75×40
BL065	720	60	26/1 560	24/1 440	65×50×30
DA090	720	60	26/1 560	24/1 440	70×60×45

9.5 海运提单

运输单据是外贸单证工作中最重要的单据之一,是出口商按规定要求装运货物后,承运人或其代理人签发的一种书面凭证。

根据运输方式的不同,承运人出具的运输单据不同,主要有海运提单、不可转让海运单、租船提单、邮包收据、航空运单、承运货物收据等。由于在对外贸易中海运所占比重最大,所以海洋运输单据尤其是海运提单使用得也较多,空运单的使用虽然也有其普遍性,但除了收货人必须要求作成记名式收货人之外,其他与海运提单基本相似,故本书仅以海运提单为例来介绍运输单据。

海运提单(OCEAN BILL OF LADING)是承运人确认已收到托运人的货物,并已装船或待以装船,而签发给托运人的收据,它由承运人单方面签发,所以是托运人与承运人之间运输合同的证明,有物权凭证的作用,卖方可通过掌握海运提单来控制货物。

9.5.1 海运提单的内容

海运提单内容由正面事实记载和背面条款两部分组成。不同船公司的提单格式各不相同,但其主要内容大致相同。

1. 提单正面内容

根据《海商法》(Maritime Code of People's Republic of China)的第 73 条的规定,提单正面应记载以下各项:①货物的品名、标志、包装和件数、重量和体积,以及运输危险货物时对危险性质的说明;②承运人的名称和营业地点;③船舶名称;④托运人的名称;⑤收货人的名称;⑥装货港和在装货港接收货物的日期;⑦卸货港;⑧多式联运提单还要增加接收货物地点和交付货物的地点;⑨提单的签发日期、地点和份数;⑩运费的支付;⑪承运人或者其代表的签字。

《海商法》第73条同时还规定,"提单缺少本款规定的一项或者几项的,不影响提单的性质"。

实践中,提单正面还通常印有以下4种契约文句。

(1) 装船(或收货)条款。说明承运人或其代理人已经收到表面状况良好的货物,并已装在指定的轮船上。如 "Shipped on board the vessel named above in apparent good order and condition (unless otherwise indicated) the goods or packages specified herein and to be discharged at the above mentioned port of discharge or as near thereto as the vessel may safely get and be always afloat" 上列外表状况良好的货物或包装(除另有说明者外)已装在上述指名船只,并应在上列卸货港或该船能安全到达并保持浮泊的附近地点卸货)。

(2) 内容不知悉条款。声明承运人或其代理人只对货物的表面状况进行核实,而对于托运人在提单上填写的货物的价值等内容不知悉,所有货物的重量、尺码、标志、品质等都由托运人提供。如 "The weight, measure, marks, numbers, quality, contents and value, being particulars furnished by the Shipper, are not checked by the Carrier on loading"(重量、尺码、标志、号数、品质、内容和价值是托运人所提供的,承运人在装船时并未核对)。但是,"不知悉条款"并不一定有效。

(3) 承认接受条款。承运人或其代理人表示承认提单是运输合同成立的证明,承诺按照提单条款的规定承担义务和享受权利,但也要求托运人、收货人或提单的持有人承诺接受提单印定的各种法律和责任条款。如 "The Shipper, Consignee and the Holder of this Bill of Lading hereby expressly accept and agree to all printed, written or stamped provisions, exceptions and conditions of this Bill of Lading, including those on the back hereof"(托运人、收货人和本提单持有人兹明确表示接受并同意本提单和它背面所载一切印刷、书写或打印的规定、免责事项条件)。

(4) 签署条款。承运人或其代理人表明签发了若干份正本提单(即"全套提单"),各份提单具有相同效力、其中一份完成提货后其余各份自行失效。提单的持有人凭其中一份提货后,其余的自动失效。该条款是承运人签发提单正本的份数和提取货物必须交出经背书的一份提单以换取货物或提货单的条款。如 "In witness whereof, the Carrier or his Agents has signed Bills of Lading all of this tenor and date, one of which being accomplished, the others to stand void. Shippers are requested to note particularly the exceptions and conditions of this Bill of Lading with reference to the validity of the insurance upon their goods"(为证明以上所述,承运人或其代理人已签署各份内容和日期一样的正本提单,其中一份如果已完成提货手续,其余各份均告失效。请托运人特别注意本提单中与该货保险效力有关的免责事项和条件)。

2. 提单背面的条款

全式提单背面印定的条款规定了承运人与托运人、收货人或提单持有人之间的权利、义务和责任豁免,是处理当事人争议的主要法律依据,一般分为强制性条款和任意性条款两类。强制性条款的内容不能违反有关国家的海商法规、国际公约或港口惯例的规定,违反或不符合这些规定的条款是无效的。任意性条款是指上述法规、公约和惯例没有明确规定,允许承运人自行拟订的条款。

各船公司的提单背面条款繁简不一,内容不尽相同,但通常都有下列主要条款:①定义条款;②首要条款;③管辖权条款;④承运人责任条款;⑤承运人的责任期间条款;⑥装货、卸货和交货条款;⑦运费和其他费用条款;⑧自由转船条款;⑨选港条款;⑩赔偿责任限额条款;⑪危险货物条款;⑫舱面货条款。

9.5.2 海运提单的缮制

海运提单的格式,每家船公司都有自己不同的格式,但各项栏目、内容基本一致。

1. 承运人(Carrier)

提单上必须表明以轮船公司身份注册的承运人,否则银行不予接受。

2. 托运人(Shipper)

托运人即发货人,信用证方式下为信用证受益人,如果受益人是中间商,货物是从产地直接装运的,则也填写实际卖方,因为根据 UCP600 规定,如信用证无特殊规定,银行将接受以第三者为发货人的提单。托收方式下该项为托收委托人。

3. 收货人(Consignee)

这是提单的抬头,是银行审核的重点项目。一般来说,提单收货人栏有以下三种填法。

1) 记名式

记名式是指在收货人栏内填写某人或某企业的。这种提单只能由提单上所指定的收货人提货,不能转让,故在实务中使用不多。例如,信用证规定"FULL SET OF B/L CONSIGNED TO AAA CO.",则提单收货人一栏中填 AAA CO.。

2) 不记名式

不记名式是指在本栏留空或填入"TO BEARER"(来人抬头)。意即谁持有提单谁就可以提货。这种提单转让时无须背书,风险较大,目前在国际上很少使用。

3) 指示式

这种提单使用最为普遍,指示提单的转让必须经过背书,可以是空白背书,也可以是记名背书。指示式又可分为"记名指示式"和"不记名指示式"两种。

(1) 记名指示式,一般有发货人指示式(TO ORDER OF SHIPPER)、银行指示式(TO ORDER OF ××× BANK)和收货人指示式(TO ORDER OF ABC COMPANY LTD.),实务中只要根据信用证的要求,制单时分别填入即可。

① 发货人指示式即在本栏填写"TO ORDER OF SHIPPER",这种提单必须由发货人背书,可以空白背书,也可以记名背书,如何背书应按信用证或合同规定办理。发货人背书后将提单交议付银行或者付款银行转寄开证行,进口商付款或者办妥融资手续后从开证行取得提单向船公司提货。例如,来证要求 FULL SET OF B/L ISSUED TO ORDER OF SHIPPER,若 SHIPPER 为 BBB CO.,则提单收货人一栏中填 TO ORDER OF BBB CO.。

② 银行指示式即在本栏填写"TO ORDER OF ××× BANK",这种提单必由 ××× BANK 背书。在信用证项下,"TO ORDER OF ××× BANK",一般大多是指开证行(THE ISSUING BANK),开证行背书后交进口商提货。信用证上的词汇常常是:"FULL SET OF B/L MADE OUT TO OUR ORDER"。这个"OUR",指的就是

开证行。例如,来证要求 FULL SET OF B/L MADE OUT TO OUR ORDER,若开证行名称为 BBB BANK,则提单收货人一栏中填 TO ORDER OF BBB BANK。

③ 收货人指示式即在本栏填写"TO ORDER OF ×××COMPANY LTD.",在信用证项下,"TO ORDER OF ×××COMPANY LTD.",一般多是指开证申请人(THE APPLICANT)。信用证上用的词汇常常是"B/L ISSUED TO ORDER OF APPLICANT"。实务中,收货人指示式使用较少,因为开证行付款后,其物权不在银行手中,而是掌握在收货人手中,故开证行不愿意接受收货人指示式的做法。

(2) 不记名指示式

不记名指示式,即在收货人一栏填写"TO ORDER",这种提单由发货人签字盖章进行背书。常见信用证规定为"FULL SET OF B/L MADE OUT TO ORDER",凭指示抬头,即"空白抬头"。本栏的填法,如是信用证支付方式下的提单,要严格按照信用证规定办理。托收方式下,本栏一般填"TO ORDER"或"TO ORDER OF SHIPPER",然后由发货人背书。注意:不能做成收货人指示式,否则代收行和发货人均无法控制货权;未经代收行同意,也不能做成代收行指示式,因为 URC522 第 10 条规定,事先未征得银行的同意,货运提单不应直接做成银行抬头或银行指示性抬头。

4. 被通知人(Notify Party)

被通知人即买方的代理人,货到目的港时承运人发送到货通知的对象。被通知人有权提货,其职责是及时接受承运人发出的到货通知,并将该通知转告真实的收货人。信用证方式下,如果信用证中有规定,应严格按信用证规定填写,如果来证中没有具体说明被通知人,则将开证申请人名称、地址填入提单副本的这一栏中,而正本的这一栏保持空白或填写买方。如果来证中规定 Notify… only,意指仅通知×××,则 only 一词不能漏掉。如果信用证未规定被通知人地址,而托运人在提单被通知人后面加注详细地址,银行可以接受,但无须审核。托收方式下一般可将合同的买方名称填入。

如果是记名提单或收货人指示提单,且收货人又有详细地址的,此栏可以不填。如果是不记名指示式提单或托运人指示式提单,此栏必须填列被通知人名称及详细地址,否则船方无法与收货人联系,收货人也不能及时报关提货,货物甚至会因超过海关规定申报时间被没收。

5. 提单号码(B/L No.)

本栏在提单右上角,提单必须注明提单号,不可漏打,该号码主要是为便于联系工作和核查。

6. 前段运输(Pre-carriage by)

如果货物不需转运,本栏空白;如果货物需转船,本栏填写第一程船的船名;如属联合运输,本栏填写海运前一段运输工具名称。

7. 收货地点(Place of Receipt)

如果货物不需转运,本栏空白;如果货物需转船,填写前一段运输的收货地点;如属联合运输,本栏填写前段运输的承运人接受货物的地点,如果海运是首程运输或属于集装箱的单一海洋运输方式,则本栏和第 6 栏可留空。

8. 船名航次(Ocean Vessel Voy. No.)

如果货物不需转运,填写实际运输船舶的船名和航次;如果货物需转船,填写第二程船的船名和航次；如属联合运输，本栏填写海运这一段的实际船名和航次。

9. 装货港（Port of Loading）

如果货物不需转运，填写装运港名称；如果货物需转船，填写中转港口名称；如属联合运输，本栏填写海运段的装货港名称。

10. 卸货港（Port of Discharge）

如果货物不需转运，填写卸货港（指目的港）名称；如属转船，第一程提单上的卸货港填写中转港名称，收货人填第二程船公司，第二程提单装货港填上述中转港，卸货港填最后目的港；如由第一程船公司出联运提单（THROUGH B/L），本栏可填最后目的港，并在提单上列明第一和第二程船名；如属联合运输，本栏填写海运段的卸货港名称。如经某港转运，要显示"VIAXX"字样。

11. 交货地点（Place of Delivery）

填写最终目的地名称。如果货物的目的地是目的港的话，空白这一栏。

若信用证或合同仅规定为"中国港口"（Chinese ports, Shipment from China to...），制单时应根据实际情况填写具体港口名称；若规定"Your port"，出口方只能在本市港口装运，若本市没有港口，则事先须洽开证人改证；如同时列明几个装运港，提单只填写实际装运的那一个港口名称；若有两个以上卸货港，只能选其一。

12. 标记与号码（Marks & Nos.）、封志号/集装箱号（Container No. /Seal No.）

本栏填写唛头，应与商业发票上的唛头完全一致。联合运输一般都采用集装箱运输，所以要填写集装箱号和封志号。如果货物装两个或两个以上的集装箱，则应分行列出各集装箱号和封志号，而且还要列出每个集装箱各自不同的件数、毛重和尺码。如果既无集装箱号，又无唛头时，填写"N/M"。

13. 包装种类与件数（No. & Kind of Packages）

本栏填写实际货物的包装数量和包装单位，应与唛头中件号的累计数相一致，并在大写合计数内填写英文大写文字数目，若有两种以上不同包装单位，应分别填写，再合计。散装货，只填"IN BULK"。对于集装箱整箱货，一般须在本栏要加注"SHIPPER'S LOAD COUNT & SEAL, SAY TO CONTAIN"字样，以表示承运人对此不负责任。如果联运提单上没有"ON BOARD"字样，一般也在本栏加注"SHIPPED ON BOARD"或"ON BOARD"字样。

14. 商品名称（Description of Goods）

应按信用证规定的名称以及其他单据如发票名称来填写，如果品名繁多、复杂，可以用概括性的商品的统称，不必列出详细规格，但不得与信用证中货物的描述有抵触。填写此栏时应注意避免不必要的描述，如信用证上商品是 Shoes（鞋子），就不能擅自详细描述成 Men's canvas shoes（男式帆布鞋）或 Ladies' casual shoes（女式轻便鞋）等。如果信用证规定以法语或其他语种表示名称时，应按其语种表示。

15. 毛重和体积（Gross Weight & Measurement）

若信用证无特别规定，则只填总毛重和总体积。毛重包括货物的毛重和集装箱的皮重，若为集装箱货，体积则按集装箱计，一般一个 20 英尺的集装箱体积为 67CBM。如裸装货物没有毛重只有净重，应先加 Net weight 或 N.W.，再注具体的净重数量。FOB 价格条件下可免填体积。

16. 运费支付（Freight & Charges）

本栏只填运费支付情况，一般不填写运费的具体数额。此栏应根据价格条件填写，一般有 PREPAID 和 COLLECT 两种。

17. 正本提单签发份数（Number of original Bs/L）

托收方式下，正本提单的份数一般 1～3 份均可。信用证方式下，按信用证规定，可是一份，也可是两份、三份。

18. 签发地址与日期（Place and date of issue）

签发地址通常是承运人收受货物或装船的地址，提单签发的日期不得晚于信用证规定的装运期，对提单正面条款中已有装船条款（Shipped on board the vessel named above...），提单签发日期即被视为装船日期。如果提单上没有预先印就"已装船"（Shipped on board...）字样的，则必须在提单上加注装船批注（On board notation）。

19. 承运人签署（Signed for or on behalf of the carrier）

正本提单都必须有承运人或其代理人的签章才能生效。若信用证要求手签，也须照办。根据《UCP600》第 20 条的规定，提单必须注明承运人的名称，然后由承运人或作为承运人的具名代理人或其代表，或船长或作为船长的具名代理人或代表签署，且以上任何人的签字或证实均须表明其身份。

例 9－1 承运人签字的提单。

　　提单上部为：COSCO

　　提单签字处：COSCO

　　　　　　　（签字）×××

　　　　　　　AS CARRIEER 或 THE CARRIEER

例 9－2 承运人代理人签字的提单。

　　提单上部为：COSCO

　　提单签字处：ABC SHIPPING COMPANY

　　　　　　　（签字）×××

　　　　　　　AS AGENT FOR AND/OR ON BEHALF OF THE CARRIER COSCO

例 9－3 船长签字的提单。

　　提单上部为：COSCO

　　提单签字处：COSCO（或不注或注船名）

　　　　　　　（签字）×××

　　　　　　　AS MASTER 或 THE MASTER

例 9－4 船长代理人签字的提单。

　　提单上部：COSCO

　　提单签字处：ABC SHIPPING COMPANY

　　　　　　　（签字）×××

　　　　　　　AS AGENT FOR AND/OR ON BEHALF OF THE MASTER ×××
　　　　　　　OF THE CARIER COSCO

20. 其他

提单上还应注明 ON BOARD 字样，正本要注明 ORIGINAL，有时还要注明货物的交接方式，如 CY－CY、CFS－CY 等。

【相关单证】

单证 9-5　海运提单样本

Shipper			B/L　NO.
		COSCO	
		中国远洋运输（集团）总公司 CHINA OCEAN SHIPPING (GROUP) CO. CABLE：COSCO BEIJING TLX：210740 CRC CN	
Consignee		**ORIGINAL** **BILL OF LADING**	
		RECEIVED in apparent good order and condition except as otherwise noted the total number of containers or other packages or units enumerated below for transportation from the place of receipt to the place of delivery subject to the terms and conditions hereof. One of the bills of Lading must be surrendered duly endorsed in exchange for the goods or delivery order. On presentation of this document duly endorsed to the Carrier by or on behalf of the Holder of the Bill of Lading, the rights and liabilities arising in accordance with the terms, and conditions hereof shall, without prejudice the any rule of common law or statute rendering them binding on the Merchant, become binding in all respects between the Carrier and the Holder of the Bill of Lading as though the contract evidenced hereby had been made between them. IN WITNESS Whereof the number of original Bills of Lading stated under have been signed, all of this tenor and date, one of which being accomplished, the other(s) to be void	
Notify Party			
Pre-carriage by	Place of Receipt		
Ocean Vessel Voy. No.	Port of loading		
Port of Discharge	Place of Delivery	Final Destination (of the goods-not the ship)	
Marks & Nos. Container. Seal No.	No. of containers of P'kgs	Description of Goods	Gross Weight kgs.	Measurement
TOTAL NO. OF CONTAINERS OR PACKAGES' (IN WORDS)				
FREIGHT & CHARGES	Revenue Tons	Rate	Per	Prepaid	Collect
Ex. Rate：	Prepaid at	Payable at	Place and date of Issue	
	Total Prepaid	No. of Original B (s) /L	Signed for the Carrier	

LADEN ON BOARD THE VESSEL

　　　　　　　　　　　　　　　　　　　　　　AS CARRIER
　　DATE　　　　By _____　(TERMS CONTINUED ON BACK HERE OF)
　(COSCO STANDARD FORM 11)　　CHINA OCEAN SHIPPING (GROUP) CO.

海运提单（背面）

1. **DEFINITIONS** herein the term "Shipper" occurs hereinafter. It shall be deemed to include also Receiver, Consignee. Holder of this Bill of Lading and Owner of the goods.

2. **JURISDICTION** All disputes arising under and in connection with this Bill of Lading shall be determined by the court in the People's Republic of China.

3. **DEMISE CLAUSE** If the ship is not owned by or chartered by demise to the corporation by whom this Bill of Lading is issued (as may be the case notwithstanding anything that appears to the contrary) this Bill of Lading shall take effect only as a contract with the Owner or demise charterer as the case may be as principal made through the agency of the said corporation who act as agents only and shall be under no personal liability whatsoever in respect thereof.

4. **HAGUE RULES** This Bill of Lading shall have effect in respect of Carrier's liabilities, responsibilities, rights and immunities subject to the Hague Rules contained in the International Convention for the Unification of Certain Rules Relating to Bills of Lading 1924.

5. **PACKING AND MARKS** The Shipper shall have the goods properly packed accurately and clearly marked before shipment. The port of destination of the goods should be marked in letters of 5 cm high, in such a way as will remain legible until their delivery.

6. **OPTIONAL STOWAGE** (1) The goods may be stowed by the Carrier in containers or similar articles of transport used to consolidate goods (2) Goods stowed in containers other than flats, pallets, trailers, transportable tanks or similar articles of transport whether by the Carrier or the Shipper, may be carried on or under deck without notice to the Shipper. Such goods whether carried on or under deck shall participate in general average.

7. **DECK CARGO, PLANTS AND LIVE ANIMALS** Cargo on deck, plants and live animal are received, handled, carried, kept and discharged at Shipper's or Receiver's risk and the Carrier shall not be liable for loss thereof or damage thereto.

8. **FREIGHT** (1) Freight and charges shall be deemed earned on receipt of the goods by the Carrier and shall be paid by the Shipper and non-returnable and non-deductable in any event. Freight payable at destination together with other charges is due on arrival of the goods at the place of destination and shall be paid before delivery of the goods. (2) For the purpose of verifying the freight basis, the Carrier reserves the right to have the goods and the contents of containers, trailers or similar articles of transport inspected in order to ascertain the weight, measurement, value or nature of the goods. In case the particulars of the goods furnished by the Shipper are incorrect, the Shipper shall be liable and bound to pay to the Carrier a sum either five times the difference between the correct freight and the freight charged or to double the correct less the freight charged, whichever sum is the smaller, as liquidated damages to the Carrier.

9. **LIEN** The Carrier shall have a lien on the goods and any documents relating thereto for all sums payable to the Carrier under this Bill of Lading and for general average contributions to whomsoever due and for the cost of recovering the same, and for that purpose shall have the right to sell the goods by public auction or private treaty without notice to the Shipper. If on sale of the goods, the proceeds fail to cover the amount due and the cost incurred, the Carrier shall be entitled to recover the deficit from the Shipper.

10. **TIME BAR, NOTICE OF LOSS** In any event the Carrier shall be discharged from all liabilities under this Bill of Lading unless suit is brought within one year after the delivery of the goods or the date when the goods should have been delivered. Unless notice of loss of or damage to the goods and the general nature of it be given in writing to the Carrier at the place of delivery before or at the time of the removal of the goods into the custody of the person entitled to delivery thereof under this Bill of Lading, or if the loss or damage such removal shall be prima facie evidence of the delivery by the Carrier of the goods as described in this Bill of Lading. In the case of any actual or apprehended loss or damage the Carrier and the Shipper shall give all reasonable facilities to each other for inspecting and tallying the goods.

11. **THE AMOUNT OF COMPENSATION** (1) When the Carrier is liable for compensation in respect of loss of or damage to the goods, such compensation shall be calculated by reference to the invoice value of the goods plus freight and insurance premium of paid. (2) Notwithstanding clause 4 of this Bill of Lading the limitation of liability under the Hague Rules shall be deemed to be CHY 700 per package or unit. (3) Higher compensation may be claimed only when, with the consent of the Carrier, the value for the goods declared by the Shipper which exceeds the limits laid down in this clause has been stated in this Bill of Lading and extra freight has been paid as required. In that case the amount of the declared value shall be substituted for that limit. Any partial loss or damage shall be adjusted pro rata on the basis of such declared value.

12. **LOADING, DISCHARGING AND DELIVERY** The goods shall be supplied and taken delivery of by the owner of the goods as fast as the ship can take and discharge them, without interruption, by day and night. Sundays and Holidays included, notwithstanding any custom of the port to the contrary and the owner of the goods shall be liable for all losses or damages incurred in default thereof. Discharge may commence without previous notice. If the goods are not taken delivery of by the Receiver in due time from alongside the vessel, or if the Receiver refuses to take delivery of the goods, or in case there are unclaimed goods, the Carrier shall be at liberty to land such goods on shore or any other proper places at the sole risk and expense of the Shipper or Receiver, and the Carrier's responsibility of delivery of goods shall be deemed to have been fulfilled. If the goods are unclaimed during a reasonable time, or wherever the goods will become deteriorated, decayed or worthless, the Carrier may, at his discretion and subject to his lien and without any responsibility attaching to him, sell, abandon or otherwise dispose of such goods solely at the risk and expense of the Shipper.

13. **LIGHTERAGE** Any lighterage in or off ports of loading or ports of discharge shall be for the account of the Shipper or Receiver.

14. **FORWARDING, SUBSTITUTE OF VESSEL, THROUGH CARGO AND TRANSHIPMENT** If necessary, the Carrier may carry the goods to their port of destination by other persons or by rail or other means of transport proceeding either directly or indirectly to such port, and to carry the goods or part of them beyond their port of destination, and to transship and forward same at Carrier's expense but at Shipper's or Receiver's risk. The responsibility of the Carrier shall be limited to the part of the transport performed by him on the vessel under his management.

15. **DANGEROUS GOODS, CONTRABAND** (1) The Shipper undertakes not to tender for transportation any goods which are of a dangerous, inflammable, radio-active, and/or any harmful mature without previously giving written notice of their nature to the Carrier and marking the goods and the container or other covering on the outside as required by any laws or regulations which may be applicable during the carriage. (2) Whenever the goods are discovered to have been shipped without complying with the subclause (1) above or the goods are found to be contraband or prohibited by any laws or regulations of the port of loading, discharge or call or any place or waters during the carriage, the Carrier shall be entitled to have such goods rendered innocuous, thrown overboard or discharged or otherwise disposed of at the carrier's discretion without compensation and the Shipper shall be liable for and indemnify the Carrier against any kind of loss, damage or liability including loss of freight, and any expenses directly or indirectly arising out of or resulting from such shipment. (3) If any goods shipped complying with the subclause (1) above become a danger to the ship or cargo, they may in like manner be rendered innocuous, thrown overboard or discharged or otherwise disposed of at the Carrier's discretion without compensation except to general average, of any.

16. **REFRIGERATED CARGO** (1) The Shipper undertakes not to tender for transportation any goods which require refrigeration without previously giving written notice of their nature and particular temperature range to be maintained. If the above requirements are not complied with, the Carrier shall not be liable for any loss of or damage to the goods howsoever arising. (2) Before loading goods in any insulated space, the Carrier shall, in addition to the Class Certificate, obtain the certificate of the Classification Society's Surveyor or other competent person, stating that such insulated space surveyor or other competent person fit and safe for the carriage and preservation of refrigerated goods. The aforesaid certificate shall be conclusive evidence against the Shipper, Receiver and/or any Holder of Bill of Lading. (3) Receivers have to take delivery of refrigerated goods as soon as the ship is ready to deliver, otherwise the Carrier shall land the goods at the wharf at Receiver's or Shipper's risk and expense.

17. **TIMBER** Any statement in this Bill of Lading to the effect that timber has been shipped "in apparent good order and condition" does not involve any admission by the Carrier as to the absence of stains, shakes, splits, holes or broken pieces, for which the Carrier accepts no responsibility.

18. **BULK CARGO** As the Carrier has no reasonable means of checking the weight of bulk cargo, any reference to such weight in this Bill of Lading shall be deemed to be for reference only, but shall constitute in no way evidence against the Carrier.

19. **COTTON** Description of the apparent condition of cotton or cotton products does not relate to the insufficiency of or torn condition of the covering, nor to any damage resulting therefrom, and Carrier shall not be responsible for damage of such nature.

20. **OPTIONAL CARGO** The port of discharge for optional cargo must be declared to the vessel's agents at the first of the optional ports not later than 48 hours before the vessel's arrival there. In the absence of such declaration the Carrier may elect to discharge at the contract of carriage shall then be considered as having been fulfilled. Any option must be for the total quantity of goods under this Bill of Lading.

21. **GOODS TO MORE THAN ONE CONSIGNEE** Where bulk goods or goods without marks or goods with the same marks are shipped to more than one Consignee, the Consignees or Owners of the goods shall jointly and severally bear any expense or loss in dividing the goods or parcels into pro rata quantities and any deficiency shall fall upon them in such proportion as the Carriers, his servants or agents shall decide.

22. **HEAVY LIFTS AND OVER LENGTH CARGO** Any one piece or package of cargo which exceeding 2000 kilos or 9 meters must be declared by the Shipper in writing before receipt by the Carrier and/or length clearly and durably on the outside of the piece or package in letters and figures not less than 2 inches high by the Shipper. In case of the Shipper's failure in his obligations aforesaid, the Shipper shall be liable for loss of or damage to any property or for personal injury arising as a result of the Shipper's said failure and shall indemnify the Carrier against any kind of loss or liability suffered or incurred by the Carrier as a result of such failure.

23. **SHIPPER-PACKED CONTAINERS ETC.** (1) If a container has not been filled, packed or stowed by the Carrier, the Carrier shall not be liable for any loss of or damage to its contents and the Shipper shall cover any loss or expense incurred by the Carrier, of such loss, damage or expense has been cause by negligent filling, packing or stowing of the container; other contents being unsuitable for carriage in container; or the unsuitability or defective condition of the container unless the container has been supplied by the Carrier and the unsuitability or defective condition would not have been apparent upon reasonable inspection at or prior to the time when the container was filled, packed or stowed. (2) The provisions of the sub-clause (1) above also apply with respect to trailers, transportable tanks, flats and pallets which have not been filled, packed or stowed by the Carrier.

24. **WAR, QUARANTINE, ICE, STRIKES, CONGESTION, ETC.** Should it appear that war, blockade, pirate, epidemics, quarantine, ice, strikes, congestion and other causes beyond the Carrier's control would prevent the vessel from safely reaching the port of destination and discharging the goods thereat, the Carrier is entitled to discharge the goods at the port and the contract of carriage shall be deemed to have been fulfilled. Any extra expenses incurred under the aforesaid circumstances shall be borne by the Shipper or Receiver.

25. **GENERAL AVERAGE** General average shall be adjusted in Beijing in accordance with the Beijing Adjustment Rules 1975.

26. **BOTH TO BLAME COLLISION** If the carrying ship comes into collision with another ship as a result of the negligence of the other ship and any act, neglect or default in the navigation or the management of the carrying ship, the Shipper undertakes to pay the Carrier, or where the Carrier is not the Owner and in possession of the carrying ship, to pay to the Carrier as trustee for the Owner and/or demise charterer of the carrying ship, a sum sufficient to indemnify the Carrier and/or the Owner and/or demise charterer of the carrying ship against all loss or liability to the other or non-carrying ship or her Owners insofar as such loss or liability represents loss of or damage to his goods or any claim whatsoever of the Shipper, paid or payable by the other or non-carrying ship or her Owners to the Shipper and set-off, recouped or recovered by the other or non-carrying ship or her Owners as part of their claim against the carrying ship or her Owner or demise charterer or the Carrier. The foregoing provisions shall also apply where the Owners, operations, or those in charge of any ship or ships or objects, other than, or in addition to, the colliding ships or objects, are at fault in respect to a collision, contact, stranding or other accident.

27. **U. S. A. CLAUSE** Notwithstanding any other term hereof the Carriage of Goods by Sea Act 1936 of the United States of America shall have been affect subject to in respect to carriage of goods to and from the United States of America. If any provision of this Bill of Lading be invalid under the Carriage of Goods by Sea Act 1936, such provision shall, to the extent of such invalidity, but no further, be null and void.

【案例】

杨光8月20日将货物从仓库提出准备装船,提单号码COS07-25061(见表9-3)。

表9-3 提单

Shipper HEBEI HENGTAI IMPORT & EXPORT CORPORATION NO. 231 HEPING ROAD, SHIJIAZHUANG, HEBEI, CHINA			B/L NO. COS07-25061		
			中国远洋运输(集团)总公司 CHINA OCEAN SHIPPING (GROUP) CO. CABLE: COSCO BEIJING TLX: 210740 CRC CN		
Consignee TO ORDER			**ORIGINAL** **BILL OF LADING** RECEIVED in apparent good order and condition except as otherwise noted the total number of containers or other packages or units enumerated below for transportation from the place of receipt to the place of delivery subject to the terms and conditions hereof. One of the bills of Lading must be surrendered duly endorsed in exchange for the goods or delivery order. On presentation of this document duly endorsed to the Carrier by or on behalf of the Holder of the Bill of Lading, the rights and liabilities arising in accordance with the terms, and conditions hereof shall, without prejudice the any rule of common law or statute rendering them binding on the Merchant, become binding in all respects between the Carrier and the Holder of the Bill of Lading as though the contract evidenced hereby had been made between them. IN WITNESS Whereof the number of original Bills of Lading stated under have been signed, all of this tenor and date, one of which being accomplished, the other(s) to be void		
Notify Party PACIFIC INTERNATIONAL INC. 129 HAYWARD WAY STREET MONTE, CA 91513					
Pre-carriage by		Place of Receipt			
Ocean Vessel Voy. No. QINLUN V. 1502		Port of loading XINGANG			
Port of Discharge LOS ANGELES		Place of Delivery	Final Destination (of the goods-not the ship)		
Marks & Nos. Container. Seal No. PACIFIC 18185 LOS ANGELES 1-225	No of containers or Packages 2250 BALES	Description of Goods		
		100% COTTON STRIPE TOWEL ART NO. ABC69 SIZE: 30″×60″	Gross Weight kgs. 10 125 KGS		Measurement 59.06M^3
TOTAL NO. OF CONTAINERS OR PACKAGES' (IN WORDS)		SAY TWO THOUSAND TWO HUNDERED AND FIFTY BALES ONLY		
FREIGHT & CHARGES FREIGHT PREPAID	Revenue Tons	Rate	Per	Prepaid	Collect
Ex. Rate:	Prepaid at XINGANG	Payable at		Place and date of Issue TIANJIN AUG. 23, 2008	
	Total Prepaid	No. of Original B(s)/L THREE (3)		Signed for the Carrier	
LADEN ON BOARD THE VESSEL DATE By _____ (COSCO STANDARD FORM 11)			AS CARRIER (TERMS CONTINUED ON BACK HERE OF) CHINA OCEAN SHIPPING (GROUP) CO.		

【技能实训】

1. 根据下列所列资料，缮制海运提单一份。

L/C NO. AND DATE: 581032, MAY 2, 2007
APPLICANT: SEABROOK INTERNATIONAL CORP. 306, WESTLAKE, OHIO 44145 USA.
BENEFICIARY: CHINA NATIONAL METALS & MINERALS I/E CORPORATION JIANGSU BRANCH
DOCUMENTS REQUIRED:
FULL SET CLEAN SHIPPED ON BOARD OCEAN BILL OF LADING MADE OUT TO ORDER AND BLANK ENDORSED NOTIFY A. W. FENTON MS. S. SEYBOLD, 6565 EASTLAND RD, CLEVELAND OH 44142 USA. MARKED FREIGHT COLLECT DATE LATEST MAY 31, 2007.
…
COVERING:
　　MEN'S SHIRT AND PANTS
　ITEM No. 7001, 220SETS, USD19.35 PER SET
　ITEM No. 7002, 780SETS, USD20.35 PER SET
　ITEM No. 7003, 420SETS, USD18.80 PER SET
　FOB SHANGHAI TO SAVANNAH, GA, USA. PARTIAL SHIPMENT ALLOWED
　TRANSHIPMENT ALLOWED
…
OTHER MESSAGES
THE S.S. IS ALLIGATOR LIBERTY, V. 07097H

PACKING: ONE SET INTO ONE P.P. BAG, 10 SETS INTO ONE CARTON
GROSS WEIGHT: 12KGS/CARTON
NET WEIGHT: 10KGS/CARTON
MEASUREMENT: 58 CM×50 CM×33CM PER CARTON

SHIPPING MARK: SEINCO
　　　　　　　　PS04E05F009
　　　　　　　　SAVANNAH
　　　　　　　　NO. 1-142

2. 根据下列所供信息，填制提单一份。

本批货物共1 200套（SET），装于300个纸箱（CTN），放在30个托盘（PALLETS）内，每套内有3个（3PCS IN ONE SET），每箱毛重28KGS，体积0.04M³，装运港：XINGANG, TIANJIN, 目的港：BREMEN, B/L NO.：SCOS4567 船名：CHANGJIANG V. 195, 提单日期：2006.8.1, 信用证内容如下。

　　　　　　　　DRESENER BANK, BREMEN BRANCH
　　　　　　　　　　　　　　　　　　　　　　DATE：JULY 4, 2006
CREDIT NO. DRE1234　　　　　　　　　　　　EXPIRY：AUG. 31, 2006
APPLICANT：ABC CORP. BREMEN.
　　　　　4523 AW. HERO ROAD, BREMEN, GERMAN
BENEFICIARY：MINGYI ARTS AND CRAFTS I/E CORP. TIANJIN, CHINA

ADVISING BANK: BANK OF CHINA, TIANJIN, CHINA
AMOUNT: DEM13 800.00 (SAY DEM SIX THOUSAND SIX HUNDRED ONLY)
DEAR SIRS,
WE OPEN THIS IRREVOCABLE DOCUMENTS CREDIT AVAILABLE AGAINST THE FOLLOWING DOCUMENTS:
…
FULL SET OF CLEAN ON BOARD BILL OF LADING MADE OUT TO ORDER AND BLANK ENDORSED MARKED "FREIGHT PREPAID", NOTIFY APPLICANT SHIPMENT FROM TIANJIN TO BREMEN LATEST ON AUG. 25, 2006.
COVERING:
1200 SETS (3 PCS OF EACH) "WILLOW PRODUCTS"
ART NO. MY0615 600SETS DEM 12.00 PER SET,
ART NO. MY0627 600SETS DEM 11.00 PER SET
CIF BREMEN
PARTIAL AND TRANSSHIPMENT ARE NOT ALLOWED

SHIPPING MARK: SCHCO
　　　　　　　　BREMEN
　　　　　　　　NO. 1-300

3. 请根据信用证相关内容及有关资料缮制海运提单。

L/C No.: 894010151719
PLACE AND DATE OF ISSUE: HONG KONG APR 04, 2007
APPLICANT: HONGJI CORPORATION LIMITED
　　　　　　UNIT 1001-3 10/F YUE XIU BLDG
　　　　　　1512 LOCKHART ROAD
　　　　　　WANCHAI HONG KONG
BENEFICIARY: BOYA IMPORT AND EXPORT CORP.
　　　　　　　120 TONGHUA ROAD, QINGDAO, CHINA
SHIPMENT: FROM QINGDAO, CHINA TO SYDNEY, AUSTRALIA BEFORE MAY 25, 2007
TRANSSHIPMENT: ALLOWED
PARTIAL SHIPMENT: NOT ALLOWED
DOCUMENTS REQUIRED:
——FULL SET OF CLEAN ON BOARD FREIGHT COLLECT OCEAN BILL OF LADING, MADE OUT TO ORDER OF SHIPPER AND BLANK ENDORSED, MARKED "FREIGHT COLLECT" NOTIFY "ID COM CO., 79-81 WALES RD, NSW, AUSTRALIA" AND THE L/C NO.
——INVOICE IN TRIPLICATE
——PACKING LIST IN TRIPLICATE
DESCRIPTION OF GOODS: 800 SETS LUGGAGE SET OF 8 PCS
MODEL NUMBER D-017 400SETS USD 20.00 PER SET
MODEL NUMBER D-025 400SETS USD 20.00 PER SET
FOB QINGDAO
OTHER MESSAGES

```
NAME OF VESSEL: S.S "DONGFENG" V. 06W01
PACKING: ONE SET IN ONE SEAWORTHY CARTON
GROSS WEIGHT: 22.00KGS EACH CARTON
NET WEIGHT: 20.00KGS EACH CARTON
MEASUREMENT: 82.5CM×25.5CM×61CM PER CARTON
SHIPPED IN TWO 40' CONTAINERS
SHIPPER'S LOAD AND COUNT: FCL/FCL
CONTAINER NO. & SEAL NO.:
    COSU2567   40' 0051
    EMCU2678   40' 0052
SHIPPING MARK: HONGJI
               BY25896
               SYDNEY
               NO. 1－800
```

9.6 装运通知

装运通知（Shipping advice/Advice of shipment），又称"装运声明"（Shipping statement/Shipment declaration）是发货人根据信用证或合同规定，在货物装船并取得提单后，发给进口方或其指定的人的有关货物装运情况的书面文件。

在实务中，发货人在装运货物后，应立即（一般在装船后3天内）通知买方或收货人有关装运情况，以便其安排具体的接货事宜，如租订仓库、安排接货运输工具、报关等。特别是在FOB、CFR或FCA、CPT等条件下，装运通知又是进口商办理货物运输保险的凭证。因此，买方为防止因卖方的疏忽而使自己不能及时投保，通常会在信用证中要求该通知的副本作为议付的单据之一。若卖方未及时通知而使买方漏保或没有及时安排接运工具，卖方应负责赔偿买方由此而产生的所有损失。

信用证中有关装运通知举例如下。

（1）ORIGINAL FAX FROM BENEFICIARY TO OUR APPLICANT EVIDENCING B/L NUMBER, NAME OF SHIP, SHIPMENT DATE, QUANTITY AND VALUE OF GOODS。

（2）SHIPMENT ADVICE WITH FULL DETAILS INCLUDING SHIPPING MARKS, CARTON NUMBERS, VESSEL'S NAME, B/L NUMBER, VALUE AND QUANTITY OF GOODS MUST BE SENT ON THE DATE OF SHIPMENT TO US.

（3）BENEFICIARY MUST CABLE ADVISE THE APPLICANT FOR THE PARTICULARS BEFORE SHIPMENT EFFECTED AND A COPY OF SUCH ADVICE SHOULD BE PRESENTED FOR NEGOTIATION.

9.6.1 装运通知的主要内容及其缮制

装运通知没有固定的格式，它可以由各出口企业根据信用证的具体要求自行缮制。装运通知的主要内容有单据名称、抬头人名称和地址、合同号或信用证号、货名、数量、金额、船名、开航日期、提单号码、发电日期等。

1. 单据名称（Name of Document）

在实务中，应与信用证规定的名称相符，通常称为 Shipping Advice，Advice of shipment 等，也有人将其称为 shipping statement/declaration。

2. 地点及日期（Place and Date）

出单日期一般与提单同日，信用证项下应按来证规定缮制，但不能超过信用证约定的时间。出单地点通常是实际发货地或收益人所在地。

3. 抬头人（To）

应按信用证规定，可以是开证申请人、申请人的指定人或保险公司等。

（1）填写开证申请人名称和地址。

（2）按信用证条款填写接受该装船通知的人的名称与地址。

（3）填写承保该批货物的保险公司的名称与地址，即与买方签发了预约保险单的保险人名称与地址。当保险人收到装船通知后，可以将预约保险单及时地转为一份正式保险单。

4. 通知内容（Contents）

主要包括所发运货物的合同号或信用证号、发票号、商品名称、数量、金额、运输工具名称、开航日期、起运地和目的地、提运单号码、运输标志等，并且与其他相关单据保持一致，如信用证提出具体项目要求，应严格按规定出单。此外通知中还可能出现包装说明、ETD（船舶预离港时间）、ETA（船舶预抵港时间）、ETC（预计开始装船时间）等内容。

5. 签署

填写出口公司的名称和法人代表或经办人的签字，如信用证要求"certified copy of shipping advice"，通常加盖受益人条形章。

9.6.2 缮制装船通知应注意的事项

（1）CFR/CPT 交易条件下签发装运通知的必要性。因货物运输和保险分别由不同的当事人操作，所以受益人有义务向申请人对货物装运情况给予及时、充分的通知，以便进口商办理保险。

（2）装运通知应按规定的方式、时间、内容、份数出单。

（3）相似概念的区别。装运通知（shipping advice）是由出口商发给进口商的；装运须知（shipping instructions）是进口商发给出口商的；shipping note/ bill 装货通知单/船货清单；装货单（shipping order，S/O），又称关单、下货纸，是由接受了托运人提出装运申请的船公司发给托运人的，是托运人用以向海关办理出口货物申报手续的主要单据之一，是命令船长接受该批货物装船的通知。

9.6.3 信用证中有关装船通知条款举例

（1）ORIGINAL FAX FROM BENEFICIARY TO OUR APPLICANT EVIDENCING B/L NO., NAME OF SHIP, SHIPMENT DATE, QUANTITY AND VALUE OF GOODS（要求受益人向开证申请人提交正本通知一份，通知上列明提单号、船名、装运日期、货物的数量和金额）。

（2）INSURANCE COVERED BY APPLICANT. ALL SHIPMENTS UNDER

THIS CREDIT MUST BE ADVISED BY YOU IMMEDIATELY AFTER SHIPMENT DIRECT TO ABC INSURANCE CO. AND TO THE APPLICANT REFERRING TO COVER NOTE NO CA364 GIVING FULL DETAILS OF SHIPMENT. A COPY OF THIS ADVICE TO ACCOMPANY EACH SET OF DOCUMENTS（要求保险由开证申请人负责，货物装运后由受益人直接发通知给ABC保险公司和申请人，通知上应注明号码为CA364的暂保单，并说明货物的详细情况。每次交单都应随附该通知副本）。

（3）BENEFICIARY'S CERTIFIED COPY OF FAX SENT TO APPLICANT WITHIN 48 HOURS AFTER SHIPMENT INDICATING CONTRACT NO., L/C NO., GOODS NAME, QUANTITY, INVOICE VALUE, VESSEL'S NAME, PACKAGE/CONTAINER NO., LOADING PORT, SHIPPING DATE AND ETA（要求受益人应在发货后48小时内发出装运通知，通知内容包括合同号、信用证号、商品名称、数量、发票金额、船名、箱/集装箱号、装货港、装运日期和船舶预抵港时间）。

（4）SHIPMENT ADVICE QUOTING THE NAME OF THE CARRYING VESSEL, DATE OF SHIPMENT, NUMBER OF PACKAGES, SHIPPING MARKS, AMOUNT, LETTER OF CREDIT NUMBER, POLICY NUMBER MUST BE SENT TO APPLICANT BY FAX, COPIES OF TRANSMITTED SHIPMENT ADVICE ACCOMPANIED BY FAX TRANSMISSION REPORT MUST ACCOMPANY THE DOCUMENTS（表明船名、装船日期、包装号、唛头、金额、信用证号、保险单号的装船通知必须由受益人传真给开证人，装船通知和传真副本以及发送传真的电讯报告必须随附议付单据提交）。

【相关单证】

单证9-6 装运通知样本

Shipping Advice

Date and place

To：

Dear Sirs：

Re：Invoice No.：　　　　L/C No.：

We hereby inform you that the goods under the above mentioned credit have shipped. The details of the shipment are as follows：

Commodity：
Quantity：
Total value：
Ocean Vessel：
Date of Shipment：
Port of Loading：
Destination：
B/Lading No.：
Shipping Marks：

We hereby certify that the above content is true and correct.

Company name
signature

【案例】

杨光在2008年8月23日取得海运提单后,随即向PACIFIC INTERNATIONAL INC发出装运通知。

河北恒泰进出口公司
HEBEI HENGTAI IMPORT & EXPORT CORPORATION
NO. 231 HEPING ROAD, SHIJIAZHUANG, CHINA

Shipping Advice

Aug. 23, 2008

To: PACIFIC INTERNATIONAL INC.
129 HAYWARD WAY STREET, MONTE, CA 91513
Dear Sirs:

Re: Invoice No.: HT07110   L/C No.: LC-710-076405

We hereby inform you that the goods under the above mentioned credit have shipped. The details of the shipment are as follows:

Commodity: 100% COTTON STRIPE TOWEL

Quantity: 4 500 DOZENS

Total value: USD 22 050.00

Ocean Vessel: Per s.s. QINLUN Voy. 1502

Date of Shipment: AUG. 23, 2007

Port of Loading: XINGANG

Destination: LOS ANGELES

B/Lading No.:   COS07-25061

Shipping Marks: PACIFIC
                  18185
                  LOS ANGELES
                  1-225

We hereby certify that the above content is true and correct.

HEBEI HENGTAI IMPORT & EXPORT CORPORATION

杨光

9.7 受益人证明

受益人证明（BENEFICIARY'S CERTIFICATE），又称受益人声明（BENEFICIARY'S STATEMENT），是一种由受益人出具的"正式有关内容的书面证明"，以证明受益人履行了信用证规定的任务或证明已按信用证的要求行事。格式如下。

BENEFICIARY'S CERTIFICATE
TO WHOM IT MAY CONCERN：　　　　　　　　　　　　DATE：××
RE. L/C NO. ××　INV. NO. ××
WE HEREBY CERTIFY THAT TWO COPIES OF NON-NEGOTIABLE B/L HAVE BEEN SENT TO THE APPLICANT BY AIRMAIL WITHIN 2 DAYS AFTER SHIPMENT DATE.

　　　　　　　　　　　　　　　　　　　　　　　×××SIGNATURE

9.7.1 受益人证明的基本内容及缮制要点

受益人证明无固定格式，通常由出口方根据信用证的具体要求自行缮制，一般包含以下内容。

(1) 单据名称。受益人证明有多种形式。因此，单据的名称因所证明事项不同而有所差异，可能是寄单证明、寄样证明（船样、样卡和码样等）、取样证明、货物产地、品质、唛头、包装和标签证明、电抄形式的装运通知、产品生产过程、商品业已检验的证明等。应严格按照信用证的规定填写。

(2) 出证日期。单据应在规定的时间内做出。如信用证有关内容是"BENEFICIARY'S CERTIFICATE STATING THAT ALL DOCUMENTS TO BE SENT TO APPLICANT WITHIN 2 DAYS AFTER THE SHIPMENT DATE."若提单日期是 6 月 25 日，则受益人证明的日期不能早于 6 月 25 日，也不能晚于交单日期。

(3) 抬头人。通常填写"To Whom It May Concern"，意指"致有关人"。

(4) 发票号码和信用证号码。表明与其他单据的关系。

(5) 证明内容。受益人证明通常以"THIS IS TO CERTIFY"（DECLARE，STATE，EVIDENCE 等）或"WE HEREBY CERTIFY"等开始，证明的内容应严格与信用证规定相符。但在信用证内通常使用将来时态，受益人制单时应对所用时态作相应的变化。如信用证规定"BENEFICIARY'S CERTIFICATE EVIDENCING THAT TWO COPIES OF NON-NEGOTIABLE B/L WILL BE DESPATCHED TO APPLICANT WITHIN TWO DAYS AFTER SHIPMENT"，在具体制作单据时应将要求其里的"WILL BE DESPATCHED"改为"HAVE BEEN DEPATCHED"；对"BENEFICIARY'S CERTIFICATE STATING THAT CERTIFICATE OF MANUFACTURING PROCESS AND OF INGREDIENTS ISSUED BY ABC CO. SHOULD BE SENT TO SUMITOMO CORP"的要求，"SHOULD BE SENT"应改为"HAD/HAS BEEN SENT"。

(6) 签署。因属于证明性质，按有关规定，证明人（受益人）必须签字，一般注明出证人的公司名称和经办人签字。

9.7.2 常见受益人证明举例

(1) 寄单证明 (BENEFICIARY'S CERTIFICATE FOR DESPATCH OF DOCUMENTS),是最常见的证明。信用证有时规定,在货物装运后,受益人应立即直接邮寄某些单据给收货人或其指定的人,并出具有关证明即寄单证明,以证实已按信用证的规定办事。作为议付单据之一,寄单证明可以由出口公司或受益人出具,内容一般包括所寄单据的名称、份数、寄出时间、寄送方式和寄送对象等。格式如下。

CERTIFICATE

TO WHOM IT MAY CONCERN: DATE:××

RE: SHIPPING DOCUMENTS UNDER L/C NO. ×××

WE CERTIFY THAT A SET OF NON-NEGOTIATIBLE DOCUMENT UNDER L/C INCLUDING A COPY OF B/L, A COPY OF INVOICE, A COPY OF PACKING LIST HAVE BEEN MAILED TO THE APPLICANT.

BY EMS WITHIN 48 HOURS AFTER SHIPMENT.

×××SIGNATURE

如若信用证规定:ORIGINAL BENEFICIARY'S SIGNED CERTIFICATE TOGETHER WITH THE COURIERS RECEIPT CERTIFYING THAT THE FULL SET OF ORIGINAL DOCUMENTS HAVE BEEN SENT TO ××× CO. BY AIRMAIL/DHL/SPEED POST 5 DAYS AFTER B/L DATE. 此时,受益人除了出具由其本公司出具的书面寄单证明外,还要随附信用证指定的快递公司出具的邮寄 (POST RECEIPT) 或快递收据 (SPEED POST RECEIPT)。

(2) 寄样证明 (BENEFICIARY'S CERTIFICATE FOR DESPATCH OF SHIPMENT SAMPLE)。有些信用证要求,受益人在货物装船时,需取样向买方寄样,并签发寄出船样、样卡、码样等情况的证明,这类证明为寄样证明。如 CERTIFICATE TO SHOW THAT THE REQUIRED SHIPMENT SAMPLES HAVE BEEN SENT BY DHL TO THE APPLICANT ON OCT. 10, 2005。

(3) 包装和标签证明 (BENEFICIARY'S CERTIFICATE FOR PACKING AND LABEL)。除在合同或信用证中对包装或唛头进行明确规定外,有些国家通常还要求受益人另外出具书面的证明。例如,对伊拉克出口,必须有包装、唛头证明;对港、澳出口,必须在包装上刷制"请勿用钩"字样,并出具证明;对澳大利亚、新西兰出口,通常要求出具包装清洁完好的证明。如 BENEFICIARY CERTIFICATE STATING EACH EXPORT PACKAGE TO BE MARKED WITH "MADE IN CHINA"。

9.7.3 信用证中有关受益人证明条款举例

(1) BENEFICIARY'S CERTIFICATE STATING THAT THREE SETS COPIES OF NON-NEGOTIABLE SHIPPING DOCUMENTS TO BE AIRMAILD DIRECTLY TO THE APPLICANT IMMEDIATELY AFTER SHIPMENT (受益人证明三套不可

议付的装运单据须在装运后立即航空径寄开证申请人）。

(2) BENEFICIARY'S CERTIFICATE CERTIFYING THAT BENEFICIARY HAS FAXED THE SHIPPING DOCS (B/L, INVOICE, PACKING LIST, PHYTOSANITARY CERTIFICATE) WITHIN 2 WORKING DAYS AFTER SHIPMENT DATE TO APPLICANT AND THE RELATE CERTIFIED TRUE COPY OF FAX（受益人证明发货后两日内传真发送有关单据给申请人，传真报告应证实并向银行提交）。

(3) TWO SETS OF SHIPPING SAMPLES AND ONE SET OF NON-NEGOTIABLE SHIPPING DOCUMENTS MUST BE SENT TO APPLICANT BY SPEED POST/COURIER SERVICE WITHIN 5 DAYS FROM THE DATE OF BILL OF LADING AND A CERTIFICATE TO THIS EFFECT FROM BENEFICIARY TOGETHER WITH RELATIVE SPEED POST/COURIER RECEIPT MUST ACCOMPANY THE DOCUMENTS（两套船样和一套不可议付的装运单据须在提单日后5日内通过邮局快递寄给开证人，受益人证明应表明已照此行事，相应的邮政快递收据必须随议付单据提交）。

【案例】

杨光与8月24日通过敦豪快递公司向PACIFIC INTERNATIONAL INC. 寄出全套不可议付货运单据，制单时缮制了如下的受益人证明。

河北恒泰进出口公司
HEBEI HENGTAI IMPORT & EXPORT CORPORATION
NO. 231 HEPING ROAD, SHIJIAZHUANG, CHINA

BENEFICIARY'S CERTIFICATE

Aug. 27, 2008

To Whom It May Concern,

Dear Sirs：

Re：Invoice No.：HT07110   L/C No.：LC-710-076405

WE HEREBY CERTIFY THAT ONE COMPLETE SET OF NON-NEGOTIABLE SHIPPING DOCUMENTS HAVE BEEN SENT TO APPLICANT BY DHL WITHIN 2 DAYS AFTER SHIPMENT.

HEBEI HENGTAI IMPORT & EXPORT CORPORATION
杨光

9.8 其他单据

9.8.1 有关运输方面的证明

1. 船籍及航程证明

船籍证明（Ship's Nationality Certificate）是用以说明载货船舶国籍的证明。有时买方出于政治原因，对装货船舶的国籍予以限制，要求卖方仅装某些国家或不装某些国家的船舶，并要求卖方提供相应证明。航程证明（Itinerary Certificate）是用以说明载货船舶在航程中停靠港口的证明。出于政治原因或为了避免航行途中货船被扣的风险，买方有时对装货船舶的航行路线、停靠港口予以限制，要求船只不经过某些地区，或不在某些港口停靠，并要求卖方提供相应证明。

为了抵制以色列，大多数阿拉伯国家商人开来的信用证中都会要求出具此类证明，往往规定装运的船只不能是以色列国籍，而且全部的航程不能在以色列港口停靠或加水加油。例如，来证中规定：shipment must be effected not Israeli vessel and not call at any Israeli ports, and not blacklisted vessel.

船籍及航程证明可由船公司或其代理出具，如果来证规定可由受益人出具，则卖方在向船公司了解了该船的情况后，也可自行签发，其格式可由出口企业自行制定。内容可根据信用证上的字句来填写，或将信用证中要求的内容写明，最后由出口公司签字盖章。格式如下。

CERTIFICATE

SHANGHAI JAN. 21, 2003

TO WHOM IT MAY CONCERN：

　　RE：INV. NO. ××, L/C NO. ××

　　THIS IS TO CERTIFY THAT M. S. /S. S. ××× FLYING THE PEOPLE'S REPUBLIC OF CHINA FLAG, WILL NOT CALL AT ANY ISRAELI PORTS DURING THIS PRESENT VOYAGE, AND SHE IS ONT BLACKLISTED BY THE ARAB COUNTRIES.

×××SIGNATURE

2. 货装集装箱证明

有些来证规定装集装箱船只，若信用证中没有要求出具具体书面证明时，只要提单上能表示出是集装箱运输，就无须提供单独的书面证明，但如果信用证有下列条款，如 shipment to be made by container vessel and beneficiary's certificate to this effect is required。此时受益人就须要出具一份证明，以便顺利议付。其内容及格式如下。

CERTIFICATE

TIANJIN FEB. 12, 2003

TO WHOM IT MAY CONCERN：

　　RE：INVOICE NO. , ×× L/C NO. ×××

THIS IS TO CERTIFY THAT SHIPMENT OF THIS CAPTIONED INVOICE HAS BEEN EFFECTED BY THE CONTAINER VESSEL "S. S ×××".

×××SIGNATURE

3. 船龄证明

有些国家有时对卖方所装运货物船只的使用年限有一定的规定，如印度、孟加拉国、巴基斯坦、科威特等，如来证要求货物须在中国香港转船，二程船的船龄不得超过15年，不能驶入科威特港等。若信用证中有此类条款，则卖方须提供书面的证明。此种证明一般由中国香港的运输代理签发。其格式如下。

CERTIFICATE

TIANJIN FEB. 12, 2003

TO WHOM IT MAY CONCERN:

RE: INVOICE NO. ××

WE HEREBY CERTIFY THAT THE GOODS UNDER THE ABOVE INVOICE SHIPPED BY S. S. JINJIANG V. 4. B/L NO. 165 WILL BE TRANSSHIPPED AT HONGKONG VIA AN ON-CARRIER NOT OVER 15 YEARS OLD, AND IS ALLOWED TO ENTER KUWAIT PORT FROM HONGKONG.

×××SIGNATURE

4. 船级证明及班轮公会船只证明

有的国家特别是印度的信用证常常对装运货物船只的船级有一定的要求，如要求提供英国劳合氏船级社（LLOYDS）签发的船级证明等。由于我国目前各口岸的劳合氏船只很少，我国出口商对于这一点能否做到很难掌握，所以此类条款一般不能接受。若不能不接受时，则在允许转船的情况下，必须安排在中国香港转船，并由中国香港的劳合氏船级社代表其伦敦公司签发证明。其格式如下。

CERTIFICATE

TO WHOM IT MAY CONCERN:

RE: HAIXING V. 81, B/L NO. ×××

WE HEREBY CERTIFY THAT THE ABOVE ON-CARRYING VESSEL IS A CONFERENCE LINE VESSEL COVERED BY INSTITUTE CLASSIFICATION CLAUSE.

×××SIGNATURE

5. 船长收据

在近洋运输中，货到单未到的情况下，信用证会规定，货装船后，正本或副本单据须交装货船只的船长，随船带给收货人。在议付时则须提交船长收据作为证明。如信用证规定，ORIGINAL INSPECTION CERTIFICATE OF QUALITY MUST BE SENT TO THE MASTER OF THE CARRYING VESSEL, AND THE MASTER'S RECEIPT REQUIRED FOR NEGOTIATION.

此种情况下，须将"质检证"的正本交给船长，并由船长出具收据，证明后才能进行议付。此类信用证多见于日本。其格式如下。

RECEIPT

TIANJIN FEB. 12，2003

RECEIVED FOR SHIPPERS，××× CO. LTD.，THE FOLLOWING DOCUMENTS WHICH PRESENT MASTER IS REQUIRED TO TRANSMIT TO THE CONSIGNEE，××× CO.，LTD.：

2 COPIES OF B/L；

2 COPIES OF INVOICE；

2 COPIES OF PACKING LIST.

SIGNATURE

6. 船公司的运费账单

在 CIF 和 CFR 条件下，有时信用证会要求提供有关运输费用方面的数据，尤其是伊朗的信用证（欧洲国家一般无此要求）。在不必费时费力的情况下，我国出口商可事先向船公司或其代理言明，并将船公司收账的运费账单复印即可。如 FREIGHT NOTE, INVOICE FOR FREIGHT 等。

若信用证条款规定必须在商业发票上加注运、保费及 FOB 金额，还应注意三者所使用的货币币种应与发票一致。

9.8.2 其他

1. 借记通知单

有时信用证金额不足，保险加成的规定超过合同规定需追加保险费或因保险责任扩展而发生超额保费时，由于这些费用应由买方负担且金额较小，如要修改信用证，有时会影响货物及时出运和议付结汇，或者修改费及利息损失也许大于应收款项，因此一般采用借记通知单通知对方，请对方把款项汇来或征得对方同意，在佣金中扣除。此时需出具借记通知单。

2. 扣佣通知书

当佣金不要求在商业发票上表示出来时，需另外出具扣佣通知书或称贷记通知书表示扣佣金额。此时汇票金额应为发票额减去扣佣通知的金额。

3. 出口地无领事证明

有些国家在信用证中常规定，出口货物的单据要由其驻中国使领馆在上面认证或签证后，才能到银行交单议付，否则须出具出口地无领事证明。在我国一般可由出口公司签发出口地无领事证明，并由当地贸促会盖章加以证明。

在国际贸易中，当买方或信用证要求一些与货物的包装、运输等有关的单据时，为满足其要求，卖方应在事先了解对方的要求后，及时与有关部门联系，了解能否办到，并及时出证，若不能满足买方的要求，应及时与买方联系更改或更换。虽然这类单据并不是出口贸易中必不可少的单据，但从结汇的角度来看，一旦这些单据成为信用证要求的单据，就与其他单据同样重要，要认真对待。

第10章

【本章导读】

出口收汇核销

出口退税

【学习目标和要点】

出口企业办理完货物装运，顺利收结货款，就完成了出口业务活动的主要部分，但根据国家有关政策规定，企业还要及时向国家外汇管理部门和税务部门办理出口收汇核销和出口退税手续。通过本章的学习，学生应了解出口收汇核销及出口退税的一般流程，并学会填写出口收汇核销单。

出口收汇核销及出口退税

10.1 出口收汇核销

出口收汇核销制度是外汇管理部门在海关的配合和外汇指定银行的协助下,对出口货物从报关出运直至出口收汇的全过程进行跟踪监管,以证实货物出口后是否有相应的外汇收回国内或按规定使用的一项外汇管理制度。建立出口收汇核销制度是国家加强出口收汇管理,确保国家外汇收入,防止外汇流失的一项重要措施。

外贸出口单位在办理有关货物的出口通关手续时,应到当地的外汇管理部门申领经外汇管理部门加盖"监督收汇"章的核销单,凭此及出口报关单和其他所需的文件证明办理报关手续,货物报关后,由海关在核销单和有该单编号的报关单上加盖"放行"章,货物出口结汇后,出口单位必须在外汇管理部门规定的期限内办理出口收汇核销手续。

出口收汇核销实行出口收汇核销员制度,出口单位领取出口收汇核销单、办理出口收汇核销手续,应当由本单位的核销员负责办理。

10.1.1 出口核销的范围

除经批准外,一切出口贸易项下的货物均应办理出口核销手续。具体可分为收汇贸易、不收汇贸易和其他贸易三大类。

收汇贸易包括一般贸易、进料加工、来料加工、来件装配、有价样品;不收汇贸易包括易货贸易、补偿贸易(实物补偿)、实物投资、记账贸易;其他贸易包括寄售、出境展销(览)、承包工程等,收款和不收款或自用、损耗、赠送、出售、退还兼有的贸易。

10.1.2 出口收汇核销流程

出口企业如果是首次申领核销单,必须持有关材料到企业注册地外汇管理部门办理核销备案登记。在备案登记前,企业应到海关办理"中国电子口岸"入网手续(见图10-1),申领"中国电子口岸"企业法人IC卡和"中国电子口岸"企业操作员IC卡。IC卡分企业法人卡和企业操作员卡。企业法人卡又称公章卡,是企业在中国电子口岸中唯一代表企业身份的IC卡。企业操作员卡用于企业内部人员身份认证,持卡人可以在中国电子口岸进行具体操作,并对填写、修改的电子文件进行个人数字签名。未申领IC卡的企业不能进入此系统,无法办理相关出口收汇核销业务。

办理核销备案登记时,应当向外汇局提供下列材料:①单位介绍信、申请书;②《中华人民共和国进出口企业资格证书》或《中华人民共和国外商投资企业批准证书》或《中华人民共和国台港澳侨投资企业批准证书》正本及复印件;③《企业法人营业执照》(副本)或《企业营业执照》(副本)及复印件;④《中华人民共和国组织机构代码证》正本及复印件;⑤海关注册登记证明书正本及复印件;⑥外汇管理部门要求提供的其他材料。

1. 申领核销单

出口核销工作从申领核销单到收汇核销,均通过"中国电子口岸执法系统"的子系统"出口收汇系统"完成。

第 10 章　出口收汇核销及出口退税

图 10-1　中国电子口岸"出口收汇"系统主页

　　出口单位在到外汇管理部门领取核销单前,应当根据业务实际需要先通过"中国电子口岸出口收汇系统"向外汇管理部门提出领取核销单申请,然后由本单位核销员持本人"中国电子口岸"操作员 IC 卡及其他规定的凭证到外汇管理部门领取核销单(见图 10-2)。

　　2. 外管管理部门发放外汇核销单

　　外汇管理部门根据出口单位申请的核销单份数和出口收汇核销考核等级向出口单位发放核销单,并将核销单电子底账数据传送至"中国电子口岸"数据中心。

　　3. 口岸备案

　　企业在出口货物报关前,必须先通过"中国电子口岸出口收汇系统"向报关地海关进行核销单的口岸备案(见图 10-3)。经备案的核销单方能用于出口货物报关申报,否则,报关地海关无法及时获得该核销单电子底账数据。未进行报关前备案的核销单不能用于出口报关。

　　4. 核销单数据传输

　　备案后,"中国电子口岸出口收汇系统"向海关内部网传输核销单数据。

　　5. 出口报关申报

　　出口企业使用中国电子口岸报关申报系统进行电子报关申报,系统向海关内网传输企业申报的出口报关单数据,再凭已缮制的核销单、注明核销单编号的出口报关单和其他有关单据,向海关正式申报。企业要如实向海关申报成交方式,按成交方式申报成交价格、数量、运费、保费以及合同协议号等内容,保证报关数据的真实性和完整性。

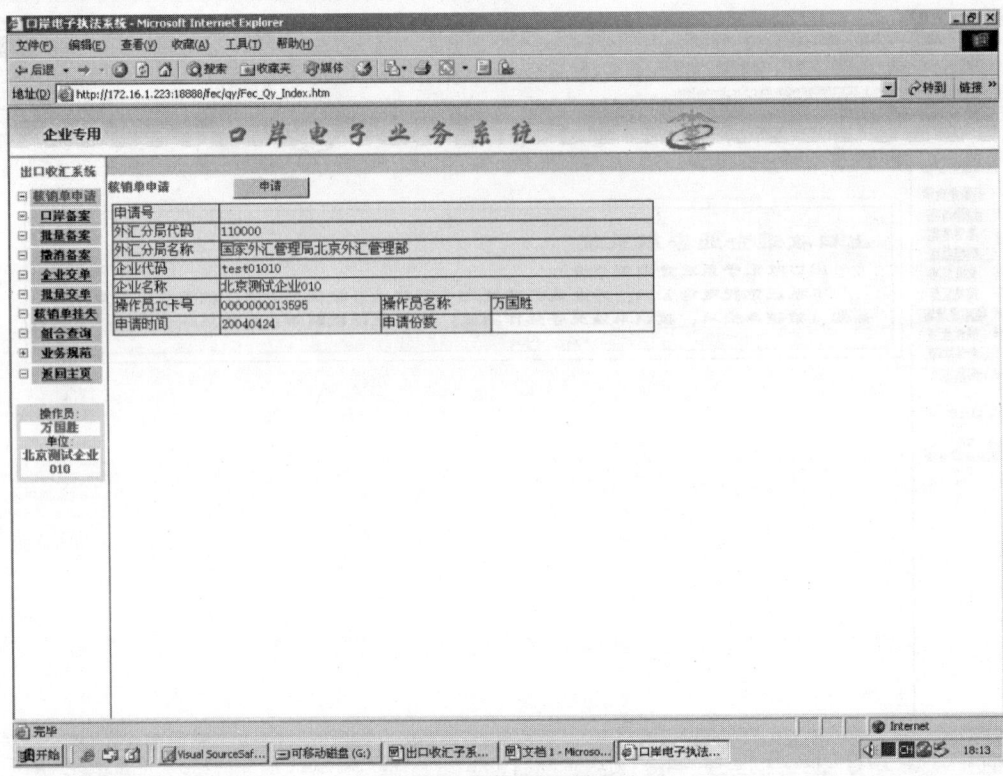

图 10-2　核销单申请

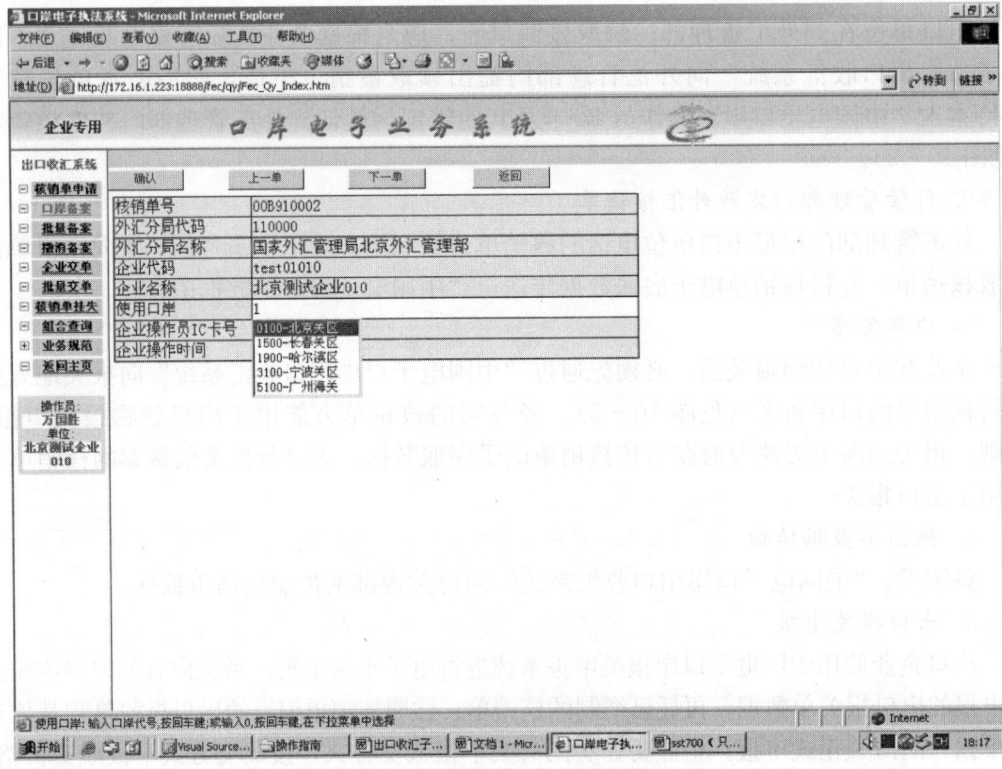

图 10-3　口岸备案

6. 出口结关报关单数据传输

海关审核报关单数据无误后,在核销单"海关签注栏"处加盖"验讫章",与盖有"放行章"的报关单一并退还出口企业,并向中国电子口岸数据中心传输已结关出口报关单电子数据。

7. 向外汇管理部门交单

出口单位在报关出口后通过"中国电子口岸出口收汇系统"将已用于出口报关的核销单向外汇管理部门交单(见图10-4)。系统亦会将企业已交单确认的出口结关报关单数据传输至外汇管理部门。

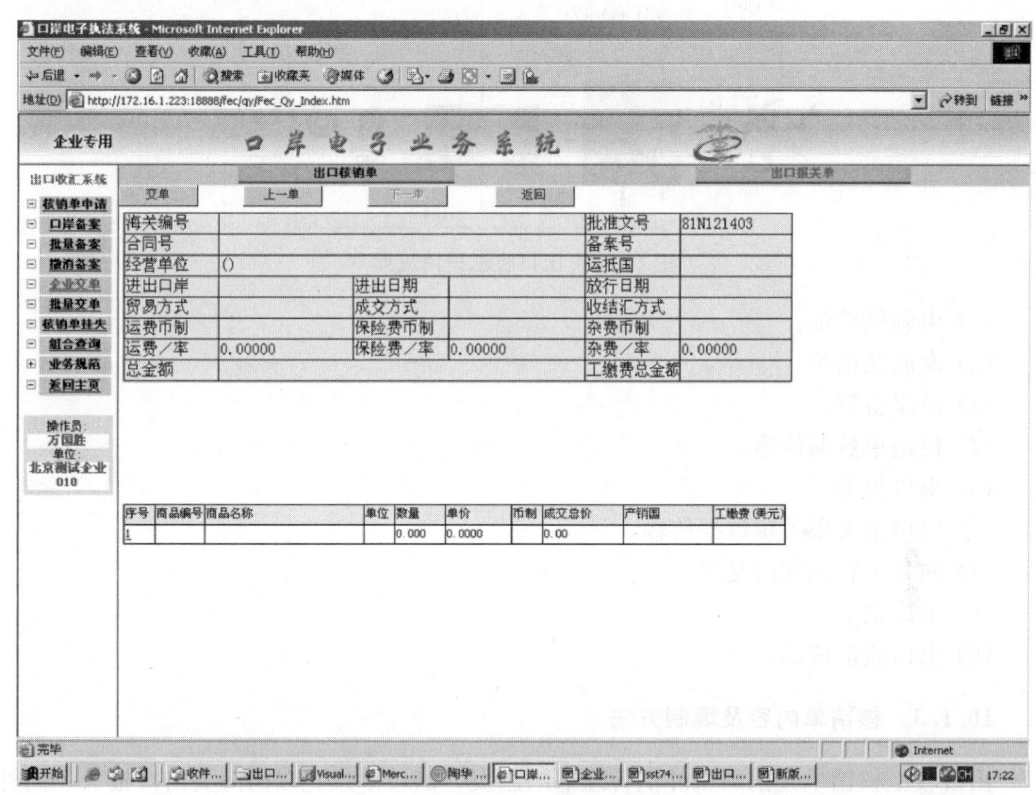

图 10-4 企业交单

8. 出口结汇

货物出口后,出口企业应当按照出口合同约定的收汇时间和方式以及报关单注明的成交总价,及时、足额地收回货款。即期收汇项下应当在货物报关出口后 180 天内收汇,远期收汇项下应在远期备案的收汇期限内收汇。收汇后,银行向出口单位出具出口收汇核销专用联(结汇水单或收账通知),并在其上填写有关核销单编号。

9. 出口收汇核销

出口企业收汇以后,凭经海关签章的核销单、结汇水单(收账通知)、出口货物报关单(外汇核销联)以及其他规定单据(如来料加工、来件装配出口还须提供加工合同和登记手册),到外汇管理部门办理核销。外汇管理部门通过"出口收汇核销系统"及其他相关系统查询出口结关报关单数据,核对企业提交的纸面单据,对核销单进行核销,并在核销单上加盖"已核销"章,并将其中的出口退税专用联交出口单位办理出口退税之用。

外汇管理部门定期将已核销电子数据上传至"中国电子口岸"数据中心,供商务、海关、税务等相关主管部门查询使用。

综上所述,出口收汇核销的具体流程如图10-5所示。

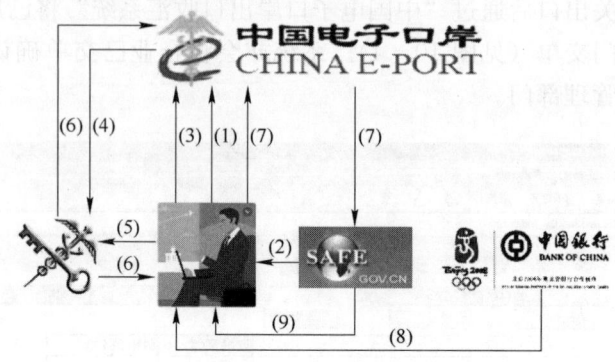

图10-5 出口收汇核销流程

(1) 申领核销单。
(2) 发放核销单。
(3) 口岸备案。
(4) 核销单数据传输。
(5) 出口报关。
(6) 出口结关报关单数据传输。
(7) 向外汇管理部门交单。
(8) 出口结汇。
(9) 出口收汇核销。

10.1.3 核销单内容及填制方法

出口收汇核销单是由国家外汇管理部门制发,出口单位凭以向海关出口报关、向外汇指定银行办理出口收汇、向外汇管理部门办理出口收汇核销、向税务机关办理出口退税申报的有统一编号及使用期限的凭证。它由存根、正本及出口退税联构成。

1. 存根联

(1) 出口单位,填写出口公司名称,并加盖公章。
(2) 单位代码,填写出口公司在外汇管理部门备案的代码。
(3) 出口币种总价,填写货币种类和数额。
(4) 收汇方式,如L/C、D/P、D/A和T/T等。
(5) 预计收款日期,根据不同的收汇方式,估算收汇的大概日期。
(6) 报关日期,与报关单上填报日期相同。
(7) 备注,填写收汇方面需要说明的事项。

2. 出口收汇核销单正本

(1) 出口单位,同存根联。

(2) 单位代码，同存根联。

(3) 银行签注栏，用以表明出口商委托结汇银行收账的情况。包括类别、币种金额、日期、公章4栏，并由银行盖章。

① 类别，填写受托银行或解付银行对结算业务的归类，分为信用证、托收和自寄单据三种方式。

② 币种金额，填银行扣除议付等银行费用后的实际收汇金额。

③ 日期，填写收结汇日期。

(4) 海关签注栏，即在报关时，经审核放行后，海关在此栏加盖海关"验讫放行"章，签注放行日期。

(5) 外汇局签注栏，即在货物已出口、出口单位收到货款后，向外汇管理部门办理核销时，由外汇管理局加盖"已核销"章。

3. 出口退税专用联

(1) 出口单位，同存根联。

(2) 单位代码，同存根联。

(3) 货物名称、数量、币种总价，按报关单填写。

(4) 报关单编号，填写海关在报关单右上角批注的编号。

(5) 外汇局签注栏，即出口结汇后，由外汇管理部门核销盖章注明以后，才能办理申请退税工作。

【相关单证】

单证10-1　出口收汇核销单样本

10.2 出口退税

出口退税是世界各国鼓励出口的一种通行做法，符合 WTO 规则，是产品出口后，由税务机关将其出口前在生产和流通环节中已征收的增值税和消费税退还给出口企业，从而使出口商品以不含税价格进入国际市场，在同等税收条件下参与国际竞争的一种政策制度。我国从 1985 年 4 月 1 日起对出口产品实行退税制度。

出口企业中，一般都是由专职财务人员负责办理出口退税事宜，程序如下。

10.2.1 办理出口退税登记

1. 申请出口退税登记

企业在取得有关部门批准其经营出口产品业务的文件和工商行政管理部门核发的工商登记证明后，应于 30 日内持企业出口经营批件（复印件）和工商营业执照（副本），到当地主管退税业务的税务机关办理退税登记，领取《出口企业退税登记表》。

2. 申报和受理退税登记

企业领到《出口企业退税登记表》后，即按登记表及有关要求填写，加盖企业公章和有关人员印章后，连同出口产品经营权批准文件、工商登记证明等证明资料一起报送税务机关，税务机关审核《出口企业退税登记表》及相关文件，受理登记后，由税务机关填写相关内容。如退税公式、退税方法、申报方式等作出明确规定。

3. 核发《出口企业退税登记证》

税务机关接到企业的正式申请，经审核无误并按规定的程序批准后，核发给企业"出口退税登记证"。

10.2.2 出口退税申报

1. 核对海关电子信息

出口企业收到海关签退的出口货物报关单后，通过"电子口岸"核对海关报关单电子信息（见图 10-6 和图 10-7）。

2. 退税申报

出口企业须在海关放行日期（即报关单右下角海关签发的验讫放行日期）后 90 天内备妥退税单据，办理申报手续。申报时，出口企业将有关进货和出口凭证信息录入企业申报软件，申报系统对申报数据进行检查、汇总后，生成本次申报（见图 10-8）。然后，企业将事先生成的退税预申报软盘连同有关退税凭证，报送税务机关。

产品报关出口后，若出口企业逾期未提出退税申请，税务部门一律不办理产品的出口退税。

3. 审批出口退税

税务部门收到退税申请资料，按有关规定审核无误后，安排退税资金，将出口退税资金划转出口企业。

第 10 章 出口收汇核销及出口退税

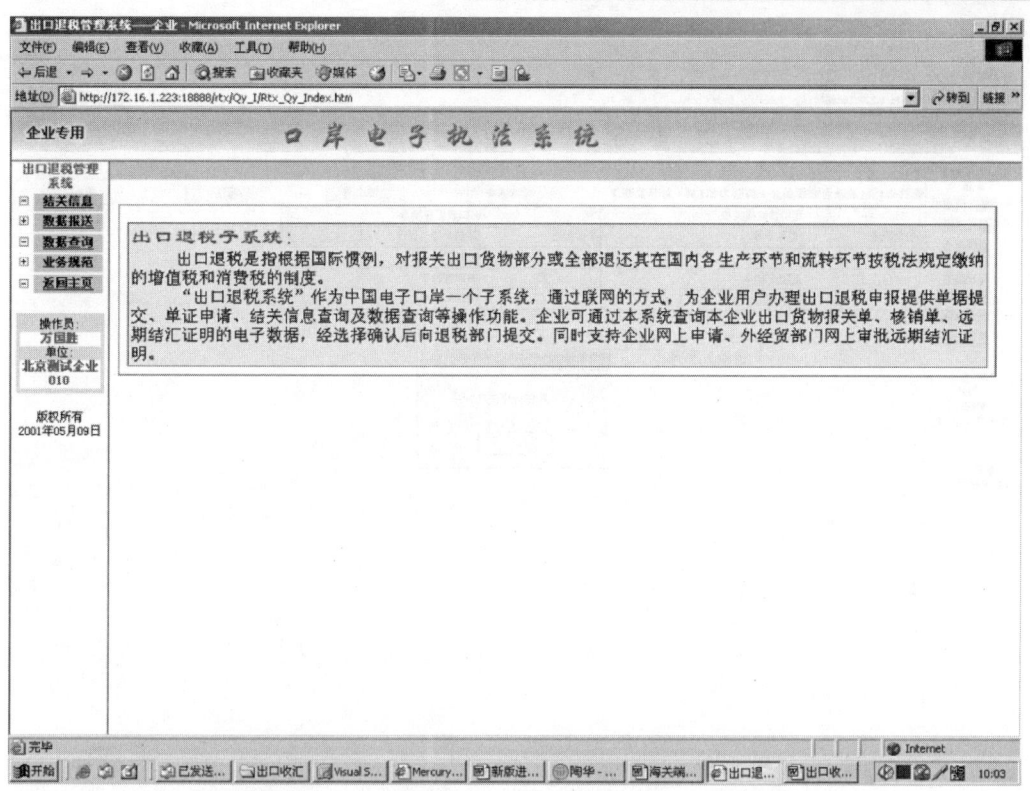

图 10-6 中国电子口岸"出口退税管理系统"主页

图 10-7 中国电子口岸"出口退税系统"结关信息

图 10-8　中国电子口岸"出口退税管理系统"报送数据

10.2.3　出口退税所需单证

出口退税所需单证主要包括以下几种。
（1）采购出口货物的增值税专用发票。
（2）盖有外汇管理部门核销章，办完核销手续的出口收汇核销单（出口退税专用）。
（3）盖有海关验讫放行章的出口货物报关单（出口退税专用联）。
（4）出口商业发票。
（5）税收（出口货物专用）缴款书或出口货物完税分割单。
（6）出口退税进货凭证申报表。
（7）出口货物退税申报明细表。
（8）出口退税汇总申报表。
（9）出口货物销售明细账。
（10）退税申报软盘。

【技能实训】

1. 登录国家外汇管理局、国家税务总局，学习有关出口收汇核销、出口退税相关政策规定。
2. 了解中国电子口岸"业务指南"，下载学习"出口收汇（企业端）操作手册"（http://www3.chinaport.gov.cn/down/url.jsp? fid＝eport/chukou/shouhui2.rar）和"出口退税操作手册"

(http://down.chinaport.gov.cn/eport/tuishui/zhinan.rar)。

3. 根据下列资料填写出口核销单（见表 10-1）。

表 10-1 出口收汇核销单样本

出口收汇核销单 存根	出口收汇核销单	出口收汇核销单 出口退税专用
（　）编号：	（　）编号：	（　）编号：
出口单位：	出口单位：	出口单位：
单位代码：	单位代码：	单位代码：
出口币种总价：	银行签注栏：类别／币种金额／日期／盖章	货物名称／数量／币种总价
收汇方式：		
预计收款日期：		
报关日期：		
备注：		
	海关签注栏：	报关单编号：
此单报关有效期截止到	外汇局签注栏： 　年　月　日（盖章）	外汇局签注栏： 　年　月　日（盖章）

（出口单位盖章）（海关盖章）　　　　　（出口单位盖章）（海关盖章）　　　　未经核销此联不得撕开

远大公司常年经营化工产品制造与出口，与日本慧通株式会社成交 50 公吨"CR-50 钛白粉"，总价为 USD86 329.00，结汇方式为信用证。该企业在外汇管理部门的备案号码为 130653823，核销单编号为 3210839200，报关单编号为 892728003。

参考文献

[1] 祝卫. 出口贸易模拟操作教程. 上海：上海人民出版社, 2002.

[2] 孟祥年. 国际贸易实务操作教程. 2版. 北京：对外经济贸易大学出版社, 2005.

[3] 吴国新, 李元旭. 国际贸易单证实务. 2版. 北京：清华大学出版社, 2008.

[4] 余心之, 徐美荣. 新编外贸单证实务. 北京：对外经济贸易大学出版社, 2005.

[5] 余世明, 冼燕华. 国际商务模拟实习教程. 广州：暨南大学出版社, 2007.

[6] 张宝顺. 国际商务模拟操作. 北京：对外经济贸易大学出版社, 2006.

[7] 严思忆, 李宝柱, 陈波. 国际货物贸易单证实务. 北京：对外经济贸易大学出版社, 2007.

[8] 广银芳. 外贸单证制作实务. 北京：清华大学出版社, 2007.

[9] 张援越, 王瑞华, 王桂英. 报关与报检实务. 北京：北京理工大学出版社, 2007.

[10] 王斌义. 报检报关操作实务. 北京：首都经济贸易大学出版社, 2006.

[11] 孟恬, 马君. 国际货物运输与保险. 北京：对外经济贸易大学出版社, 2008.

[12] 全国国际商务单证培训认证考试办公室. 国际商务单证理论与实务. 北京：中国商务出版社, 2009.

[13] 海关总署报关员资格考试教材编写委员会. 报关员资格全国统一考试教材. 北京：中国海关出版社, 2009.

[14] 程同春, 程欣. 新编国际商务英语函电. 南京：东南大学出版社, 2007.

[15] 黎孝先. 国际贸易实务. 4版. 北京：对外经济贸易大学出版社, 2007.

[16] http://www.customs.gov.cn/publish/porta10/.

[17] http://www3.chinaport.gov.cn/.

[18] http://www.mofcom.gov.cn/.

[19] http://www.jctrans.com/.